Nicholas Belfield Dennys

The Folk-lore of China

And its Affinities with that of the Aryan Semitic Races

Nicholas Belfield Dennys

The Folk-lore of China
And its Affinities with that of the Aryan Semitic Races

ISBN/EAN: 9783744768665

Printed in Europe, USA, Canada, Australia, Japan

Cover: Foto ©Thomas Meinert / pixelio.de

More available books at **www.hansebooks.com**

THE

FOLK-LORE OF CHINA,

AND ITS AFFINITIES
WITH THAT OF THE ARYAN AND SEMITIC RACES.

BY

N. B. DENNYS, Ph.D., F.R.G.S.,

M.R.A.S.; AUTHOR OF "A HANDBOOK OF THE CANTON VERNACULAR," &c.

" Unus utrique error, sed variis illudit partibus."
—Horac

LONDON:
TRÜBNER AND Co., 57 & 59, LUDGATE HILL.
HONGKONG:
"CHINA MAIL" OFFICE.

1876.

[*All rights Reserved.*]

To

REAR ADMIRAL

THE HON. FRANCIS EGERTON, M.P.

&c., &c., &c.

A SLIGHT TOKEN OF THE RESPECT AND GRATITUDE
OF THE AUTHOR.

PREFACE.

The following compilation consists of a series of Articles contributed to the *China Review*, and now republished with a few additions and corrections. Of their many defects no one is more sensible than the author, who has moreover necessarily been debarred from access to numerous authorities which a residence at home would have placed within his reach. It is nevertheless hoped that this slight contribution to a better knowledge of Chinese popular beliefs, arranged as it is in a more compendious form than was hitherto accessible, will find some favour.

The author desires to express his obligations to the Rev. J. Chalmers, M.A., and to Mr. Christopher T. Gardner, of H.M. Consular Service, Canton, who very kindly placed valuable manuscript notes at his disposal. Most of his numerous obligations to previous publications are acknowledged in the foot-notes.

N. B. D.

HONGKONG, *November*, 1876.

CONTENTS.

CHAPTER I.
INTRODUCTORY.

Attention of Late Bestowed on the Study of Folk-lore—China Presents a most Interesting Field of Enquiry—Little as yet Done to bring together what is Known upon the Subject—Similarity between Chinese and Western Beliefs—Our Own Recent Emancipation from Superstition—The Myth-making Faculty Common to all Mankind—Previous Allusions to Chinese Folk-lore—Arrangements of Subjects—Chinese Folk-lore Extensive—Probable Derivation from the Cradle of the Aryan Races—Importance of Popular Beliefs in Chinese Estimation,...................pp. 1-8.

CHAPTER II.
BIRTH, MARRIAGE, AND DEATH.

Superstitions as to Day and Hour of Birth—Practices to Ascertain Sex of Expected Child—Frightening Away Demons—Three Children at a Birth—Binding the Wrists—Cutting the Cord of the Feet—Rocking an Empty Cradle—Ceremonies after Birth—Worshipping the Measures—Superstitions as to Marriages—Wedding Rings—Betrothal Ceremonies—Using the Sieve—Rubbing the Bride's Feet—The Marriage Veil—Worshipping Heaven and Earth—Shears, Honey &c.—Bridal Candles—Lucky Numbers at Weddings—Bride Cake or Bread—Touching the Threshold—Shoes—Sitting on the Dress—Death—Purchase of Coffins beforehand—Burial Clothes—"Saining" a Corpse—Cash from the Corpse's Sleeve—Reversing the Body—Opening the Roof—White and Black Cocks—Watching Spirits—Watching the Dead—Clothes, Arms, Food, &c., for the Dead—Offerings after Death.—Throwing Earth upon the Coffin—A Lucky Place for a Grave—White the Mourning Colour—Aversion to Disturbing a Grave,................pp. 8-27.

CHAPTER III.
DAYS AND SEASONS.

Lucky and Unlucky Days—The Chinese Sabbath—Persian Derivation—Congratulating the Moon—Unlucky Days in Each Month—Tabular Arrangement of Ditto—New Year's Day—The "First Foot."—St. Swithun's Day in China—An Obscured Moon,...pp. 27-32.

CONTENTS.

CHAPTER IV.

PORTENTS OR OMENS, AUGURIES, LUCKY NUMBERS, AND DREAMS.

Upsetting the Oil Jar—Crows, Magpies and Ducks—Dogs and Cats—Crowing Hens—Swallows—Owls—Setting an Even Number of Eggs—Superstitions as to Mirrors—Crooked Paths—Eclipses, Comets, and Stars—Bells—Drawing Water at Certain Hours on a given Date—Omens of Personal Sensation, Itching, Shivering, Sneezing &c.—A Shaky Finger—Trousers—Sitting in a Warm Chair—Meeting a Funeral or Coffin—People with Joined Eyebrows—Itching of the Palm and Specks on the Nails—The First Words heard after making a Resolution—Casting Lots—Lucky Numbers, 3, 5, and 7—Numerical Categories—Even Numbers, Lucky—Chinese beliefs as to Dreams—Comparison of Chinese and Japanese Superstitions as to Dreams,............ ....pp. 33-45.

CHAPTER V.

CHARMS, SPELLS, AMULETS, AND DIVINATIONS.

Attempted Cure of Diseases by Charms and Incantations—Magic Mirrors—Fire-Crackers as Charms—Exorcising the Spirit of an Executed Criminal—Firing Cannon at the Pei-ho—Shooting Arrows at a Tidal Wave—Iron Plates Sunk as Charms—Anti-Demoniacal Powers of Certain Woods—The Bamboo, Peach, Willow and Plum—Charms Affixed to Buildings—Coffin Nails—Cats in Clay as Charms—Stone Lions—Coins under Door Sills—Cash Swords—Triangles—The "Evil Eye"—The *Svastica* or Thor's Hammer—The Eight Diagrams—Arrows on the Roof—Stone Slabs—Red Cloth—Murderer's Knives, the Classics and Fishing Nets &c.—Drawings of Reptiles or Animals—Taking a Hair of the Dog that Bit You—Lustrations by Spittle—Characts or Written Charms—Red and Yellow, Lucky Colours—Ashes of Burnt Paper Charms taken in Tea, &c.—Amulets—Lucky Cash—Lock and Hook Amulets—Bells as Amulets—Divinations—Divining Sticks—Spirit Rapping—Somnambules or Media—Form of Incantation—Divination by Willow-wood Images—Mesmerism—Chinese *Sortes Virgilianæ*—Divination by Paper Slips—Trained Birds—Chiromancy or Palmistry—Physiognomy—Divination by Leaves, ...pp. 45-63.

CHAPTER VI.

SUPERSTITIONS AS TO VARIOUS SUBJECTS.

The Hare and Its Attributes—Discovery of Drowned Bodies—Casting Salt into the Water—The last Piece left upon a Plate—Fêng-shui—Value of Human Blood and Flesh as Medicinal Aids—Chinese Cannibalism and its Reason—Blood Bread Sold at Peking after Executions—Blood of Unborn Infants—Restorative Properties of Human Flesh—Ancient Rain Stones—Gymnastics; Curious Belief as to Effects of Practising Them—Bridges and the Beliefs Concerning Them—Curing Swellings—How to Prevent Water from Boiling over and Eggs from Cracking—Cinnebar and Vermilion as Antidotes to Sickness—Superstitions as to the Female Principle and Silkworms—Signs by Corpses if Dissatisfied, ...pp. 64-71.

CHAPTER VII.

GHOSTS, APPARITIONS, AND SUPERNATURAL BEINGS.

Prominent Part played by Ghosts on the Chinese Stage—The False Ghost at Chinkeang—Chinese Terms for Ghosts; Their Shapeless Form—Candles Burning Green in the Presence of Ghosts—Apparition at Shanghai—The Ghost from the S. S. *Fusing*—The Foochow Gun-boat Ghost—Ghosts of Suicides and of Women who Die in Child-bed—Ghosts of Murdered People—Haunted Houses—Sanding Floors to Detect Ghostly Visitants—Intelligence of Ghosts—Pauper Ghosts—The *Shen* of Offence—The Ghost in a Chinese Farce—Idol Ghosts—Ghosts Permitted to Revisit the Earth—Charms against Malevolent Ghosts—Animal Ghosts, ...pp. 71-79.

CHAPTER VIII.

WITCHCRAFT AND DEMONOLOGY.

Antiquity of Witchcraft in China—Witches not Persecuted in China—Summoning Genii—Chinese Ideas of Genii—Taoistic and Confucian Opinions respecting them—Celebrated Genii—Isles of the Genii—Clay Images of Persons whom it is desired to Injure—Paper and Feathers as used by Wizards—The *Mao-shan* and *Shan-ching-kwei*—Demon Monsters—Taoistic Chiefs of the Genii—People possessed by Spirits—"Devil Dancers"—Reputed Powers of Christian Converts as Exorcists—Charm against Witches—Cats and Witchcraft—Hares, &c.—Tigers—Carp, &c.—Dragons—Foxes and Demonology—Curious Fox Stories—Fox Myths amongst the American Indians and Japanese—Stones possessed by Spirits, ...pp. 79-96.

CHAPTER IX.

ELVES, FAIRIES, AND BROWNIES.

Chinese Ideas regarding Fairies—Fairy Haunts—Storm Fiends—Rip van Winkle Legends and Fairies—The Fairy Home—Brownies—The *Shan-sao*—Stealing the Fairy Dress—Fairy Flies and Bees—Chinese Kelpies—The Goddess of the Palace of the Moon—Fairy Tales—The word *Shen* and its meanings, ...pp. 97-102.

CHAPTER X.

SERPENTS, DRAGONS, FABULOUS ANIMALS, AND MONSTERS.

The Serpent and Universal Legend—Healing Qualities of Serpents' Flesh—Human Beings assuming Serpent form—British Parallels—The Fuhkien Snake Story—Serpent Worship and its Temples—Serpents as River Gods—Precious Stones in the Heads of Serpents—The Snake and the Butcher's Block—Dragons and their Serpent Origin—Serpent Worship in India and China—Five-Clawed Dragons—British Dragons—Chinese Description of the Dragon—River Dragons—Domestic Dragon Worship—Ah Tseung and the Bob-tailed Dragon—Chinese Version of St. George and the Dragon—The Phœnix and Unicorn—The Blood-yielding Baboon—Sea Serpents and Strange Fish—Mermaids and their Original Home—Popular Beliefs respecting the Straits of Hainan, ...pp. 102-115.

CONTENTS.

CHAPTER XI.
SUPERSTITIONS REGARDING THE POWERS OF NATURE.

The Sun, Moon and Stars, and Beliefs regarding them—The Lunar Goddess, Frog, Toad, Hare, &c.—Planetary Influences—Cosmical Phenomena and Native Records—The "Old Man of the Moon"—The Goddess of the Moon—The Lunar Hare and its Legend—The Moon and Tides—The Sun and Chinese Beliefs regarding it—Stars and Planets, Chinese Legends respecting them—The Mirage—Meteors and their Portentous Attributes—Thunder and Lightning—The God of Fire—A Peking Legend—"Fire Pigeons"—Mountains and their Presiding Divinities—Legends respecting the Formation of Islands—The Rain God and his Misdeeds—A would-be "Rain-priest"—Superstitions as to Tides—Earthquakes—Natural Hairs—Blood from the Sky—The Legend of Lake Man—Emission of the *Chiao*—Blood from the Earth—Dragons and Waterspouts—Human Beings Transformed into Stone—A Fall of Chinese Manna,..pp. 115-128.

CHAPTER XII.
LEGENDS OF LOCALITY, HOUSEHOLD TALES, &c.

Numerous Legends current amongst the Chinese—The Yangtsze and Yellow River—The Entrance to Purgatory—The Demons of Teng-chow—Imprisoned Genii—The Golden Cup of Hercules and Pei-tu—The Valley of the White Deer—Spirits of the Gorges—Transformed Dogs—The Source of the Hwang Ho—Mountain of the Genii—The Legend of the Bell—*Pro patriâ mori*—A Chinese Ali Baba—The Loadstone—Magic Tombs—Good Deeds Rewarded—Words Engraved upon the Heart—Punch and Judy Shows and their Origin—Legendary Origin of Tea—Origin of the Cocoa-nut—Mercury and the Philosopher's Stone—The Judgment of Solomon—Magic Bread—The Swan Maidens and a Lewchewan Legend—Use of Household Tales and Legends for Comparative Purposes—Chinese Story Radicals,..pp. 129-145.

CHAPTER XIII.
FABLES AND PROVERBIAL LORE.

Chinese Fables numerous—Absence of Native Collections of Fables—Indo-Chinese Fables—Mr. Thom, and his Translation of Æsop—The Earliest Chinese Fable—Comparative Antiquity of the Fable in China and Greece—The Cat and the Mice—Offering a White Pig—Men and Snakes—The Ass and the Oxen—The Tiger and the Monkey, Ass, Fox, &c—The Geese and the Tortoise—The Brother's Boots—The Crows and the Owls—The King and the Mill Horses—Borrowing Trouble—The Blind Man and the Lame Man—The Folly of Avarice—Proverbs, their Extensive Use in China—Writings of Messrs. Lister and Scarborough—A Comparison of well-known Chinese and English Proverbs—The Chinese word for "Heaven"—Conclusion,..pp. 146-156.

ERRATUM.

In the footnote, page 84, the paragraphs quoted are wrongly attributed to Mr. C. T. Gardner. They are by an unknown writer in a Shanghai journal.

THE FOLK-LORE OF CHINA.

I.—INTRODUCTORY.

The attention which has of late been attracted to the study of European and Asiatic folk-lore happily renders unnecessary any apology for an effort to bring to the knowledge of English readers the vast, and as yet almost unworked, field of which it is the design of these pages to treat. The numerous and in many cases able works recently published have not only placed at the disposal of students a vast mass of facts bearing on the science, but have so fully vindicated its claims to the consideration of the ethnologist and philologist, that any introductory essay in the same direction is unnecessary. The labours of Professor Max Müller, the Brothers Grimm, Baring Gould, Kuhn, Kelly, Thorpe, Dasent, Wilson, Ralston, and Spence Hardy, of Muir, Bleeke, and others, have satisfactorily paved the way for successors in the field. The widespread traditions of the Aryan family, down to the homely superstitions of our own peasantry, the myths of Oceanica and the popular tales of Scandinavia, have alike received illustration, and often erudite comment from capable pens. In endeavouring to do for the folk-lore of China what has been so well done for that of other countries I shall in one respect enjoy an exceptional advantage. No serious attempt has yet been made to prove its kinship with the familiar beliefs of the Aryan races; and the following pages may therefore claim, on the score of novelty alone, an attention which might otherwise be denied them.

That a population so enormous as that which owns the nominal sway of the Dragon Throne—variously estimated at from 250,000,000 to 400,000,000—should present a field of most interesting enquiry, is less strange than that so few enquirers should as yet have essayed to explore it. The extreme difficulties of the language and the fact that few who study it for even conversational purposes do so except for a specific end, and to fulfil some defined duty, have doubtless mainly contributed to this state of affairs. Whatever the cause, however, the fact remains that the folk-lore of the oldest and most populous nation of the globe, rich in the traditions of a period to which modern history is but a thing of yesterday, has been hitherto almost ignored by even the most successful students of Chinese. Those least acquainted with the people and their customs need not be assured that in China, as in most other parts of the world, there are certain subjects regarding which quaint and curious superstitions, beliefs and practices obtain amongst the populace. Unlike the civilized nations of Europe and America, however, China numbers amongst believers in the truth of these superstitions a vast public of some pretensions to education—such as it is— and of social position in the eyes of their countrymen. The doings of every Chinaman, from Emperor to coolie, are affected and guided by astrological portents, divinations, etc., in which even the more highly educated, who affect to despise them, place a *practical* trust. The half-cynical disbelief of the mandarin and literate, becomes firm conviction in the peasant; and China presents the now-a-days singular spectacle of an entire nation, numbering over three hundred millions of souls, whose everyday life is framed to meet the exigencies of a puerile system of superstition.

It must not, however, be supposed that these superstitious beliefs differ to any material extent from those current amongst humanity elsewhere. The variations will be found to lie rather in detail than in principle; and just as white replaces black for the mourning colour, but leaves untouched the custom of adopting a special costume as a sign of grief, so it will be found that a variation or even apparent contradiction in the beliefs we are about to deal with are in like manner the outcome of motives common to the inhabitants of almost all countries alike. Thus, the Scottish custom of opening the windows of the room in which a person has died, to give the soul free egress, is, in some parts of China, paralleled by the practice of making a hole in the roof. The Lancashire superstition as to the "first foot" on New Year's Day finds its Chinese counterpart in the dislike expressed to meeting a woman or a Buddhist priest under such conditions. I forbear to here enlarge upon such agreements in superstition, as they will be found treated of at length in the following pages. The one grand distinction between Chinese and European folk-lore lies, as above intimated, in the different powers they exert over the respective communities. In the one case it is either a matter only of amused indifference or of interested research to all but the lowest classes of the population. In the other it represents an all-pervading system of regulations believed in or complied with by high and low alike. We must not, however, forget at how very recent a date we, who now pride ourselves on our civilization and enlightenment, were emancipated from the thraldom of similar and equally oppressive beliefs. To turn for a moment to the page of western history, we find that the belief in omens, divinations, &c., has, ever since the earliest times, influenced communities beside whom we incline, with somewhat undue arrogance, to term the Chinese "barbarous." St. Chrysostom and many of the early fathers inveighed against popular superstitions in no measured way. In the eighth century we find a Council of Church dignitaries, Pope Gregory III., Charlemagne and his successors, and the abbots and bishops of Scotland and France, vehemently denouncing beliefs similar in all respects to those in vogue in China. The great Martin Luther himself believed in superstitions as gross as any recorded.* We turn with abhorrence from the story of Matthew Hopkins, the witch-finder, and cannot forget that, almost within the memory of our own great grandfathers, the Puritans of the New World outvied in their superstitious bigotry the worst absurdities recorded in Chinese annals. It is well to recall these matters to mind, because the enlightenment of the present day is apt to sneer too unreservedly at the blind gropings after truth of less favoured races. The popular folk-lore of Norway, Germany and Britanny presents features quite as quaint as those we shall come across in dealing with their Asiatic congeners.

Nor, when we leave the domain of what we may term domestic folk-lore—superstitions as to days and seasons, charms, omens, lucky numbers, &c.,—and ascend to that of myths and legends, is the parallelism between Chinese and Aryan belief less striking and interesting. We miss of course all that can be traced to Christianity; but the powers of nature have appealed as strongly to the wonder and dread of the sons of Han as they did to the races of whom we ourselves are the successors and heirs. "Language," says a recent writer, "in its immature phases, has created, without any conscious exercise of imagination, most of the old-world, pathetic legends, which, different garbs notwithstanding, meet us like familiar friends in the early records of nations so widely divergent that it would be hard to discover any other trace of kinship." I will not here pause to ask how fully this applies to Chinese. The myth-making faculty is in any case the common heritage of mankind; and narrow as are the limits within which it has been exercised by the Chinese, and grotesque as are the forms assumed by its productions, they evidence the same yearning to idealise the mysterious powers of the universe, the same poetic faculty, if more rudely expressed, as has characterized mankind since the Chaldean astrologers kept their lonely vigils, and found in the star-studded heavens materials for the mythic beliefs of the long-forgotten past.

In view then of the interesting and almost limitless field of research presented by the superstitious beliefs of nearly a third of the human race, it is, as I have said, more than remarkable that no one has yet essayed the task of compiling some record of their peculiarities. Scattered allusions to them undoubtedly pervade a large number of recent contributions to our better knowledge of China, while certain subjects have been dealt with more at length—in some cases with much ability. Mr. T. Watters has struck a rich vein of curious information in his articles on Chinese notions respecting Pigeons, Doves, and Foxes; while Mr. Stent, in his paper on Chinese Legends, has given some interesting examples of

---

* Luther himself believed in the existence of a stone (the *œtita*), which superstition gave out was to be found in eagle's nests, and which possessed the power of detecting thieves! It is not, we imagine, generally known that Luther was grossly superstitious—but he was. It is, we think, in the *Colloquia Mensalia*, edited by Lauterbach, that Luther is said to have expressed his belief in, among other traditions, the following—that three toads spitted on a stick extracted poison from wounds; that the swan sang sweetly before death; that the electors of Germany could touch for the scrofula, and that the 38th year of man's life was one of peculiar danger to him.—*Englishman*.

the romances or tales which are current among the Chinese. As Mr. Stent says, almost every place in China has some legend attached to it, the whole constituting a mass of material for collectors of folk-lore, not only interesting from its own quaintness, but useful for comparison with the legends of other nations.* Mr. Kingsmill's discussion of the mythical origin of the Chow Dynasty, Dr. Eitel's account of the curious Buddhist fable which includes the Hwang-ho among the sacred rivers flowing from the Himalayan Lake, and Mr. Mayers's sketch of the rise and growth of the cult of the god of Literature in China, all contain curious and suggestive matter on this head. They deal however only with portions of the subject.

A writer in the year 1798 remarked that " the study of popular antiquities (of which folk-lore is an important branch) though the materials of it lie so widely diffused, and indeed seem to obtrude themselves upon every one's attention, does not appear to have engaged so much the notice of enquirers into human life and manners as might have been expected." But the last seventy years have witnessed an activity in this direction which would allow of the formation of a small library of works dealing only with such matters. It is time that China were added to the list of countries whose folk-lore has been recorded for comparative purposes. And any shortcomings of execution on the part of the present writer will, it is hoped, be condoned on the score of its being the first attempt to deal systematically with the vast array of material at disposal.

Any arrangement of subjects is of course arbitrary; but I shall endeavour to follow what seems to me the most natural order of sequence; and I must here be pardoned for devoting a short space to explaining what I conceive that order to be. The unstudied arrangement of many able works on European folk-lore, although perhaps adding additional charm to their perusal on the part of the general reader, somewhat militates against their use for handy reference by those who care to study them for the sake of comparison. It is therefore much to be desired that some general system could be agreed upon by those who care to make this entertaining subject a matter of serious research. With some diffidence I adopt an arrangement which deals in the first instance with superstitions personal to the individual, such as those relating to birth, marriage and death—superstitions which we find equally disseminated amongst the most degraded and the most civilized peoples of the earth. To these succeed the beliefs accorded to the good or evil luck attaching to days or seasons. Next to them come the credence placed in lucky numbers, portents, auguries and dreams, succeeded by the popular beliefs in charms, spells and divinations. These are followed by accounts of popular superstitions—such as those relating to drowned men, the last piece of edible left upon a plate, the virtues of human blood, &c. Entering the domain of the more technically supernatural, but still dealing with beliefs immediately affecting the happiness or misery of mankind, we come to witchcraft and demonology,—sprites, elves and fairies, such as those who, to quote a native composition, " come in clouds and go in mist;" who make use of " grass that when cut makes horses, or beans that when scattered become fighting men."†

* See *Report N. C. B. R. A. S.*, 1873.   † Wade's *Wen ta pien*, Ch. XVIII.

Ghosts and apparitions are naturally connected with the foregoing. The next section refers to dragons, serpents, fabulous animals, and monsters, which play as important a part in the popular legends of China as in those of Christendom. Long before our patron saint St. George slew the monster so long depicted on the now extinct five-shilling piece, a doughty Chinese champion (a lady, by the way) had performed a similar feat, and had been also embalmed in popular memory; while the snake, regarded with not less awe as an incarnation of the supernatural in China than in Europe, figures conspicuously in her legendary lore. Natural phenomena, such as typhoons, earthquakes, floods, &c., which I next deal with, have naturally, here as elsewhere, been attributed to supernatural influence from time immemorial. Legends form the next division of our subject, commencing with those of locality; for the hills and vales of Cathay have their haunted spots, and its cities too have their haunted houses. Legends of Locality and Household Tales conclude this branch of the subject, a selection of the best known, and those of an essentially popular nature, being alone given. Fables and Proverbial Lore complete the series; but the latter has been too fully dealt with in separate works and essays to render more than passing reference to its characteristics necessary.

Briefly tabulated, then, the Chapters will be arranged in the following order:—

A—SUPERSTITIONS AS TO PERSONAL FORTUNE.
    Birth, Marriage, Death.
    Days and Seasons.
    Portents, Auguries, Dreams, Lucky Numbers.
    Charms, Spells, Amulets and Divinations.

B—SUPERSTITIONS AS TO VARIOUS SUBJECTS.

C—SUPERSTITIONS INVOLVING THE INTERFERENCE OF SUPERNATURAL POWERS.
    Ghosts, Apparitions and Supernatural Beings.
    Witchcraft and Demonology.
    Elves, Fairies and Brownies.
    Serpents, Dragons, Fabulous Animals and Monsters.
    Superstitions regarding the Powers of Nature.

D—LEGENDARY FOLK-LORE.
    Legends of Locality, Household Tales, &c.

E—FABLES AND PROVERBIAL FOLK-LORE.

That it is difficult in all cases to draw the precise line in classification, those who have paid any attention to the subject will readily understand; and the most that can be done is to adopt some system which, however faulty, is handy for reference.

The word "Folk-lore" can be applied to many of the domestic traditions of China only as a matter of literary convenience. The word which, according to Mr. Kelly, was invented (or rather first used in its generic sense) by the late editor of *Notes and Queries*,* is indeed the only one in the language which satisfactorily expresses the subject of which it treats, and has met with general acceptance. But there is this difference between most of the folk-lore of the Aryan races and that of China. In the former case it chiefly relates to legends and superstitions handed down from generation to generation by word of mouth; in the latter it necessarily includes much that is to be found in print at every native bookstall. Old Moore's and Zadkiel's Almanacks represent this sort of literature in England, but do not of course contain a tithe of what is current amongst the people. In China such literature flourishes like a rank weed, to the partial destruction of aught else more useful and ennobling. In addition to these native "authorities," a vast amount of material relating to the subject is to be found in the columns of the foreign and native newspapers. The aid thus afforded has been fully availed of in the following chapters, though it must not of course be supposed that there does not also exist a large amount of veritable lore, a knowledge of which has been perpetuated in the ordinary conversational way. The cheapness of the press has indeed proved in China a powerful help in preserving much that might otherwise have died out. The precise form of any superstition can therefore be frequently traced, thanks to this conservative element, and differing versions of popular myths are easily referred to their true origins.

It does not appear that the great teachers of China have done much, except in an indirect way, to encourage popular superstitions. But faint references—and those chiefly to ceremonial matters—are to be found in the classics, nor does popular belief credit Confucius, Mencius, Lao-tzŭ, and others with more than inferential approval of the superstitions current in their own day. The principle of filial reverence for age has probably contributed more than anything else to imbue the minds of the people with a respect for anything, from a porcelain bowl to an aphorism or proverb, which savours of antiquity; and folk-lore shares with ethics the benefits of the national bias. As regards details, the folk-lore of China is much the same as that of Europe, with here and there some unexpected contradictions. Many of these superstitions are, and of course must be, equally childish, whether finding their home in a Cornish hamlet or a Chinese town; but it is none the less interesting to find that they often exist in almost identical shape in places so far asunder. To the mind of the present writer they convey far deeper assurances of a common origin between differing races than the often untrustworthy resemblances of isolated words in their respective tongues.

It will probably be found that the theory which refers the greater portion of the folk-lore of Europe to the Oriental cradle of the Aryan races, from whence it was disseminated by their migrations westward, is equally applicable to the folk-lore of China. The first-named supposition has been ably supported by Kelly and his brother workers, and if, as is believed, equally strong grounds can be shewn for adopting the second, a contribution of some importance to ethnology,

---

* Kelly's *Indo-European Traditions and Folk-lore*, Preface, p. ix.

INTRODUCTORY.

and indirectly to philology, will have been made. And it is difficult, when the domestic superstitions of Scotland or the tales of New England witchcraft, the drear legends of Iceland or the myths of Thuringia are found to be almost identical with beliefs in little-known China,—when the almond-eyed mother of Kwangtung is found repeating to her offspring the mystic nonsense uttered by her Hindoo or Turkish sister, as she too, under other skies, listens to the prattle of childish tongues—it is, I say, difficult to deny that a strong case has been made out for a common fount whence the folk-lore of at least two continents has flowed Eastward and Westward in ever-accumulating streams. I need not here refer to such essentially related peoples as the Japanese, Tibetans, Mongolians, &c., whose superstitions are so analogous to those of the Chinese as to be fairly classed under the same head. Such information as has been available respecting them, will be found collated in its proper place.

I have slightly touched in a preceding paragraph upon the unusually widespread belief accorded in China to signs and omens, legends, charms, &c., and a passing remark as to the extent to which this belief obtains may not be out of place. The Court of China, like courts elsewhere, sets the fashion in this as in other matters, and both the marriage of the late Sovereign and the recent accession of the new infant Emperor has afforded an apt illustration of how thoroughly superstition is interwoven with the political system of the country. Thus, at the marriage of Tung-chi with Ah-lu-te, the young lady received amongst the bridal gifts ten pieces of green and white jade called *ju-i**—"Heart's delight." They were of mystic import, being supposed to possess the power of conferring joy and happiness on their owner.† The lucky days for the various ceremonies were fixed by the court astrologers, and nothing was done without reference to their predictions. Such phrases as "so and so being a lucky day, His Imperial Majesty will proceed &c.," are of constant occurrence in the court circulars. But the burdens laid upon the august inhabitants of the "Forbidden City" are but light compared to those borne by the rest of the people. Whether it be to build a house or assume office, to marry a wife or open a school, to set out on a journey or complete a bargain, nothing can be done by any Chinese without reference to Geomancy. Nor are more homely details less under the control of superstitious belief. Every act connected with birth, marriage or death, the bringing up of children and the enterprises of manhood, are alike referred to some detail of this curiously all-pervading system. The superstitions indeed exist amongst ourselves, those really affected by them being only the most ignorant of the population. But in China all are, or assume to be, firm believers in the occult influences of the charm or incantation which custom decrees shall be used. The veriest "Lancashire witch" was no more a slave to her own belief in witchcraft than are average Chinese to their faith in the virtues of divination. Folk-lore therefore assumes in China a place almost unknown to it elsewhere, and no student of the manners and customs of its people can overlook its influence on their every-day life.

* 如意. † *Marriage of the Emperor of China:* By L. M. F., p. 25.

II.—BIRTH, MARRIAGE AND DEATH.

In China, as throughout the western world, curious superstitions attach to human life in all its various stages. The hour and day of an infant's birth are as much a matter of solicitude to the Chinese female as to the "wise woman" of our own North-country hamlets.* The queer-looking almanacks to be found amongst the stock of every native bookshop or stall, invariably contain a series of figures representing a fanciful deity, whose title may be rendered as that of the Emperor "Four Quarters" or "All the Year Round," each figure having one of the horary characters placed on some portion of its person. Thus, during the spring quarter the sign for from 11 to to 1 o'clock a.m. appears on the forehead; that for from 9 to 11 o'clock on the shoulder; that for from 1 to 3 o'clock upon the stomach; etc. (See illustration). When a child is born these diagrams are consulted, and according as the hour mark occurs upon the forehead, shoulders, hands, legs or other portion of the body, so they augur the future destiny of the child. Thus title and degree will be the lot of him who is born at noon. The child who makes his appearance between 9 and 11 o'clock will have, in the familiar words of the gypsy, "a hard lot at first, but finally great riches." Toil and sorrow, however, will be the portion of the unlucky baby who first sees the light between 3 and 5 a.m., or p.m., and so on.†

The following verses have been kindly placed at my disposal by a friend, who has taken the trouble to put into rhyme some of the doggrel that accompanies the diagrams above referred to:—

THE RHYME OF THE EMPEROR "ALL-THE-YEAR-ROUND."

> In birth, the Emperor's *forehead* shows
> A fate that never sorrow knows,
> Plebeians that rich and honoured be
> And rise to title and degree,
> The rank they seek is still bestowed;
> Nobles that follow a worthy lord
> And women, chaste and well-beloved,
> Wed and breed scholars true and proved.

---

* Children born between midnight and dawn are thought by the North country folk to be endowed with a sort of second sight, "so that they see spirits," or, as a nurse puts it, "are bairns that see more than other folk."—See Henderson's *Notes on Folk-lore*, p. 3.

† If the Chinese lay great stress on the *hour* of birth, we no less attribute to the *day* a talismanic influence over the future of the newborn child; as witness the goodwives' rhyme:—

> Monday's child is fair of face,
> Tuesday's child is full of grace,
> Wednesday's child is full of woe,
> Thursday's child has far to go,
> Friday's child is loving and giving,
> Saturday's child works hard for its living,
> But the child that is born on the Sabbath day
> Is blythe and bonnie, and good and gay.

Or, as another version has it:—

> Born on a Sunday a gentleman,
> Born on a Monday fair of face,
> Born on a Tuesday full of grace,
> Born on a Wednesday sour and glum,
> Born on a Thursday welcome home,
> Born on a Friday free in giving,
> Born on a Saturday work hard for your living.

The Emperor's *hands* in birth portend
The gains that handicraft attend

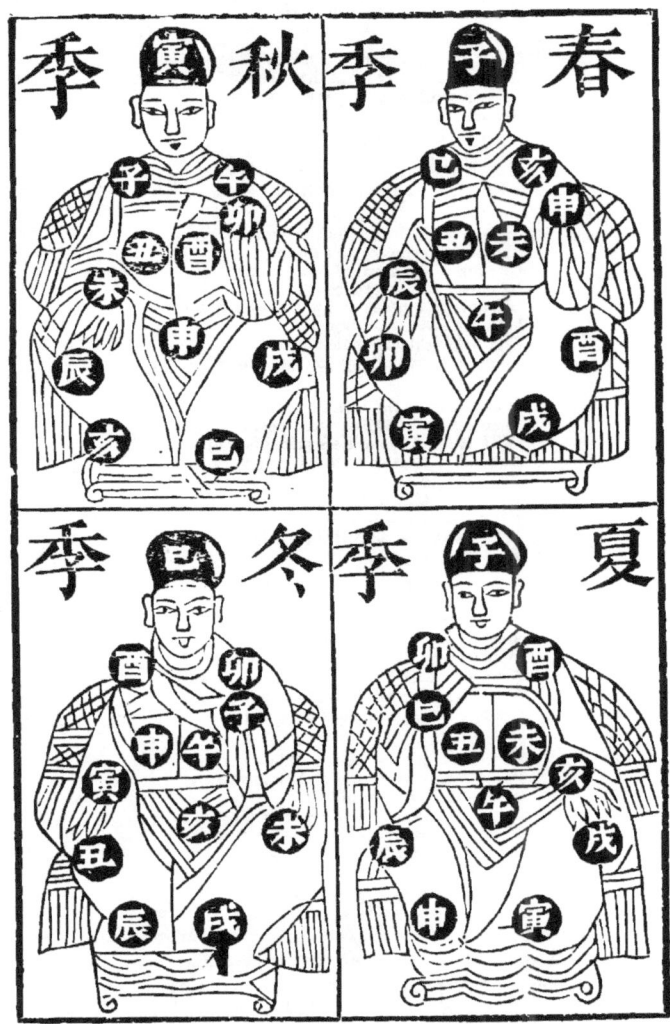

Abroad, a welcome rich and free,
As home, a well-found family;

One year shall yield a plenteous store,
Next year shall make that plenty more,
Wealth shall flow in on every side,
Wealth with old age shall still abide.

The Emperor's *shoulders* mean, I trow,
An heir to goodly gifts that grow
To more and more as years draw on,
Grandsons and sons to honour come,
Rank comes too when the time is fit,
Old age brings fields and farms with it;
If kith and kin at first were cold
" Bitter, then sweet," is truth of old.

When on the *belly* falls the sign,
Shalt have enough, as I divine,
Of clothes and food, of acts or arms,
Of music and the pageant's charms;
Old age with peace and joy shall crown
Mid-age's office and renown,
And a delightsome halo spread,
Increasing, round thy honoured head.

If on the *loins* the sign be found,
Then rank with wealth and years is crowned,
With honour when life's prime is told
And eld y-blessed with yellow gold,
Yea, though arisen from low degree
His fate is true nobility;
His scions, an illustrious band
Who make a name within the land.

But on the *leg*—the meaning there
Is toil and sorrow, want and care,
Nor clothes nor food enough shall be,
May all thy kin be kind to thee!
Who day by day must drudge and toil
Nor be content for all thy coil.
Yet, when thy bitter youth is past,
Old age shall bring thee bliss at last.

The Emperor's *foot* means this—at last
Peace comes from vigil and from fast,
A life-time of tranquillity!
Have nought to do with rent or foe;
Widowed—renew not married life;
Widower—seek no second wife;
Thy path a wilderness unblest,
Flee to a cell and be at rest!

The practices resorted to previous to the birth of children, either to secure that blessing or to ascertain the sex of the expected infant, form in themselves a curious chapter. An idea that adopting a girl belonging to another family will increase a woman's own likelihood of having children herself, is based upon the belief that each living woman is in the unseen world represented by a tree; and that, just as grafting succeeds with trees, so adoption (which represents the same process in family life) may succeed as regards children. Another superstition is that each woman is represented in the other world by a vase containing a flower. A sorceress is hired to proceed thither and "change the earth." A third way of securing children is to obtain from the temple of the Goddess of Children a shoe which has been worn by her. This is taken home and, being placed beside the image or tablet of the goddess, receives equal worship; and, should the desired object be attained, a pair of shoes exactly resembling the one obtained must be returned to the temple. Sometimes several are taken from an equal number of temples, and in that case the goddess from whom the last shoe was received is rewarded with most offerings. A flower is in other cases taken from one of the temple vases in place of a shoe, and is supposed to be nearly as efficacious.

Shortly before the birth of the child in Fuhkien a ceremony is performed by a priest, with the intention of frightening away the demons who are supposed to haunt the mother for the purpose of destroying her life in childbirth. "The priest recites the classics proper to the occasion. Ten or twenty pieces of a kind of grass cut up about an inch long, and several likenesses of the crab cut out of common paper, are put in a censer and burned. Or sometimes several live crabs, after being used in the ceremony are taken and turned into the street—by way of frightening or propitiating the spirits. The reason why crabs are used is that the name of one of these demons sounds like that of crab, in the local dialect."*

The formula for ascertaining the sex of a coming child is not very far removed from the children's amusement of prophesying by buttons, commencing "Tinker, Tailor, Soldier, Sailor, &c." The mother adds to the number of her age in years that of the month, day and hour she was born: thus if twenty years old and she was born in the sixth hour of the third day of the second month, she would have a total of thirty-one. She then takes a series of pictures of the thirty-six assistants of the Goddess of Children, sold for fortune-telling purposes; and according to the sex of the child in the arms of the thirty-first concludes that her own child will be a boy or a girl. If the number of her age, &c., exceed thirty-six, she commences to count the first picture from number thirty-seven. Childless women also resort to a similar process to ascertain whether they will or will not have children. Those curious to ascertain the religious ceremonies made use of prior to birth may be referred to Mr. Doolittle's work on Chinese Social Life.

It may be noted, in passing, that the Chinese make but little provision whatever for the birth of female children, which are deemed beneath the notice of augury or portent. At the birth of a child of either sex, however, amongst the boating population, a piece of red coloured cloth is hung from the awning of the sampan in which the birth has taken place.†

---

* Doolittle's *Social Life of the Chinese*, Vol. I., p. 117.

† The ring of the door is bound with a *white* linen cloth in Holland—See *Brand's Pop. Antiq.*, vol. 2, p. 72. This appears to have had a superstitious origin quite distinct from the practice into which it has degenerated in England of "muffling" the knocker, so that its use may not disturb the mother and child.

A superstition obtains in the southern provinces that if three children appear at a birth one of them will eventually become a noted rebel, and it hence becomes a question of "Which is Papa going to keep?" if the luckless father would avoid that direst of Chinese curses, a thoroughly bad son. To decide the question a "wise man" is sent for, by whose directions the three infants are taken into a perfectly dark room. The wise man then takes three pieces of string, each of a different colour, such as white, red and black, and entering the room ties one of these pieces of string round a wrist of each baby. The one that is found when brought out into the light to have the red string on its wrist is drowned like a puppy.* Presuming however that the little one has not had such ill-luck as to be the odd one of three, it still undergoes within an hour or two of birth the ceremony of "binding the wrists." A cash or charm is tied to this part of the arm by means of red cords, which are not untied for some ten or twelve days. Others attach miniature toys, such as a mallet, drum, bell, &c., the red cords being about two feet long altogether, with one foot of loose string between them. Sometimes, however, the cord or tape alone is used, being replaced when dirty, but worn altogether for several months or even a year.† This of course has reference to the dread lest evil spirits should harm the child, and the impelling motive finds expression in other countries in a not quite dissimilar way. Thus the Danish women place amulets (garlic, salt, bread and steel) over the cradle of a new-born infant before depositing it therein;‡ while a superstition formerly obtained both in England and the Highlands that a child should not be left alone until it was christened lest it should be stolen or changed by fairies.§ A practice common amongst nurses is to pass a knife edge downward between the feet of a child just as it commences to run alone. This is called "cutting the cord of his feet," and is supposed to facilitate his learning to walk.‖

There is a curious little piece of folk-lore, common alike to the Middle Kingdom and our own fatherland, which I lighted upon by accident. A wide-spread superstition exists at home against rocking a "toom," or empty cradle.¶ Now, strangely enough, Chinese nurses in the South of China have precisely the same

---

* The Romans admired the number 3, and numerous Western superstitions are based on its being regarded as a "lucky number."—See *Predictions Realized*, by H. Welby, p. 15.

† Doolittle's *Social Life of the Chinese*, p. 121. Mr. Doolittle refers the tying of the wrists to a different motive. "It is," he says, "thought that such a tying will tend to keep the child from being troublesome in after life and from meddling with what does not belong to it, just as though he or she was bound. When boys or girls are naughty or troublesome they are often asked *if their mammas did not bind their wrists?* Implying that if their wrists had been properly bound when an infant they would have been restrained from misconduct in subsequent life." I am disposed, however, to refer the *origin* of the custom to the belief I have stated in the text, though the Chinese of to-day may look upon it rather as symbolical than efficacious as regard demons.

‡ Brand's *Pop. Antiq.*, vol. II. p. 78.

§ The modern Greeks entertain a similar belief referring to the first eight days of a child's life.

‖ *Social Life of the Chinese*, vol. I. p. 127.

¶ The first verse of a fragment given in Henderson's *Folk-lore of the Northern Counties* says:—
"Oh rock not the cradle when the baby's not in,
For this by old women is counted a sin,
It's a crime so inhuman it may na' be forgi'en,
And they that would do it ha'e lost sight of heaven."

belief. A little four-year old girl, who is a very intimate acquaintance of mine, not long ago began rocking the cradle in which her newly-born sister was usually laid to sleep. An amah who saw her, rushed at the child, exclaiming "You no makee rock so fashion! That baby b'long die, s'posie rock." As it happened the infant did die, as was fully expected by the medical attendant: but of course the amah found in the anticipated fact a verification of her prediction, and farther enquiry has satisfied me that the superstition is identical with and quite as widespread as our own. The resemblance of belief here certainly seems something more than accidental.

The ceremonies observed shortly after the birth of a child are curious. A package of seed, rush (such as is used for candle wicks), cat's and dog's hair, onions or garlic, a pair of chopsticks, and some charcoal, is in Fuhkien tied up with red string in a piece of red paper and suspended on the outside of the door where the mother is lying.* In the extreme South some of these articles are omitted. "A pair of the trousers of the child's father are put on the frame of the bedstead in such a way that the waist shall hang downward or be lower than the legs. On the trousers is stuck a piece of red paper, having four words written upon it intimating that all unfavourable influences are to go into the trousers instead of afflicting the babe. The hair on the package outside the bedroom door is to keep the noises which may be made for eleven days by the dogs and cats in the vicinity from frightening the babe. The coal is to aid in making it hardy and vigorous. The onions are to cause it to be quick-witted and intelligent. The pith (rush) is explained as contributing to make it fortunate or successful in life." † On the fourteenth day the parcel and trousers respectively are taken away. Odd as the custom above referred to may seem, it is exactly parallelled by those prevailing in both Germany and Scotland. In the former country it is usual to lay in the cradle a package of snapdragon, blue marjoram, black cumin, a right shirt sleeve and a left stocking; while, on the authority of Mr. Henderson, it may be noted that in Scotland "the little one's safeguard is held to lie in the juxtaposition of some article of dress belonging to its father." ‡ Of the hair of cats or dogs I shall have more to say in a future chapter. But I may remark that a superstition as to the curative and evil-warding power of hair exists at this day in both Wales and Gloucester. §

There is a custom called "Worshipping the Measures" frequently performed by Chinese during the eighth month if they have sickly children. The "measures" are two constellations in the Northern and Southern hemispheres respectively. They are generally identified as the four stars α, β, γ, δ, in the dipper (*Ursa Major*) and ζ, λ, μ, σ, and τ in *Sagittarius*. For the purpose under notice they are represented as two old men, the "Northern Measure" being the god of longevity, who keeps the book in which is recorded the date of each person's death, while the "South Measure" is the god of emoluments. Longevity

---

* *Social Life of the Chinese*, Vol. II. p. 120.
† *Ibid.*
‡ Henderson's *Folk-lore of the Northern Counties*, p. 6.
§ Brand's *Popular Antiquities*, Vol. III. pp. 288-89.

and riches are thus to be secured by worshipping them. The legend in which this custom is based is thus given :*—"A long while ago a certain lad on going into the street one day met an old man who proved to be a celebrated fortune-teller named Kwan-lo. He addressed the lad saying: 'You are a fine boy. What a pity that your life is to be so short.' The lad at once asked him how long it was to be, and he told him that he was to die at the age of nineteen. This frightened the lad, who was already near that age, and he went home crying and told his mother what he had heard. She in turn was very sad also, but told the lad to go and enquire further of the fortune-teller. He did so and was instructed to take a plate of preserved venison and a bottle of wine and carry them to the top of a certain mountain where he would find two old men playing chess. He was told to place the venison and the wine down by them without saying a word, and then wait patiently till they had finished the game, when he might advance and make known his requests. The lad proceeded to do as he was instructed, and was surprised to find two men engaged in a game of chess. After he had silently placed the food and drink by them they kept on playing until they had finished the game without noticing the lad. They then seemed hungry and began to eat of the provisions they saw by their side. After they had done eating and drinking the lad advanced and told his story, weeping while talking, and besought them to save him from dying at so early an age. They heard the lad and then took out their records, and found on examination that his life was indeed nearly finished. They however took a pen and interpolated before the nineteen the Chinese figure for nine, thus making the record read ninety-nine. They then ordered the boy to return home and tell the old man he met in the street that he must not do in like manner again; that the time appointed by heaven was not to be divulged to mortals. The lad thanked the old gentlemen, who were no other than the '*North Measure*' and '*South Measure*,' went home and narrated what had occurred."

The superstitions regarding marriage are as plentiful in China as we should expect to find them amongst a people in which its ceremonies are held in such extreme honour. Of the outward symbols of the married state there is, as we all know, a great importance attaching to the wedding ring. Now it is very certain that the Chinese did not take the idea of wearing wedding rings from us. Yet we find that in certain parts of China, and in Java, the custom of sending the "measure of the finger-ring" previous to marriage is well known. Turning to Chinese annals we find the preparing of a "united-hearts' finger-ring" mentioned amongst the preliminary ceremonies to marriage. More than that, just as the purchase of the ring is considered by us as having morally bound the intended bridegroom, so in parts of China it affixes *legal* responsibility upon him; a failure to carry out the marriage then subjecting him to the penalties of breach of promise of marriage.† Bearing in mind the symbolic nature of a ring in the western world—that of something without end—it is interesting to find a value attached to it out here similar to that we ourselves endow it with at home. In

---

* *Social Life of the Chinese*, Vol. I. p. 131.

† See *Notes and Queries on China and Japan*, Vol. IV. pp. 12, 13.

Durham, for instance, the breaking of the wedding ring forbodes death, and its loss, the loss also of the husband's affection. Not less interesting is it to find that, while our north-country good-wives throw a plateful of *shortcake* over a newly-made bride as she returns to her future home,* the Chinese go through the same ceremony with rice, which is a sign of abundance.† As regards the lucky day for marrying, the Chinese have numerous portents. The first, sixth, and tenth of the month are laid down in the Imperial almanacks‡ as the most suitable, but marriages of course take place on almost all days except those specially noted as "uncanny."

The ceremonies of betrothal are of course deeply interwoven with superstitious observances. When children are thus engaged, a pair of fowls, a pair of ducks or geese, and a few pounds of vermicelli, are sent by the bride's to the bridegroom's family, who retain the male birds and return the hens. Widows who re-engage themselves are prohibited from wearing gaudy—that is, red or other bright-coloured—skirts, and must confine themselves to black, white or blue. A curious superstition also hinges, in the case of betrothals put an end to by the death of the intended bride, on shoes. The bridegroom goes to the house of mourning and asks for the last pair which she wore previous to death. These he takes home and burns incense to for a space of two years, believing that her spirit will be present, enticed thither by the shoes. In thus doing he acknowledges her as his (intended) wife. As most readers will know, betrothals are managed by go-betweens, who settle the match on behalf of the parents without consulting the principals. The first thing to be examined by the agent is the horoscope of the girl in order to compare it with that of the future husband, and, if all preliminaries are happily arranged, certain articles and presents are interchanged which are mostly intended to have a symbolical meaning. If any unlucky accident happens during the three days allotted for final consideration, the negociation is broken off. If all be right, there are provided, in addition to the betrothment cards, four large needles and two red silk threads, and two of the former threaded with one of the threads are stuck into each card. The red thread is supposed to represent that with which the feet of all mortals are in the spirit-world tied to those who are fated to be husband and wife—in other words, it represents unalterable fate. A similar thread is used to tie together the cups out of which the bride and bridegroom drink. I am unable in the authorities at my command (some twenty works on the Folk-lore of various countries) to trace any resemblance to this custom elsewhere.

---

* Henderson's *Notes on the Folk-lore of the Northern Counties*, p. 22.

† In some parts of England wheat was cast on the head of the newly-made bride. The same practice obtains in Sicily. This was also a Hebrew custom. In Russia, when the priest has tied the nuptial knot at the altar, his clerk or sexton throws upon the bride's head a handful of hops, wishing she may prove as fruitful as the plant thus scattered.

‡ Ovid notes the month of May as unlucky for marriages, and the old Roman Calendars forbade them on Feb. 11, June 2, Nov. 2, Dec. 1, &c. For much curious information on this subject see Brand's *Popular Antiq.*, Vol. 2, p. 168.

"*If you marry in Lent
You will live to repent,*"

says an old English north-country rhyme, and numerous are our other sayings about fortunate days for the all-important ceremony.

A curious ceremony is frequently observed shortly before a marriage takes place. The wedding garments of the bride, and in some cases those of the bridegroom, are placed in succession in a sort of bamboo sieve which is then passed over a fire kindled in a brazier. In Fuhkien it is customary while this operation is being performed to repeat sentences like the following: "A thousand eyes, ten thousand eyes we sift out; gold and silver, wealth and precious things we sift in."* The ceremony is supposed to have a purifying effect, evil influences being thereby warded off. No female must, however, touch the bride's clothes after undergoing this process until she is married—especially a pregnant woman or one in mourning. Another superstitious custom consists in placing five cash of the reigns of five different emperors under the bed mat, and hanging up five bundles of boiled rice (each bundle consisting of five smaller ones) tied with red string to the curtain frame.

Amongst the beliefs which, so far as I can ascertain, are peculiar to the Chinese, is one which relates to the first interview of a bride and bridegroom. On such occasions the bride's assistants often request the bridegroom to rub the feet of his future spouse under the belief that his compliance will prevent her feet from aching in future.†

The ceremonies which take place after the first meeting of the bride and bridegroom recall in a minor degree certain superstitions which obtain elsewhere than in China. Thus the bride's face is hidden by a long white veil not unlike that worn by Egyptian women when they venture abroad. This points to a motive similar to that inducing amongst the old Anglo-Saxons the use of the "care cloth," made of white linen, which was held over the pair as the nuptial benediction was pronounced, to hide the blushes of the bride. If the bride was a widow, this was dispensed with, and similarly in the rare event of a Chinese widow re-marrying she dispenses with a veil. The bride and bridegroom after their first interview go through an act of worship known as "worshipping Heaven and Earth." A table is set out, and on it are placed some lighted candles, a lighted censer, and the following articles: two miniature white cocks made of sugar, five kinds of dried fruit, a bundle of chopsticks, a foot measure, a mirror, a pair of shears and a case containing money scales.‡ The fruits are frequently placed on a platter of willow wood, which, as every one knows, is supposed to possess supernatural properties in places other than China. The precise signification of the shears is not very clear to the Chinese themselves, but they regard them as typifying industry. It is odd, however, to find that knives known as "bride knives" formed part of the wedding outfit of our great-great-grandmothers. Mirrors, says Brand,§ "were formerly used by magicians in their superstitions and diabolical operations, and there was an ancient kind of divination by the looking glass." As regards the white cock, I shall have more to say about this bird under the heading of superstitions connected with deaths. When its images made of sugar are used as above described, an attendant breaks off a portion of each and gives them to the newly-married pair to eat. All the

* *Social Life of the Chinese*, Vol. I. p. 74.
† *Ibid.*, Vol. I. p. 94.
‡ *Social Life of the Chinese*, Vol. I. p. 86.
§ *Popular Antiquities*, Vol. III. p. 95.

articles displayed are intended to be omens of prosperity and future harmony. Upon the same table as these are shewn on, are placed two oddly-shaped goblets, which are filled with a mixture of wine and honey, of which both bride and bridegroom partake. Honey plays a similar part at Sicilian marriages, a spoonful of the pleasant, but sticky, liquid being administered to each of the contracting parties by two of the attendants directly the marriage ceremony has been performed.

The candles placed upon the offering table are speedily transferred to the bride's chamber, where, however, they are shortly replaced by others intended to continue burning during the night. I have not been able to trace any analogous custom at Western weddings, but the idea underlying the use of candles in this respect by the Chinese is as old as the oldest superstition. It is thought to be extremely unlucky if one or both of these bridal candles be accidentally extinguished, as it would denote the speedy death of one or both of the parties. Nor should the wax and tallow of which these candles are made melt or trickle down the sides, the tricklings being an emblem of tears, and signifying either that the husband and wife will not agree together, or that they will have much sorrow. If both candles burn about the same time, it foreshadows the death of the bride and bridegroom at an advanced age within a short period of each other. If one burns much longer than the other, it means that either the wife or the husband will long survive the other. Now all this superstitious respect for flame seems to refer to a Chinese version of the Promethean Legend. It does not indeed say that fire was brought from heaven to animate man, but it makes fire typical of man's vital force, and is doubtless a dim fragment of an older legend identical with that of Prometheus. "Candle omens" of a different sort are familiar in Northern England, and amongst the Greeks the brilliancy or dulness of a candle flame was an omen of good or bad fortune. In like manner the lamps and candles used in the above ceremony, and still more directly the large lighted lanterns carried in front of all Chinese bridal processions, find a parallel in the old Roman custom of carrying torches before a bride. The gypsies of Calabria observe a similar custom, as do also, I believe, the Japanese; and there is some ground for believing that it was formerly a custom in England.*

Before leaving the subject of marriage I may note that the number three, usually considered lucky, is expressly avoided in many matters of its ceremonial. At the ceremony of worshipping ancestral tablets and relatives, the latter are invited to bow in return, four times instead of three, as the latter, "being an odd number, is regarded as inauspicious." On the other hand, the bride goes to visit

* The Jews also used lamps and torches in their marriage ceremonies or rather when the bridegroom came to conduct home the bride by night. See Kitto's *Cyclopædia of Biblical Literature*, Art. "*Lamp*."— Hymen, the god of marriage, was always figured as bearing a torch, and there are numerous references to the use of torches at marriages in the classical poets. Homer, Euripides and Virgil refer to it, and Lane in his *Modern Egypt*, I. 201, notices a similar custom in vogue amongst the Egyptians.

Apropos of lamps and lanterns, it is interesting to note that the "Feast of lanterns" is not peculiar to China. The Egyptians had a "Feast of Lamps," as had also the Jews. Josephus states that the latter was founded by Judas Maccabæus in celebration of the restoration of the Temple worship. Other Oriental nations also observe a similar festival.

her parents three days after marriage, and the bridegroom, who follows her to the house of his father-in-law, is regaled with three cups of tea and three pipes of tobacco. The sedan, by the way, in which the bride is borne on such visits has painted on it as a charm the image of a Taoist priest who, according to the legend, succeeded by his magical powers in counteracting the powers of the evil spirits who lie in wait on such occasions to harass and make ill the bride.

The use of bride-cake at weddings appears to be, in some form or other, both of remote antiquity and common to nearly every nation. "The ceremony used at the solemnization of a marriage was called confaircation in token of a most firm conjunction between the man and wife with a cake of wheat or barley." It was and is customary in Yorkshire to cut the bride-cake into little square pieces and then throw them over the bride and bridegroom's head. In China a quilt is held in front of the bride's sedan by its corners, and four bread cakes sent from the bridegroom's family for the purpose are tossed up in the air in succession and caught in the quilt. In neither case is the omen involved in this proceeding very clear, unless it be taken as an offering to the deities who preside over marriages, and in our own case retained as a custom which has lost its primary significance.

The custom of preventing the bride's feet from touching the threshold of the bridegroom's house obtains in China as in Europe. Usually the entrance is covered with red cloth for this purpose. "In some parts of the country she is lifted out of the sedan, over a pan of charcoal placed in the court and carried to her chamber."* Amongst the ancient Romans, "fire and water being placed on the threshold, the bride touched both; but starting back from the door she refused to enter, till she at length passed it, being careful to step over it without touching it."† (A wedding usage in Yorkshire, by the way, is to pour a kettle full of boiling water over the door-step just after the bride has left her old home. Without their having any apparent connection the coincidence of usages is curious.) The ancient superstition mentioned in *Popular Antiquities* was that the bride was not to step over the threshold on entering the bridegroom's house, but was to be lifted over by her nearest relations.‡

One of the most singular coincidences of Chinese with Western intention, is connected with shoes. It is customary at a marriage in South China for the bride to present her husband with a pair of shoes, by way of signifying that for the future she places herself under his control. These are carefully preserved in the family and are never given away, like other worn-out articles, it being deemed, that to part with them portends an early separation between husband and wife. Now, in a work published in 1610, mention is made of an ancient custom, " when at any time a couple were married, the sole of the bridegroom's shoe was to be laid on the bride's head, implying with what subjection she should serve her husband." A writer in an old number of the London *Notes and Queries* (quoted by Mr. Henderson) remarks:—The throwing shoes after the Bride and Bridegroom . . . is usually said to be "for luck," but is rather a symbol of re-

---

* *Middle Kingdom*, Vol. II. p. 59.   ‡ Brand's *Pop. Antiq.*, Vol. II. p 169.
† Platt's *Customs of Nations*, p. 278.

nunciation of all right in the bride by her father or guardian, and the transference of it to her husband. In the Story of Ruth you will recollect that her kinsman plucked off his shoe, as a sign of his renunciation of his claim to marry her. "Over Edom have I cast out my shoe" (Ps. lx. 8), meaning "I have renounced Edom," is an another illustration. So that the ceremony now observed by Chinese brides has in all probability a reference to that current of old in Palestine and at the present day known throughout England.

Those acquainted with Scandinavian folk-lore will have noted how many points relating to marriage turn upon the bride's endeavours to get her husband to do something implying future subjection to her will. Thus if a Swedish bride drop her handkerchief, and the bridegroom, from politeness, stoops to pick it up, his act is regarded as an omen that he will play second fiddle during his married life.* Now the Chinese girl does something very similar, when, it being time for the bridegroom and herself to sit down together, she endeavours to sit upon a part of his dress; † in which case he may conclude that

"I'll be no submissive wife
No not I!"

pretty fairly expresses the bride's thoughts. If he sits on *her* skirt, however, the omen is reversed, though from what is known of Chinese brides it may be concluded that they do not often succeed in being the "one" into which the two are made.‡ There is a point about the selection of the husband or wife which I may, by the way, notice. In China marriages are forbidden between people of the same family name, even though they are not in any way connected. Now in Yorkshire it is very unlucky to marry a man whose name begins with the same letter as the bride's.§ May not the two ideas have a common origin?—both being evidently at one time founded on the idea of blood-relationship. That "Matches are made in heaven" is a confirmed belief in China.

---

* Thorpe's *Mythology*, Vol. II. p. 108.
† *Social Life of the Chinese*, Vol. I. p. 88.
‡ "It's all very well to say that 'the two are made one'—the question is, *which one*."—*American paper*.
§ "If you change the name and not the letter,
You change for the worse and not for the better."
Henderson's *Folk-lore of the Northern Counties*, p. 26.

As a specimen of the absurd stories connected with weddings which obtain credence amongst the Chinese, I copy the following from a Shanghai *Evening Courier* of a few months back:—In some district of Chekiang, name and time not stated, a bride, long betrothed, on attaining the age of 18 made the usual preparations for marriage. At length the bridal chair arrived to convey her to her future home. Her friends went before her to open the door of the chair, but on doing so they started, screamed and ran away, saying there was a large snake in the chair. The bride, possibly thinking they were only in jest, went herself and looked into the chair, and saw, not a snake, but a large sheathed knife. Nothing daunted, she took the knife, put it in the box containing the lighter portions of her *trousseaux*, and ordered the chair-coolies to proceed. The marriage ceremonies being in due time completed, the young couple retired, and the bridegroom then observed that his bride had a moody and terrified look. Questioning her as to the cause, she told him the incident of the chair, the snake and the knife. He asked to see the knife: she gave it to him. He drew it from its sheath, but he had no sooner done so than his head fell off! The bride raised an alarm; the family crowded in. She told what had happened; they refused to belief her, and declared that she herself was the murderess. The Magistrate was sent for; he came, and on hearing the bride's story, asked to see the knife, and, as in the husband's case, when he drew it from the sheath, his head at once

Superstitions connected with death have in all countries obtained credence, and we need not therefore be surprised to find that China abounds with them. "Born hardly, die hardly," is as much a Chinese as an English saying. Even the strange idea (as we deem it) of purchasing a coffin before death is a ¦not uncommon practice in many parts of Germany,* and may be found existing, in remote country districts in England, so that the idea of securing a comfortable coffin is not so purely Chinese as some might think.† There is a striking similarity between many Chinese ceremonies and superstitions connected with the burial of the dead, and our own. One peculiar superstition of the Borders is, that for a cat or dog to pass over a corpse is fearfully ominous. The Chinese have a belief that if a pregnant female animal pass over the dead person, the corpse will rise up and pursue those nearest to it, and if it overtakes any one, strangle him.‡

A home belief in the efficacy of burying the dead in woollen clothes, and originating in an Act passed in the reign of Charles II. "for the encouragement of the woollen and paper manufactures of the kingdom," has its parallel in China. They here think that every one should be buried in his best clothes, but in some localities except the use of *satin* or a *girdle*, on account of the characters which signify those articles being pronounced in the local dialect the same as words signifying "to cut short—sons," and so implying the speedy death of the sons of the family. The usual rule is to select silk, crape, or the finest cotton for grave clothes,§ care being always taken to put two more articles of dress on the

fell on the floor. The newly-made widow was then told to see whether she could wield the knife with safety. She took it, and approaching a large tree made a cut at it. It was cut through by that single blow, while the woman remained unharmed. Here the legend ends abruptly, as inconsequential in its finish as it is grotesque in texture. Yet it is astonishing what excitement was caused in the teashops of the City and Settlement for some days by the telling and hearing of the story.

* A recent home paper contains the following:—In a village not far from Berlin, an old couple lived very quietly upon their little property. Both had carefully purchased their coffins some years ago, as is often the case among country folks. The coffins were placed in a stable, and were used as receptacles for different things, especially for storing up baked fruit, and other articles to be kept for winter use. Not long ago the man died suddenly. The son, who was a soldier quartered at Berlin, hastened at the summons to pay the last respects to his father's remains. In the meantime, the mother had, with the help of another son who lived with her, put all the articles together in one of the coffins, and in the other had duly placed the mortal remains of her husband. By some mischance the first-named coffin was buried, and the mistake was only discovered after the funeral, which, to the great distress of the family, had to be repeated.

† Two or three amusing stories are told of Yorkshire people who kept their coffins ready for use. One of these relates to a man with a projecting Roman nose, who had a place cut away in the coffin-lid to fit it: and another case was that of an old lady who had two holes cut in the sides to let his Satanic Majesty have free egress should he happen to get inside.

‡ A cat was not permitted to come near a corpse in Scotland. *Brand's Antiquities*, Vol. II. p. 233. "All fire is extinguished where a corpse is kept, and it is reckoned so ominous for a dog or a cat to pass over it, that the poor animal is killed without mercy.—Pennant's *Tour in Scotland*.

§ We know an old lady, as blithe a body as ever lived in this world, who, years ago, prepared becoming garments ready for her last journey. David Garrick's widow religiously preserved her wedding-sheets, that they might serve her for a shroud. In 1763 a young married lady was, at her express desire, buried in all her wedding finery, consisting of a white *negligée* and petticoats, quilted into a mattress, pillow, and lining for her coffin; her wedding-shift

upper than on the lower part of a corpse: thus it will have 3 jackets and 1 pair of trowsers, 5 jackets and 3 pairs trowsers, and so on, the very rich being buried in as many as nine upper garments. The corpse is then bound with long strips of cloth, two of which must be white and one red. After swathing, the ends are tied in an "auspicious knot;" and as many of these knots are tied at various places on the body as the material used will allow.

I have already alluded to the custom of using lights at marriages and traced a faint resemblance to a European custom in that observed by the Chinese. But as regards burials the parallel is much more exact. In the lowlands of Scotland a candle is waved thrice round a corpse as it is "sained" or blessed. In China candles are kept burning round the coffin after the body has been laid out, "to light the spirit of the dead upon his way," and a similar custom appears to have obtained amongst almost every people in the European world.* As everybody knows, the coffins of those lying in state are surrounded by wax tapers, which are kept burning until the day of interment. A candle used to be set upon a dead body in Northumberland, and a similar practice prevailed in the Isle of Man; while the modern Jews set a light at the head of one recently departed. Still more exact is the analogy between the Chinese custom of carrying torches before the dead at funerals and that which always existed amongst the ancient Jews, and until very recent times obtained amongst ourselves. Brand, in his *Popular Antiquities*, Vol. II., p. 276 *et seq.*, gives a long account of the uses of torches and lights in this connection.

Amongst the curious superstitions attaching to death in China is one that, if two "cash" be placed in the sleeve of the dead man and then shaken out, the result of the "toss" will signify the feeling of the departed. Thus, if both turn up obverse or reverse, it is concluded that the defunct is perfectly satisfied, while, if one be obverse and the other not, it signifies that something has been wrongly done. These cash are religiously preserved for similar use after the corpse is buried, when a mode of divination by tossing is resorted to, if it be desired to learn the wishes of the dead man as to family arrangements, the respect paid to his manes, &c. It is also customary in China to carefully reverse the direction of the body before putting it into the coffin—a practice to which I cannot find any Western parallel.

was her winding-sheet, and she wore a fine point-lace tucker, handkerchief, ruffles, and apron, and a lappethead of the same costly materials. Diamond earrings were placed in her ears, gemmed rings on her fingers, and a valuable necklace round her neck; white silk stockings, and silver-spangled shoes with stone buckles completed her costume. A Norfolk gentleman preserved such a happy recollection of matrimonial life, that when, at the age of ninety-one, he lay on his death-bed, he gave instructions that he should be buried in his wedding-shirt, which he had carefully kept for the purpose; that garment being supplemented with his best suit of clothes, his best wig, his silver-buckled shoes, black wrist ribbons, and his favorite walking-cane. Margaret Coosins, who was buried in Cuxton Churchyard, Kent, in 1683, ordered her body to be attired in scarlet satin, put in a mahogany coffin having a loose lid, and placed upon trestles in a vault under a pyramidal monument, the glass doors of the vault being covered with green silk curtains. Another example of vanity strong in death was afforded us a few years ago, when a wealthy court milliner left strict injunctions behind her that her body should be enfolded in point-lace.—*Chambers' Journal.*

* Moresin says a candle was an Egyptian hieroglyphic for life.—*Brand's Antiquities*, Vol. II. p. 236.

During the blessing or "saining" of a corpse in Scotland all the windows of the house are opened so as to give the soul free egress. In Fuhkien (where the windows are not quite so large as in European houses) they carry out a similar idea by making a hole in the roof.* Even the superstitious respect accorded to the cock, as capable of being influenced from the unseen world (evidenced by the carrying of a white cock or its paper image on Chinese coffins, so as to allure the soul of the departed to enter it) finds a parallel in western Europe. The Ischortzi of Ingria (Finland) burn a white cock on the festival of St. John when they visit the tombs of their departed friends. A French receipt, by the bye, for raising the devil given by Mr. S. Baring-Gould directs one to go to where four cross-roads meet, with a black cock under your arm; call out *Poule noir!* three times and the devil will come and take the cock and leave you a handful of money. Scandinavian lore also is full of allusions to the same bird.

A superstition prevails amongst the Chinese regarding "watching spirits" to which I am tempted to accord a rather lengthy notice. The unwillingness of the natives to help a drowning man, or any one in absolute peril of life, is based upon a belief that the ghost of the last man killed always acts as watchman of the purgatory into which, according to Chinese belief, the spirit of the departed first enter, and from which he can only be relieved by the arrival of a fresh defunct. If, therefore, a man's life be saved, the spirit of the person who died last before him is, in a manner, cheated out of his relief, and will assuredly haunt the person whose misplaced humanity has condemned it to a fresh term of dismal servitude. Now this belief in a "watching spirit" is essentially Gaelic: and the following extract from a recent issue of the *Inverness Courier* shews a parallelism so close as to be very singular. A correspondent writes:—"I was sailing past the beautiful island of St. Mungo, in Loch Leven, the burial place for many centuries of the people of Nether-Lochaber and Glencoe, when the following conversation took place between myself and an old man who managed the sails while I steered. It was all in Gaelic, of course, but I give the substance in English:—'You were at the funeral on the island the other day, sir?' interrogatively observed my companion. 'I was, indeed,' I replied. 'John——,' he continued, naming the deceased, 'was a very decent man.' 'He was a fine old Highlander, shrewd and intelligent,' I replied, 'and, what is more, I believe a very good man.' 'Donald——,' naming a person we both knew, 'is very ill, and not likely to last long.' 'I saw him to-day,' I observed, 'and I fear that what you say is true: he cannot last long.' 'Well, sir, it will be a good thing for John——(the person recently buried): his term of watching will be a short

---

* *Middle Kingdom*, Vol. II. p. 262. This superstition appears to be perhaps the most wide-spread of any connected with death. When a death takes place, in many parts of Europe, all the doors and windows should be unfastened, as it is thought that the first pains of purgatory are inflicted by the soul squeezing through the closed doors. We have something like this in Swift's "*Journey from this World to the Next*," where the spirits, conversing on their way to the throne of "Micros," relate to each other how they had to wait till an open door or window in the house in which the death had taken place, enabled them to get free from it. There is a curious superstition in Devonshire that the departure of life is delayed where any lock is closed in the dwelling or any bolt shot. See *Popular Antiquities*, Vol. II. p. 231.

one.' 'I don't understand what you mean;' I observed, with some curiosity. 'The man is dead and buried; what watching should he have to do?' 'Why, sir, don't you know that the *spirit* of the last person buried in the island has to keep watch and ward over the graves till the spirit of the next person buried takes his place?' 'I really did not know that,' I replied. 'Is it a common opinion that such is the case, and do you believe it yourself?' 'Well, sir, it is generally believed by the people; and having always heard that it was so, I cannot well help believing it too. The spirit whose watch it is is present there day and night. Some people have seen them; my mother, God rest her! once pointed out to me, when I was a little boy, an appearance, as of a flame of light on the island, slowly moving backwards and forwards, and she assured me it was the watching spirit going his rounds.' 'What particular object has the spirit in watching?' I asked. "Well, I don't exactly know,' was the answer. ' He just takes a sort of general charge of the Island of the Dead, until his successor arrives.' I have since found that a belief in this superstition is common among the old people. The spirit or ghost is supposed to be to a certain extent unhappy and impatient of relief while in the discharge of this office, and thus, it is considered that the sooner after a funeral there is occasion again for the opening of a grave, the better it is for the spirit of the last person interred, who then, and not till then, passes finally and fully to his rest."*

* The following extract from the same journal merits reproduction:—"In many parts of the Highlands it is believed to this day that the last person buried has to perform the duty of sentinel over the churchyard, and that to him the guardianship of the spirits of those buried before is in some degree committed. This post he must occupy until a tenant of the tomb releases him. It is not esteemed an enviable position, but one to be escaped if possible; consequently, if two neighbors die on the same day, the surviving relations make great efforts to be first in closing the grave over their friend. I remember an old nurse, who was mourning the death of a sweet girl she had reared, exclaiming with joy, when she heard, on the day after her funeral, of the death of a parishioner; ' I thank God my dear darling will have to watch the graves no longer!' A ludicrous but striking illustration of this strange notion occurred some years ago in the parish of A———. An old man and an old woman, dwelling in the same township, but not on terms of friendship—for the lady, Kate Ruadh, was more noted for antipathies than attachments—were both at the point of death. The good man's friends began to clip his nails, an office always performed just as a person is dying. He, knowing that his amiable neighbor was, like himself, on the verge of the grave, roused himself to a last effort and exclaimed: 'Stop, stop; you know not what use I may have for all my nails in compelling Kate Ruadh to keep Faire Chlaidth in place of doing it myself.'" In the statistical account of Scotland, xiv., 210, Parishes of Kilfinichen and Kilviceuen, County of Argyle, we read: "The inhabitants are by no means superstitious, yet they still retain some opinions handed down by their ancestors, perhaps from the time of the Druids. It is believed by them that the spirit of the last person buried watches round the churchyard till another one is buried, to whom he delivers his charge." In the same work, xxi., 114, it is said: "In one division of the country, where it is believed that the ghost of the person last buried kept the gate of the churchyard till relieved by the next victim of death, a singular scene occurred when two burials were to take place on the same day. Both parties staggered forward as fast as possible, to consign their respective friend in the first place to the dust. If they met at the gate, the dead was thrown down until the living decided by blows whose ghost should be condemned to porter it." It was the duty of the last person interred to stand sentry at the graveyard gate from sunset until the crowing of the cock every night until regularly relieved. This, sometimes, in thinly-inhabited parts of the country, happened to be a tedious and severe duty; and the duration of the "Faire Chlaidth" gave the deceased's surviving friends much uneasiness.

The Chinese idea of watching the dead—a duty which amongst them devolves upon the eldest son and his brothers until the coffin is removed for interment, finds expression also amongst ourselves. Mr. Henderson, in his *Folk-lore of the Northern Counties*, says: "The corpse must be watched till its burial by one of its kindred and a stranger, who may be relieved, when weary, by another relation and another stranger." In China the incense stick which is straight (emblematical of the "straight road" which the spirit of the deceased ought to travel) must not be allowed to go out lest the spirit lose its way. With us the "Saining Candle" must be kept burning during the night.

The idea of furnishing the dead with food, arms, clothing, money, etc., is essentially Chinese, but by no means confined to them. Mr. D. Forbes states that the Aymara Indians supply the dead with food and clothing.* Horses are sacrificed at the funerals of the Red Indians, and dogs used to be at the funerals of the Aztecs, while camels formed the funeral sacrifices of the Bedouins. The Chinese, less extravagant, consume paper models of money, animals, and boats, with a similar object; and the reminder of the Stygian ferry in the use of paper junks is at least odd.† The belief that the spirits of the dead pass over routes used by the living is in like manner a superstition common to both East and West. The ceremonials observed in this country to facilitate their passage, and the beatings of gongs to frighten away evil spirits are equally observed by the Kasi Indians, who, when the funeral cortege happens to pass a puddle, lay down a straw for the dead man's soul to use as a bridge. An ancient Chinese practice is, by the way, curious. They used to bury the dead in the same position as the fœtus assumes in the womb. I have nowhere met with any modern mention of this custom. According to the Chinese ritual the relations of one deceased assume mourning (made of white hempen cloth) *seven* days after his death. Though in our own case there is probably no superstitious origin in the custom it may be noted by way of coincidence that we usually bury people after the expiration of that interval, which is the first time the mourners appear publicly clad in the habiliments of woe.

A number of curious practices connected with burial and mourning are without doubt purely Chinese. Thus, on the sixtieth day after death, the family place on a table a number of plates containing offerings of food, &c., accompanied by the never-absent incense. Besides these they place on the table a wash-bowl full of water in which is floating half a duck's egg. A paper and bamboo duck, astride of which is a paper human image, is then placed on the water beside it. The image personifies the deceased, the duck his means of transport and the egg-shell a boat. The use of both duck and boat to cross the Chinese Styx is not very clear, but they are probably intended to give the deceased a choice of conveyance. A yet more inexplicable practice is that of placing a paper image of the departed in a wheeled sedan-chair of similar material, to which is attached

---

* Ethnological Review, Vol. II. No. 3, p. 231.

† In Madagascar as amongst the natives of the Carribbees, New Guinea and Kergistan, it is believed that the dead can use the things destroyed as offerings to their manes, such as guns, &c., &c.

a paper crane as if in the act of drawing the sedan. Langed in front of the crane are numerous articles of dress, money &c. (all of course in paper), and in some way the crane is supposed to convey both the spirit of the deceased and the goods on their onward passage.

Our own custom of throwing earth upon the coffin when the solemn words "earth to earth, ashes to ashes" are pronounced by the clergyman, is closely paralleled in China. Directly the coffin has been lowered, the sons of the deceased hasten to scatter earth into the grave. This earth they have previously put into the lap of their sackcloth mourning garments, and they manage to shake it out so as to fall upon the coffin if possible."* The idea thus symbolized is in both cases the same. It is, by the way, to be noted that, in China, when husband and wife are buried side by side, the grave of the husband must be on the left side (the place of honour.) The water coming from a hill on which a grave has been dug is esteemed peculiarly lucky for use and is termed "dragon's water"—in reference to the term usually applied to the hill near to or on which, when possible, sites for graves are always selected.† The superstitious aversion shewn in China to permitting a corpse to enter or be buried within the walls of a city has obtained at various times in many parts of the Western world. The Moors never bury their dead within the bounds of an inhabited place, and the inhabitants of Thibet used, it was said, to be similarly particular, always exposing them on the tops of mountains.

Most who have read anything about China are aware of the great importance attached to selecting a lucky place for a grave. Dr. Williams, in writing on this subject, laments the way in which the Chinese are befooled by the doctrines of *Fung-shuey* in this regard; but we are not so certain that Englishmen, at best, can afford to look down upon China from any very high elevation. A spot free from water and white ants, and commending a good view, while at the same time under favorable geomantic influences, is what the Chinese aim at. Our people of the Border counties, more enlightened, (?) prefer the South side of a churchyard as the "holiest ground," reserving the North for suicides and stillborn infants. A rare tract, published in 1589, sneers at a deceased man because he would not be laid East and West 'for he ever went against the hair." The South wind, says the same authority, ever brings corruption with it.‡ It is quite certain that traces of a very widespread superstition as to the depth, direction and general lucky aspect of graves still exists in England, though now-a-days surviving only in remote districts.

A native practice universally quoted in Europe as illustrative of the contradiction between Chinese customs and our own is that of wearing white for mourning—white being, in China, "an emblem of evil or sorrow." But the practice is not so opposed to European ideas as some may think. At the funerals of unmarried persons of both sexes, as well as infants, the scarves, hatbands

---

* For much here given I am indebted to the *Social Life of the Chinese,* Vol. I. p. 188 *et seq.* Mr. Chris. T. Gardner, of H. B. M. Consulate, Canton, has also kindly furnished me with several useful notes and memoranda.

† See Eitel's *Fung-shuey.*

‡ *Pop. Antiq.*, Vol. II. p. 282.

and gloves given in England as mourning used always to be white. The Chinese do not present mourners with these adjuncts of the funeral, but give in place of them white "crying cloths" or, as we should say, pocket handkerchiefs. It may be interesting here to note also that black is not of universal use even in the West. The Egyptians use yellow, the Syrians, Armenians and Cappadocians light sky-blue, and the Ethiopians grey. Henry VIII. is referred to in Hall's *Chronicle* as wearing white mourning for the unfortunate Anne Boleyn; while Plutarch (Langley's Translation) writes that, "The women in their mournynge laide a parte all purple, golde, and sumtuous apparell, and were clothed both they and their kinsfolk in white apparell." * * * "Of this ceremonie, as I take it (adds the translator) the French quenes toke the occasion, after the death of their housebandes, the kynges, to weare onely white clothying." The motives however of the Italians in adopting this colour were diametrically the opposite of those influencing the Chinese.—"The white colour was thought fittest for the ded, because it is clere, pure, and sincer, and leaste defiled."

The student of Chinese folk-lore will search in vain for any expression of the old superstition regarding female apparitions as harbingers of decease.* The Chinese theory of death is that it takes place in accordance with the reckoning of Heaven, exercised through the power of the God or Goddess controlling the special disease from which the patient suffers. To this latter, therefore, prayers and offerings are addressed, and if they prove unsuccessful the petitioners comfort themselves by remarking that it is the decree of fate. The absence of supernatural ghostly portents in this connection amongst a people so superstition-ridden as the inhabitants of the Middle Kingdom is quite as curious as the existence of its numerous beliefs.

Finally, it may be interesting to point out that the extreme dislike entertained by the Chinese to disturbing a grave, based on the supposition that the spirit of the person buried will haunt and cause ill-luck or death to the disturbers, has been felt amongst Englishmen. Aubrey, referring to the disinterment of the body of Mary, Queen of Scots, says, "it always bodes ill to a family where bodies are removed from their graves. For some of the family will die shortly after, as did Prince Henry and I think Queen Anne." The Chinese also, like ourselves, deem certain hours of the twenty-four more fatal to life than

---

* Why is Death commonly harbingered by apparitions in female shape, according to the superstitions of the East and the North, as well as of classical antiquity? The Greeks held that human life was controlled by the Fates. The Northmen had their Valkyriur, or female choosers of the slain. The companions of Anastasius in the prison at Constantinople saw "the frightful hag, the harbinger of the plague, hovering with her bat's wings over their drear abode, and with her hooked talons numbering one by one her intended victims." And now we are told that the thieves of our Indian cities have found out a way of utilizing this weird fancy. Some "old offenders," in female disguise, go about the streets of Madras exactly at twelve at night and knock at the doors of houses inhabited by natives. "There is a strange belief among the uneducated natives that the she-devil Dengue (the name of the prevailing epidemic) raps at their door at that hour of the night, and that if any inmate opens he will be struck dead by her." The unsuspecting natives —forgetting the hour—open, see the ominous figures, and "many of them drop down in a fainting fit." The visitors make the best of the occasion.—*Pall Mall Gazette*.

others. Recorded statistics in England give them as from 5 to 6 a.m., (maximum) 11 p.m. to 12 midnight, and 9 to 10 a.m. The Chinese hold that noon and midnight are the two most fatal periods.*

III.—DAYS AND SEASONS.

The superstitions of the Chinese concerning lucky and unlucky days are so numerous that, though they scarcely exceed, they certainly equal those which, some 300 years ago, existed amongst our own ancestors. To commence with those referring to periods rather than dates, we may note that the *seventh* day is reputed to possess much the same mystic properties by the Chinese as it was by the Western ancients. This may arise from its being an astronomical period —the moons phases being always spoken of as changing every seven days. But whatever the reason, both the seventh day and the period it begins or terminates is constantly observed in Chinese ceremonies. Thus, for example, the seventh, fourteenth, twenty-eighth and thirty-fifth days after a person's death are specially set aside for mourning observances. The *seventh* day is critical in fevers; and the seventh evening of the seventh month is the great worshipping time for women. But, more than this, we find that the Chinchew edition of the Imperial Almanack invariably marks the Christian Sabbath with a character, signifying "rest or quiet," though simply taken by the natives to mean unauspicious for work. Dr. Carstairs Douglas thus wrote on this subject in Vol. 4 p. 38 of *Notes and Queries on China and Japan:* "In the edition of the Imperial Almanack published at Chinchew (Tsʻuên-cheu-foo) and at Amoy and all the country round, the Christian Sabbath is *invariably* marked by the character *mih* (pronounced in Amoy *bit*), which means 'secret,' 'quiet' or 'silent.' . . . . I have not met with any heathen who can throw any light on the meaning or history of this remarkable character as it stands in the Almanack, though I have made enquiries both among the literati and at the office in Chinchew where it is published. The only trace of its meaning (excepting of course the plain and unmistakable sense of *the word itself*) as used by the Chinese at present, is that it is always placed in that part of the page which contains the *inauspicious* elements of each day, which make it unlucky for doing work. This seems clearly to prove that the original use of the phrase was to indicate 'a day of rest.'" Dr. Douglas then goes on to shew that the assumption of its having

* I find the following paragraph in an old newspaper, but cannot verify its statements:—The least mortality is during the mid-day hours, mainly from 10 to 3 o'clock. About one-third of the total deaths noted were children under five years of age, and they show the influence of the latter still more strikingly. At all the hours from 10 in the morning until midnight the deaths are at or below the mean; the hours from 10 to 11 A.M., 4 to 5 and 9 to 10 P.M., being minima, but the hour after midnight being the lowest maximum; at all the hours from 2 to 10 A.M. the deaths are above the mean, attaining their maximum at from 5 to 6 P.M., when it is 45½ per cent. above.

been introduced by the Jesuits is scarcely tenable, inasmuch as it is *not* found in the almanacks published at Peking, where Jesuit influence was greatest; while if its introduction were so recent it would not probably have found its way into the category of the criteria of lucky and unlucky days, which are always supposed to rest on the highest antiquity. The discussion was finally set at rest by Mr. Wylie, who explained "mih" as being a transcript of the Persian "*mitra*" for Sunday introduced into the Chinese Calendar through Indian astronomers.*
It is noteworthy that the day always coincides with the Christian, and not the Jewish Sabbath.

The fifteenth day of the eighth moon is a day on which a ceremony is performed by the Chinese which of all others we should least expect to find imitated amongst ourselves. Most people resident in China have seen the moon-cakes which so delight the heart of the Chinese during the eighth month of every year. These are made for an autumnal festival often described as "congratulating" or "rewarding" the moon. The moon, it is well known, represents the female principle in Chinese celestial cosmogony, and she is further supposed to be inhabited by a multitude of beautiful females; the cakes made in her honour are therefore veritable offerings to this Queen of the Heavens. Now in a part of Lancashire, on the banks of the Ribble, there exists a precisely similar custom of making cakes in honour of the "Queen of Heaven"—a relic, in all probability, of the old heathen worship which was the common fount of the two customs.

The Chinese carry out the idea of lucky days to a remarkable extent. While we now saddle only one day in the *week* with ill luck, they have selected a number of days in each *month* as uncanny for work, or even amusement.† On

---

* Dion Cassius, who wrote in the third century of our era, gives the explanation of the nature of the Egyptian week, and of the method in which the arrangement was derived from their system of astronomy. It is a noteworthy point that neither the Greeks nor Romans had in his time used the week, which was a period of strictly Oriental origin. The Romans only adopted the week in the time of Theodosius, toward the close of the fourth century, and the Greeks divided the months into periods of ten days [as the Chinese do also]; so that, for the origin of the arrangement connecting the days of the week with the planets, we must look to the source indicated by Dion Cassius. It is a curious illustration of the way in which traditions are handed down, not only from generation to generation, but from nation to nation, that the Latin and Western nations, receiving the week along with the doctrines of Christianity, should nevertheless have adopted the nomenclature in use among astrologers. —*Contemporary Review.*

† It must not however be supposed that in the "Good old Times" our ancestors were one whit better than the Chinese, and I quote the following in full from "*Predictions Realized*" as giving a good means of comparison between the belief of "Christian England" and "Heathen China" in the 17th century.

In an old MS., the writer, after stating that the most learned mathematicians have decided that the 1st of August, the 4th of September, and the 11th of March, are most injudicious to let blood; and that philosophers have settled that the 10th of August, 1st of December, and 6th of April are perilous to those who surfeit themselves in eating and drinking,—continues as follows assigning reasons why certain days should be marked as infelicitous:—

"I will repeat unto you certain days yet be observed by some old writers, chiefly the ancient astrologians who did allege that there were 28 dayes in the yeare which were revealed by the Angel Gabriel to the good Joseph, which ever have been remarked to be very fortunate dayes either to purge, let blood, cure wounds, use marchandises, sow seed, plant trees, build houses, or taking journies, in long or short voyages, in fighting or giving of battaile, or skirmishing. They also doe alledge

the 7th and other days you must not start on a journey, change your dwelling place, plant or sow, go to school for the first time, repair your house, purchase landed property, &c. The superstition as to not starting on a journey seems to be common to all nations. We know the origin of Friday being an unlucky day amongst ourselves, as being that of the Crucifixion.* But it is evident, that an older superstition is the basis of the tradition, and a thorough investigation would probably give us some common starting point for both the Aryan and Mongolian families.

A book in popular circulation in Southern China called the 黃歷通書 (hwang-li-tung-shu) gives an exhaustive return of lucky and unlucky days, from which I extract the following information. It must be premised that the 365 days of the year are divided into sets of twelve days, each being under the supposed influence of a certain planet, a certain zodiacal sign,† a certain terrestrial element and one of the twenty-eight "lunar mansions." There is a further series of twelve terms, expressing the lucky or unlucky characters of given days

that children who were borne in any of these dayes could never be poore; and all children who were put to schooles or colledges in those dayes should become great schollars, and those who were put to any craft or trade in such dayes should become perfect Artificers and rich, and such as were put to trade in Marchandize should become most wealthy, the dayes be these: the 3d and 13th of January ye 5th and 28th of Feb., ye 3d, 22d, and 30th of March, the 5th, 22d, and 29th of April, ye 4th and 28th of May, ye 3d and 8th of June, the 12th, 13th and 15th of July, ye 12th of August, ye 1st, 7th, 24th and 28th of September, the 4th and 15th of October, ye 18th and 19th of November, ye 23d and 26th of December. And thus much concerning ye dayes which are by ye most curious part of ye learned remarked to be good and evill."

In the *Book of Knowledge*, we find the following " Evil Days :"—

"Astronomers say that six days of the year are perilous of death; and therefore they forbid men to let blood of them, or take any drink; that is to say, Jan. 3, July 1, October 2, the last of April, August 4, the last day going out of December. These six days with great diligence ought to be kept, but namely [? mainly] the latter three, for all the veins are then full. For then, whether man or beast be knit in them within seven days, or certainly within fourteen days, he shall die, And if they take any drinks within fifteen days, they shall die; and if they eat any goose in these three days, within forty days they shall die; and if any child be born in these three latter days, they shall die a wicked death. Astronomers and astrologers say that in the beginning of March, the seventh night, or the fourteenth day, let the blood of the right arm; and in the beginning of April, the 11th day, of the left arm; and in the end of May, 3d or 5th day, on whether arm thou wilt; and thus, of all the year, thou shalt orderly be kept from the fever, the falling gout, the sister gout, and lose of thy sight."

A Book of Presidents (precedents), published in London in 1616, contains a Calendar, many of the days in which have the letter B affixed: "which signifieth such dayes as the Egyptians note to be dangerous to begin or take anything in hand, as to take a journey or any such like thing." The days thus marked are :—

January 1, 2, 4, 5, 10, 15, 17, 19.
February 7, 10, 17, 27, 28.
March 15, 16, 28.
April 7, 10, 16, 20, 21.
May 7, 15, 20.
June 4, 10, 22.
July 15, 20,
August 1, 19, 20, 29, 30.
September 3, 4, 6, 7, 21, 22.
October 4, 16, 24.
November 5, 6, 28, 29.
December 6, 7, 9, 15, 17, 22.

* We often hear the warning given by old dames to young people never to go courting on Friday; but, on the other hand, Good Friday is stated to be the best day in the whole year to begin weaning children.

† One of the cardinal principles of astrology was this: That every hour and every day is ruled by its proper planet. Now, in the ancient Egyptian astronomy there were seven planets; two, the sun and moon, circling round the earth, the rest circling round the sun. The period of circulation was apparently taken as the

which in the eyes of the people embody the result total of the astrological bearings of any given day. They are thus arranged and named, though it does not follow that the terms will in any given month agree with the dates here stated:—

除	滿	平	定	執	破	危	成	收	開	閉	建
1	2	3	4	5	6	7	8	9	10	11	12
13	14	15	16	17	18	19	20	21	22	23	24
25	26	27	28	29	30	..	..	..	..	..	..
Very lucky.	Neither lucky nor unlucky.	Neither lucky nor unlucky.	Very lucky.	Neither lucky nor unlucky.	Very unlucky.	Very unlucky.	Very lucky.	Neither very lucky nor unlucky, rather unlucky.	Neither lucky nor unlucky.	Unlucky.	Neither lucky nor unlucky.

The foregoing table shews the practical application of this system.

Thus it may happen that in a given month the 6th, 7th, 9th, 11th, 18th, 23rd, and 30th days of a month are very unlucky.

The 2nd, 3rd, 5th, 10th, 12th, 14th 15th, 17th, 22nd, 24th, 26th, 27th and 29th are neither lucky nor unlucky.

measure of each planet's dignity, probably because it was judged that the distance corresponded to the period. We know that some harmonious relations between the distances and periods was supposed to exist. When Kepler discovered the actual law, he conceived that he had in reality found out the mystery of Egyptian astronomy, or, as he expressed it, that he had "stolen the golden vases of the Egyptians." Whether they had ideas as to the nature of this relation or not, it is certain that they arranged the planets in order, (beginning with the planets of longest period), as follows.

1—Saturn.
2—Jupiter.
3—Mars.
4—The Sun.
5—Venus.
6—Mercury.
7—The Moon.

The hours were devoted in continuous succession to these bodies; and as there were twenty-four hours in each Chaldean or Egyptian day, it follows that with whatever planet the day began, the cycle of seven planets (beginning with that one) was repeated three times, making twenty-one hours, and then the first three planets of the cycle completed the twenty-four hours, so that the fourth planet of the cycle (so begun) ruled the first hour of the next day. Suppose, for instance, the first hour of any day was ruled by the Sun—the cycle for the next day would therefore be the Sun, Venus, Mercury, the Moon, Saturn, Jupiter, and Mars, which, repeated three times, would give twenty-one hours; the twenty-second, twenty-third, and twenty-fourth hours would be ruled respectively by the Sun, Venus, and Mercury, and the first hour of the next day would be ruled by the Moon. Proceeding in the same way through this second day, we find that the first hour of the third day would be ruled by Mars. The first hour of the fourth day would be ruled by Mercury; the first hour of the fifth day by Jupiter; of the sixth by Venus, and of the seventh by Saturn. The seven days in order, being assigned to the planet ruling their first hour, would therefore be—

1. The Sun's day (Sunday).
2. The Moon's day (Monday, Lundi.)
3. Mars' day (Tuesday, Mardi.)
4. Mercury's day (Wednesday, Mercredi.)
5. Jupiter's day (Thursday, Jeudi.)
6. Venus' day (Friday, Veneris dies, Vendredi.)
7. Saturn's day, (Saturday, *Ital.* il Sabbato.)

—*Contemporary Review.*

The 9th and 21st are rather lucky; while the 1st, 8th, 13th, 20th and 25th are very lucky.

From the explanations affixed we learn that the 6th, 18th and 30th of the month shewn, though unlucky in other respects, are lucky for hunting and fishing, calling in a doctor, or pulling down a house. The character 破 *p'o* means "to rend," "break," or "take by storm." The 7th and 19th again, to which the character 危 *wei*, signifying "danger," is prefixed are not quite so unlucky as the 6th, 10th, 18th, 22nd and 30th. The 11th and 23rd, unlucky for general purposes, are particularly so to white ants and other vermin, as those days are lucky for their destruction, filling up holes, &c., the character given 閉 *pi* meaning to "shut," "close," or "obstruct." The 2nd, 3rd, 14th, 15th, 26th and 27th are good for meeting friends, and (as well as the 9th and 21st) are peculiarly suitable for taking a baby out for its first airing.* On the 5th, 17th and 29th one can cut wood, hunt, fish, and, if you find them, catch wild animals. Not long since a party of gentlemen resident in Hongkong went over to the mainland to look for a tiger which was reported to have visited the neighbourhood of Deep Bay, but as they neglected to choose a "lucky" day their success (as the natives observed) was not remarkable. One is hardly prepared to find the 12th and 24th, noted as "neither lucky nor unlucky," recommended as propitious days for worshipping at the temples, making proposals of marriage and moving house. "Cutting out clothes," which is perhaps not a very interesting occupation at any time, is also recommended on these dates.

The 10th and 22nd in the month above given do not carry an invariably lucky status with them, it depending very much upon the month in which they occur. They are, however, always propitious for hunting and fishing. The 9th and 21st, in addition to being, as above noted, good for babies, are fortunate for building, cutting wood, seeing friends, proposing in marriage, marrying, and making and mending drains—a sufficiently incongruous selection of employments. Finally upon the 1st, 4th, 8th, 13th, 16th, 20th, 25th and 28th, anything can be done, while the 8th and 20th are the luckiest days of all.

But New Year's day is for certain things *the* day of luck. According to Chinese belief you may on this date, in almost any year, present religious offerings or vows to heaven, put on full dress, fine caps, and elegant attire; at noontide one should "sit with one's face to the south;" may make matrimonial matches, pay calls, get married, set out on a journey, order new clothes, commence repairs to a house, lay foundations, or raise up the framework of it; set sail, enter into business contracts, carry on commerce, collect accounts, pound, grind, plant, sow, &c. Nor are other superstitions connected with this auspicious day wanting. Like our own old women in the more remote country districts, the Chinese attach considerable importance to the "first-foot" or person first seen after the New Year has set in. A fair man is a lucky first-foot in the North, while a woman is peculiarly unlucky. In China a Buddhist Priest is regarded as the most ill-foreboding mortal it is possible to set eyes on as a first-foot. Another

* In some parts of England certain days are chosen for cutting a baby's nails; Friday is the most unlucky which can be selected.

similarity is to be found in the common superstition that the first words heard in the year will affect the fortune of the hearer for the coming twelve months. In Lincolnshire they arrange with the "first foot" to repeat a lucky rhyme.* In China the women go out secretly and listen to persons talking in the street. The first sentence heard is held to contain a prediction, good or bad, of the listener's luck for the ensuing year.

Another curious coincidence between Chinese and British belief is afforded in the fact that the former people have a sort of "St. Swithin's Day."† Our own popular rhyme is sufficiently well known

> St. Swithin's day, if thou dost rain,
> For forty days it will remain;
> St. Swithin's day, if thou be fair,
> For forty days 'twill rain nae mair:

and I need not more particularly allude to the legend concerning him—how the violation of his grave was followed by the "40 days rain." A correspondent of the *Shanghai Courier and China Gazette* thus writes on the 5th March 1875:— "The first prediction as to the fortunes of the New Year rested on the state of the weather on the first day of spring, which coincided with our February the 3rd. 'Heaven grant that it may not rain a drop to-morrow,' said a boatman to me on the evening of February 2nd. 'If it does,' he continued, 'the crops will be below average for a certainty; and the price of rice will go up.' 'Why so?' I asked. 'Don't you know,' he replied, "that if it rains on '*lih ch'ing*,' (the first day of spring) 'it will rain more or less for forty days afterwards.' A curious coincidence this with our St. Swithin's Day; and it is observable that the Chinese prophets, as well as the authors of the memorial prophecies of the irate Saint Swithin, make their predictions sufficiently elastic to save their credit—'*more or less* for forty days.'" It is noteworthy that the Chinese prediction is seldom verified, and that our own popular prediction is almost equally sure to be false, special observations taken at Greenwich for twenty years having shewn that rain fell in the largest number of days *when St. Swithin's Day was dry!* With amusing agreement there were more wet days than dry ones following the recent 3rd February in China, although that day was distinguished by "a bright sun and a cloudless sky!" Weather predictions in either country are evidently of equal value.‡ The Hakkas (and also many Puntis) believe that if in the night of the 15th day of the 8th month (mid-autumn) there are clouds obscuring the moon before midnight, it is a sign that oil and salt will become very dear. If, however, there are clouds obscuring the moon after midnight, the price of rice will, it is supposed, undergo a similar change.

---

* A recent article in a home Magazine on North Country folk-lore says:—Never allow a female to enter the house first on Christmas Day: it is an ill omen, and will cause loss and calamity to the family. Burn all the Christmas decorations in the shape of holly and ivy by the twelfth day, or your house will be haunted with evil spirits all the year.

† This falls with us on July 15.

‡ There is a rule generally believed in, in South Germany, that if no snow fall at Christmas there will be snow at Easter, and vice versa; the rule being "Weisse Weihnacht grüne Ostern, grüne Weihnacht weisse Ostern."

IV.—PORTENTS OR OMENS, AUGURIES, LUCKY NUMBERS AND DREAMS.

Portents or omens exert, as might be expected, a telling influence on Chinese everyday life, and implicit belief is placed in the effect which will follow certain unintentional acts on the part of any individual. Spilling the salt is held to forebode ill-luck amongst ourselves, and similarly the upsetting of the oil jar foretells misfortune to the Chinaman. The appearance and flight of birds seems, again, to have been regarded as an augury by every nation of whose social life details have come down to us, and it is not therefore surprising that the crow should in China be regarded as an omen of evil, just as it is looked upon amongst ourselves. Our North Country children cry when they see one

"Crow, crow, get out of my sight
Or else I'll eat thy liver and light;"

while a Chinese mutters an invocation against the evil harbinger, its cry being considered so unlucky that when any one about to undertake an affair hears it, he generally postpones action. On the other hand, while our old superstition concerning magpies is adverse to the appearance of a single bird—

"One for sorrow,
Two for mirth,
Three for a wedding,
And four for a birth,"

the Chinese consider the solitary visitor an omen of good luck. A duck quacking as one passes is, they hold, just the contrary. Regarding dogs the agreement of English belief with that of China is singular. For a strange dog to follow a person is regarded in most parts of our own rural districts as lucky. The Chinese say that if a strange dog comes and remains with one, it is an omen of good to his family and indicates that he will become more wealthy.* Cats, on the other hand, are inauspicious beasts, and a display of sudden attachment, such as that just noted, foreshadows poverty and distress. "May kittens should be drowned," according to English folk-lore; but I am not aware that the full-grown animal is deemed particularly objectionable except by sailors, who aver that when a cat becomes unusually frolicsome it portends a storm. Hens also come in for a share of the feeling expressed in the distich

"A whistling woman and crowing hen
Are neither fit for Gods or men."

"In China the crowing of a hen is considered ominous of something unusual about to happen in the family to which it belongs. In order to ascertain whether this event is propitious or unpropitious, the relative position of the fowl, while

---

* Social Life of the Chinese, Vol. II., p. 328.—The Æthiopians regarded the dog as a portentous animal.

crowing, is to be observed. If the hen crows while her head is toward the outside, or the front of the premises, it is an unpropitious prognostication, foreshadowing poverty or ill luck of some kind; whereas, if her head is pointing toward the rear of the premises while crowing, it is an omen of good, indicating a more prosperous state of the family. Few families will keep a *crowing* hen, even should she betoken future good, as extraordinary omens like this are deemed undesirable. The unfortunate fowl is either sold or killed as soon as possible after she has commenced to crow. It is said that if a cock should crow about ten or eleven o'clock in the evening, he is not allowed to remain on the premises long, being killed or sold, as such crowing denotes future evil to the family of the owner."* A precisely similar belief obtained amongst our own ancestors. "Moresin ranked the unseasonable crowing of a cock amongst omens," says Brand; and in Morier's *Journey through Persia*, p. 62, we read: "Amongst the superstitions in Persia, that which depends on the crowing of a cock is not the least remarkable. If the cock crows at a proper hour, they esteem it a good omen; if at an improper season, they kill him. I am told that the favourable hours are at nine, both in the morning and in the evening, at noon, and at midnight." The flight of birds, more especially swallows, is also an omen in Chinese eyes. Classical scholars do not need to be reminded how often this augury was consulted amongst the Greeks and Romans. A Chinaman never wilfully kills swallows. The French of the Mediterranean term them *ames damnées* and have also a superstitious regard for them—a queer coincidence, to say the least of it. Bats again in China afford omens of good fortune. The Chinese name of the animal is *fuk shü* (in Cantonese) or "Rat of Happiness," and its erratic dashes into a room or summer-house are held to augur coming luck to the occupants. With us, similar conduct on the part of a robin redbreast is an omen of calamity.

But these agreements of superstition are not confined to crows, dogs, bats, cocks, and hens. The owl occupies the same position in Chinese esteem as it did in ancient Roman eyes, and as it still does in Great Britain. Pliny called it "inauspicata et funebris avis," while similar epithets are applied to the bird by Ovid, Lucian, and Claudian. Chaucer described it as

"The *Oule* eke, that of deth the bode bringeth,"

and Spencer speaks of it as the bird "that whoso heares doth die." Butler, in his *Hudibras*, p. 2. Canto III. l. 707, refers to the lustration which Rome underwent because an owl had strayed into the capital. Bourne describes it as "a most abominable and unlucky bird," whose hoarse and dismal voice "is an omen of the approach of some terrible thing: that some dire calamity and some great misfortune is near at hand." Brand devotes several pages to quotations, ancient and modern, in the same sense.† Now let us see what the Chinese have to say of the bird of Minerva. "The voice of the owl is universally heard with dread, being regarded as the harbinger of death in the neighbourhood." I shall perhaps

* Social Life of the Chinese, Vol. II., p. 328. † Popular Antiquities, Vol. III., 188.

be pardoned if, for the sake of making this notice exhaustive, I quote the following from Mr. Doolittle's interesting chapter on this and kindred subjects.

Some say that its voice resembles the voice of a spirit or demon calling out to its fellow. Perhaps it is on account of this notion that they so often assert having heard the voice of a spirit, when they may have heard only the indistinct hooting of a distant owl. Sometimes, the Chinese say, its voice sounds much like an expression for "*digging*" *the grave*. Hence, probably, the origin of a common saying, that when one is about to die, in the neighborhood will be heard the voice of the owl, calling out, "*dig, dig.*" It is frequently spoken of as the *bird which calls for the soul*, or *which catches or takes away the soul.* Some assert that if its cry is dull and indistinct, as though proceeding from a distant place, it betokens the death of a near neighbor; whereas, if its notes are clear and distinct, as if proceeding from a short distance, it is a sure harbinger of the death of a person in a remote neighborhood—the more distinct the voice, the more distant the individual whose decease is indicated; and the more indistinct the voice, the nearer the person whose death is certain! It is a common saying that this bird is a transformation of one of the servants of the ten kings of the infernal regions, *i. e.*, is a devil under the guise of a bird. It is also frequently referred to as a "constable from the dark land."

To pass from birds to eggs, it may be noted that a Lancashire superstition that to set a hen on an even number of eggs will result in their being addled, or in the chickens not thriving, exists also in South China.

I have already referred to shoes in connection with birth and marriage, but can find no precise analogy to the "shoe omens" in vogue in Europe—such as the ill luck which it is feared will befall the person who puts a left shoe on a right foot and *vice versa*. Mirrors, however, share in China the superstitious respect paid to their preservation at home. To break a looking-glass is in most parts of Europe deemed a very unlucky accident. "When a looking glass is broken it is an omen that the party to whom it belongs will lose his best friend. Grose tells us that breaking a looking-glass betokens a mortality in the family, commonly the master;"[*] and Buonaparte, having once broken the glass over Josephine's portrait, could not rest till a special courier had informed him of her safety. This belief exists in full force in China. To break a mirror augurs a separation from one's wife by death, or otherwise, and is only second in ominous portent to breaking an oil jar. And this superstition of a connection existing between the mirror and its owner's life is evidenced also by its use in cases of sickness to form the head of a sort of figure made of one of the sick man's coats which, suspended to a bamboo with the end leaves still on it, is carried about in the vicinity of the house in the hope of attracting the departing soul back to its body. Mirrors are also used as charms, under which head their use will be described.

Who has not noticed or heard of the bizarre arrangements of Chinese gardens and rockeries? The motive for this laying out the pleasure grounds attached to large houses is not simply ornamental. No doubt the Chinaman is one of the most ingenious of landscape gardeners, but the crooked walks and abrupt turns not only economize space but are "lucky," inasmuch as they discourage the advent of evil spirits, who like the "broad way" in China much as they are reputed to do in Europe. Now in England, says a recent writer, "Good luck

[*] Pop. Antiq., Vol. III. p. 170.

seems to be attached to everything deformed or crooked. Thus, a crooked sixpence, all England through, is lucky; also placing crooked pins in walls is a very common custom. I never could learn the reason why, although I have known it extended to highways and lanes, such as being cautioned never to build a house in a straight lane, but always to choose (because lucky) a crooked or lane with many curves and turnings." It looks very much as if the two superstitions were identical, but fearful of being too dogmatic I leave readers to draw their own inference.

A recent English writer remarks that "throughout our history, and even in our own day among the vulgar, every eclipse or comet is regarded as the harbinger of some storm, or inundation, or some contagious disease." The sentence may stand as it is to describe the Chinese sentiment, with the slight omission of the words "amongst the vulgar;" for prince and peasant alike believe that the astrologers do not lie. But more astonishing still is it to find that an able writer, Dr. Forster, in his *Illustrations of the Atmospherical Origin of Epidemic Disorders*, gives tables occupying 40 closely-printed 8vo. pages, to shew that the visits of these scourges have really been concurrent with the appearance and approach of comets. He in fact gravely supports the theory held by the Chinese (who by the way say, the longer the comet's tail, the greater the disturbance), so far as it relates to disease. The natives consider a comet to portend war also, and as rebel fighting is generally going on somewhere in the Middle Kingdom, have no great difficulty in proving their case. Stars have, since the remotest antiquity, been held by this people to serve as portents or warnings, generally on the side of order and good government. Some eight years ago the Southern rebels had advanced from Tsao-chow to capture Chi-ning-chow, and as the city was badly defended they would have had an easy task, but for one circumstance that intervened. They fancied they saw on the Eastern road "an enormous red star of an inexplicable nature, within which was plainly visible Kwan-ti in armour, and with a helmet surmounting his fiery face and mighty beard. He darted about at the head of his legions just as he is represented as doing in paintings, and the tumult of his innumerable host was distinctly heard." The rebels were affrighted and fled, and it was officially recorded that "the spirit of Kwan-ti had preserved the city of Chi-ning-chow." As regards eclipses, the popular belief of the Chinese in the fact that the sun or moon is then being devoured by a dragon, and the means adopted of beating gongs and firing crackers to frighten the dragon away, have been held up to Western ridicule ever since books about China have been written. But precisely the same beliefs and practices prevailed amongst the Romans, Macedonians, Medes, Turks, Italians, Irish and Welsh! I need not here quote authorities at length, as they will all be found in Brand (Vol. III. p. 152-3.) But I may note that the Spartan belief that the appearance of shooting stars signified that the king had offended the gods is not very far removed from the Chinese idea that an eclipse is an omen of ill luck to the reigning emperor—a belief curiously verified but a few months back when the attack of small-pox from which the young emperor Tung Chih died was concurrent with the occurrence of a solar eclipse.

Superstitions regarding bells may be classed under the heads both of auguries and charms. The two largest bells in the empire—those at Canton and Peking—are held to possess peculiarly portentous virtues. A native account of the City of Canton states that the *kin chung* or "tabooed bell," as it is called, was cast in the beginning of the reign of Hung-wu (therefore shortly after A. D. 1468, or five centuries ago), but in consequence of a prophecy foretelling calamity to Canton whenever it should give forth sound, was deprived of a clapper and the means of access to it removed. At length one day a rash official directed a man to strike it. No sooner had its reverberating boom been heard, than upwards of a thousand male and female infants died within the city. Some evil spirit had evidently been irritated at the bell being rung, and to ward off his influence infants have, ever since, worn bells upon the clothes. But the prophecy thus vindicated was still supposed to hold good, and advantage was taken of the circumstance by our bombarding force in 1857. It was suggested to the commander of one of H. M's. ships to aim a shot at the bell, and the result was that, as calamity was indeed befalling the haughty city, the unwonted boom was once again heard. A portion of the lower rim was fractured, and the superstition thus recalled to the popular mind undoubtedly contributed to a general belief in foreign prowess.* The belief regarding the Peking bell is less deep-seated, being only to the effect that, if struck by an unauthorized hand, the rain-god will immediately visit the offence by sending down unneeded rain. Some years since, on the writer with a party of friends, visiting the great bell-temple outside the City, the Priests refused to strike the enormous specimen therein hung (it is, by the way, the largest suspended bell in the world), lest the rain-god should be offended. A small present from one of the party however induced them to let the visitors draw back the heavy wooden ram which did duty as a clapper. Strangely enough, as the first blow was struck, a heavy rainstorm came on, and the shaven-pated attendants roared out in high glee, "We told you so!" For once superstition carried the day. It is unnecessary to remind at least London readers that grave disaster to the Royal family is believed to follow the unexpected tolling of the great bell of St. Paul's. Bells, especially if blessed by a priest, were formerly thought efficacious to scare away evil spirits. Church bells have ever been regarded in a similar light; and the passing-bell tolled for a dying man was of old supposed to frighten off the demons who stood at the foot of the bed ready to seize, or at least molest, the departing soul. The latter thus got a fair start, or what sportsmen call "law." "Hence," says the authority I am quoting, "the high charge made for tolling the great bell of the Church," as being more efficacious than smaller ones heard to a less distance.

A writer in *Notes and Queries* states that a Scottish plan for securing good luck, for the space of twelve months at least, is to draw a bucket-full of water from the village well, at midnight, on New Year's eve, and, after throwing a handful of grass into it, to carry it carefully home. If the drawer

* See *Notes and Queries on China and Japan*, Vol. III. p. 22; and *Treaty Ports, &c.*, p. 169.

be a cow-keeper, he uses part of the water to wash his dairy utensils, and gives the remainder to his cows, in the rather dishonest hope that he will thereby obtain the cream of the cows of such of his neighbors as use the well, and have not been so wise as himself. Now this custom finds an exact counterpart in China. Natives living in the neighbourhood of Canton believe that water drawn on the night, or rather after midnight, of the seventh day of the seventh moon, possesses special efficacy in the cure of cutaneous diseases or fevers, if used in the cooking of gruel for a patient. It is, moreover, believed that such water will not get putrid even if kept for years, its efficacy indeed increasing with age. The date above given is reported to be that of the descent of the female genii of the Pleiades, (possibly because the constellation is formed of *seven* stars.)

Omens of personal sensation are as commonly accepted in China as in England. With us burning or itching sensations on the body forebode ill luck or calamities; thus, if you have a shivering fit, some one is walking over your destined grave; if the right ear burns, you will hear good news, but if the left, you are being defamed by an enemy. The Chinese believe that if one of the eyelids move involuntarily, it forebodes good or evil luck according to the hours at which the sensation is experienced, and the eyelid (right or left) affected. As a rule it is an ill omen. Sneezing indicates that some one is talking ill of the person so relieving himself. Any twitching of the flesh or a jumping sensation in the region of the heart always forebodes serious ill fortune (the latter symptom, by the way, often needs no prophetic interpretation); and if a man's second finger shakes, it is a sign that he will shortly be invited to a grand feast. Clothes again, especially trowsers, have ominous properties. Our own goodwives tell us that it is very unlucky to sew a button on a pair of breeches while wearing them. The Chinese give a pair of the same indispensable articles of dress to a young girl commencing to learn sewing, her successful efforts to stitch them together foreboding wealth. Our saying that if two men wash in the same bowl they will quarrel before sunset has a Chinese parallel in the belief that sitting down in a chair still warm augurs that you will shortly fall out with the last sitter.

It has always been deemed unlucky to meet a funeral in most parts of England, and the Chinese entertain an exactly similar idea, especially if the person meeting it is going to a wedding. In fact, many natives will turn back from any business visit they are about to pay if they come across either a funeral or a coffin. There is a quaint saying at home that "Trouble will never come near folks whose eyebrows meet;" and it is also alleged that ladies with overmuch down and gentlemen with overmuch hair upon their arms and hands, carry about them Nature's own guarantee that they are born to be rich some day—as rich as those happy individuals whose front teeth are set wide apart. The Chinese say that "people whose eyebrows meet can never expect to attain to the dignity of a Minister of State;" that "ladies with too much down or hair are born to be poor all their lives;" but that "bearded men will never become beggars." In fact, it is scarcely possible to take up the most ordinary magazine article on

European folk-lore without noting in almost every paragraph strange coincidences either in actual belief or in the subject of a superstition. Even the appearance of a white speck upon the finger nail or an itching sensation of the palm of the hand (both ominous of coming gifts in England) bear significance in the eyes of this mysteriously isolated people. The Chinese note that both the foregoing are omens of coming evil.

The first words heard after making a resolution are supposed in China to be ominous. Thus, if a man who has decided to do a certain thing—say, for instance, recover a debt—hears the first person he meets say *mei-yu* or *m'hai* (according to the dialect he speaks) he will defer his visit. No Chinaman will open a shop, marry a wife, or engage in any important undertaking without casting lots to see if the fates are propitious.* The method of carrying this out is as follows: Each temple in China has belonging to it about a hundred stanzas of poetry relating to a variety of subjects; each stanza is numbered and printed on a separate piece of paper; in addition to this, there are a quantity of lots made of bamboo slips about eight inches long, corresponding to the number of stanzas, and referring to them by number. The individual who wishes to make application to the god presents himself before his image on his knees, and after performing the *ko-tow* by touching the ground with his head nine times, states his name and residence, the object of his inquiries, and whether on his own or another's account. He then takes a bamboo tube containing the lots, and shakes it gently before the idol until a slip falls to the ground. He then rises from his knees and picks up this slip, and places it so that the god can see the number of the lot written on it; he then takes two pieces of wood, each having a round and a flat side. After passing these through the incense, he tosses them into the air before the idol; if they fall so that both round sides are uppermost, the answer is negative and everything is unpropitious; if they fall with one round and one flat side up, the answer is in the affirmative, and the man may go on his way rejoicing.†

A belief in what we term lucky numbers pervades the whole arcana of Chinese life and literature. Mr. Mayers, in the introduction to his admirable *Chinese Reader's Manual*, says: "In obedience it would seem to an impulse the influence of which is distinctly marked in the literary traditions of the Chaldeans, the Hebrews, and the Hindoos, a doctrine of the hidden properties and harmonies of numbers imbues the earliest recorded expression of Chinese belief. So also, it may be remarked, in the teachings of Pythagoras an abstract theory of number was expounded as underlying the whole system of existence, whence the philo-

---

* Confucius himself was not above his countrymen in this respect, for in the *Due Medium* he remarks :—" The reason of perfect ones enables them to foreknow things; if a nation be about to flourish there will be happy omens, and unlucky ones if it totter to its fall. These will appear in the divining herb *sz'*, in the tortoise, and in the airs and motions of the four members. When either happiness or misery is about to come sages will foreknow both the good and the evil. So that the supremely sincere are equal with the gods." —*Middle Kingdom*, II. 276. See Ante, page 6. This inferentially encourages a resort to "wise men" to learn future events, but can scarcely have been intended to pass approval on fortune-tellers.

† I quote this with some slight alterations from a home magazine article, as I could hardly improve on the description.

sophy of the western would become tinged with conceptions strongly resembling those which still prevail on the same subject in the Chinese mind." Mr. Mayers has here indicated the common source of many of those vulgar beliefs now known as mere folk-lore; and humble as that is in comparison with the more pretentious philosophy which he has so skilfully elucidated, it is not wholly without interest. It would seem that the popular saying "There is luck in odd numbers" meets with as much belief in China as in England. I have already noted the fact that the number 3 is, with an odd exception relating to marriage ceremonies, deemed auspicious. Thus they speak of the 3 decades of heat, the 3 powers united in nature (*t'ien, yang* and *yin*), the 3 systems of doctrine, the 3 forms of obedience, the 3 mental qualifications, the 3 powers of nature (heaven, earth and man), and so on, to say nothing of the phrases in which the same number is pressed into service to express real or assumed historical, geographical, and other facts, such as the "3 kingdoms," the "3 armies," the "3 rivers," the "3 heroes," &c.* Mr. Mayers's exhaustive "Numerical Categories," give the following number of current phrases under the first ten numerals.

Under number	2	9 phrases.
,, ,,	3	68 ,,
,, ,,	4	40 ,,
,, ,,	5	63 ,,
,, ,,	6	38 ,,
,, ,,	7	18 ,,
,, ,,	8	25 ,,
,, ,,	9	30 ,,
,, ,,	10	12 ,,

Many of these have of course a reference to popular superstitions. Five and Seven appear to be the favourite numbers in this respect. All the forces and phenomena of nature are based upon the number *five*:—we have therefore, Five active organs: the stomach, the lungs, the liver, the heart, and the kidneys. Five colours: Yellow, White, Green, Red, Black. Five varieties of taste: Sweet, Acrid, Sour, Bitter, Salt. Five elements: Earth, Metal, Wood, Fire, Water. Five planets: Saturn, Venus, Jupiter, Mars, Mercury. Five regions of heaven: Centre, West, East, South, North. And so on throughout nature. And similarly as sounds belong to the phenomena of nature, there *must* be five of them. It does not appear that any particular virtue has ever been held to reside in the number five amongst ourselves. The number seven, however, is as portentous in China as in the Western world. Besides the Sabbathaical use of the number, it enters so largely into the popular sayings of the people that one is tempted to suppose anything but an accidental or independent origin for its adoption. Thus the Chinese speak of the seven passions, the seven spirits; they wish a bride seven children; there are seven lawful reasons for divorce. The "Seven Joys" is a common tea-shop sign. There are the seven Famous Persons of the Bamboo Grove. Seven hands and eight feet is a common expression for

---

* Number three is greatly in favor for luck; school-boys insist that the third time will be fair, or will result in success. There is an old superstition or maxim, call it which we may, that three handfuls of sand on a dead body are as good as a funeral.—*Chambers' Journal*.—Falstaff, in *The Merry Wives of Windsor*, is entrapped a third time in the belief that "there is luck in odd numbers."

"too many cooks spoil the broth," and I may note that a jury is commonly termed in Hongkong (when the pidgin English word *Ju-ĥ* is not used) the "seven strangers." Except to indicate a parallel, I need hardly here specify the part which the same number plays in our own affairs. The Hebrew use of the number is familiar to all. The seven wise men, the seven hills, the seven senses, the seven churches, the seven angels, the seven planets, and some thirty other similar expressions are in frequent use amongst us. We transport rogues for seven and fourteen years and bind apprentices for seven, and we find that, of old, Selenus the mathematician, and Hippocrates, both held the Chinese idea of the seventh day being critical in diseases.

Always excepting the tabooed 13, odd numbers have ever been popular in England, in various circumstances. Thus we hold it lucky for an odd number of people to sit down to dinner. The Chinese incline to an even number, 8 being in their estimation the most fortunate. But as already noted they share with us the superstitions as to setting a hen on an odd number of eggs. On the other hand, the hair should not be combed on odd days, more especially the 1st and 15th of a month. (The coiffure of Chinese women being dressed with a glutinous substance, it is only combed out at intervals.)

Dreams have ever played an important part in the psychological history of the human race, and the belief in their portentous nature is possibly the only superstition common to all mankind. As Dr. Kitto *(Cyclopædia of Biblical Literature,* Art. *Dreams)* well observes:—"It is quite clear from the inspired history that dreams were looked upon by the earliest nations of antiquity as premonitions from their idol gods of future events; . . . . and in order to guard against imposition Moses pronounced a penalty against dreams which were invented and wickedly made use of." It is almost unnecessary to make reference to the belief reposed in these alleged warnings from another world by Western nations. The story of Mahomed's dream is known to all; and I will merely add that both the Negro and Fijian races believe them to be caused by visits of the souls of deceased friends, while such widely divergent races as the Finns and the Australian Aborigines entertain a contrary belief that the soul of the dreamer leaves his body as it enjoys or suffers imaginary pleasures or pains.* The Chinese refer all dreams to the inspiration of a god or goddess, but frequently use the divining bamboos to ascertain how they are to be interpreted. Many of the principal temples in the empire owe their construction to imaginary instructions received during sleep. A recent visitor to the city of Tai An, situated at the foot of the Tai San mountains in Shantung—one of the five sacred mountains of China—thus gives the local legend: "The common account is, that Chin Tsung, the third Emperor of T'ang Dynasty, was afflicted with a grievous boil, which the Imperial physicians could not cure. There was a Taouist Priest at Tai San called Yen He, who declared that the Goddess of the mountain had appeared to him in a dream and directed him to go to the capital and cure this boil for the

---

* The Japanese believe that some women are liable, while sound asleep and dreaming, to have their heads leave their body and roam about. It is dangerous to arouse them till the head returns!

Emperor, at the same time directing him how to proceed. He went accordingly, and gave out that he had come to cure the Emperor's boil. The Emperor hearing of it, called him in. As soon as he entered the Imperial presence, the boil called out, 'Yen He has come and my destiny is finished;' the Priest prescribed treatment, and the boil was cured. The Emperor wished to reward him with an office, but he refused, saying 'Your Majesty has not been cured by my power, but by the efficient power of the God of Tai San; you should show your gratitude by repairing the temple at Tai San.' The Emperor assented, made a large appropriation, and appointed an officer to have it rebuilt in magnificent style." I might multiply examples of this sort *ad libitum*. The memorials in the *Peking Gazette* abound with references to acts done, or crimes discovered in consequence of dreams. Mr. Doolittle notes how dreaming has been pressed into the service of Buddhism at Foochow by way of enforcing the prohibition against eating flesh. "A certain butcher one day bought three buffaloes one of which he killed. One night he began suddenly to bellow like cattle, and for a whole day remained insensible. His family in alarm called a doctor, who prescribed medicine to revive him. His family, on his recovering his senses, inquired what was the occasion of his acting thus? He answered that he saw in his dream the two buffaloes not yet killed suddenly begin to speak like men; one of them said: 'I am your father;' and the other said: 'I am your grand-father.' In a short time they became in appearance like men, and on looking carefully at them, said he, 'I saw that they were really my father and my grandfather.' The butcher was so painfully affected by these circumstances that he sent the two cattle away to the country, and changed his calling."

As an illustration of the every-day belief in dreams which comes under the observation of the least curious foreign resident in Chinese, I subjoin two stories which have within the last few months appeared in a Shanghai and Hongkong journal respectively. The first relates to the old, old subject—the discovery of treasure. "The other night a gentleman named Chang (*Anglice* Smith) went to bed and had a very remarkable dream. He thought that he was in a particular spot at the back of a certain temple in Shanghai city, and that there he came upon a hidden treasure of gold. On awaking he was so much impressed with the vivid nature of the dream that he immediately sprang out of bed, shouldered a pickaxe and wended his way to the enchanted spot. Upon reaching his destination he fell to work, and sure enough had not far to dig before he came upon a box containing five hundred taels' weight of gold, and—so runs the story—all marked with the magic name of Chang! Of course proprietorship was indisputable, and lucky Mr. Chang trotted home a richer and a happier man."

The other story appeared a very short time since in the *China Mail*, and the facts came within the writer's personal knowledge. Some time ago, a junk sailed from Hoifoong, containing a number of coolies for the barracoons of Macao. Having arrived there, the live cargo was quickly disposed of, and the Captain received as freight something over $1,000. This incited the helmsman and some of the crew to league themselves with two piratical junks to attack the boat and to rob the Captain of the money. Two or three days after, the junk left Macao on her way back to Hoifoong. On the voyage, near Chang Chow, the two pirates hove in sight, and the helmsman steered closed up to them, when the pirates boarded the junk, killed the Captain and threw him overboard. Here comes the mysterious part of the story. The master of the Luk Kee barracoon one night dreamed a dream, in which he saw the ghost of the murdered man before him, saying he had been murdered, that he was robbed of his money, and that he wished the barracoon master to complain and try to obtain redress for him, which he thought would not be difficult, as the pirates were sailing off Chang Chow. On the strength of this dream, the barracoon master complained to the Portuguese authorities, who sent out a gunboat, and the pirates were found at the spot indicated by the ghost. The crew of the attacked junk (who had come to Hongkong since the robbery) immediately went to Macao; one of them was the brother of the deceased and had been cut in several places. Whether there was any truth in the statement of the appearance of the ghost or not, the facts of the robbery and capture were correct. Here there was nothing mysterious in the fact of a friend of the junk captain dreaming that a very common contingency in Canton waters had actually occurred. Nor was it very strange that he should hit upon the most likely place to find the pirates. The Chinese however, especially in psychological matters, are not very keen in connecting cause with effect, and the lucky dreamer enjoys to this day the reputation of having been specially favoured by the Goddess of Sailors.

It does not appear that Chinese soothsayers, like their Western prototypes, divide dreams into distinct categories, or, to put it more accurately, that the fortune-telling books in circulation amongst the people agree in any standard of division. There is, however, a sort of natural order followed, as all such warnings may be divided into three classes,—those which portend good fortune, those which portend evil, and those to which no precise signification can be affixed. A very interesting paper on the subject of dreams recently appeared in the *Japan Mail;* and from this it would appear that in many respects Chinese

---

* The following is a resumé of the article in question:—

During sleep the thoughts wander into various channels and are not within the control of the dreamer. There is an old Chinese book called "Shin-rai" which contains an account of an official named "Sen mu" who divined fortunes from dreams, therefore in ancient times dreams must have been deemed of importance.

Dreams are divided into five classes.

First,—are dreams of Gods and Idols, Ancients, Ancestors &c., and olden times.

Second.—Dreams of matters unthought of in waking hours; but these dreams are usually complete, and perfectly remembered upon awaking. This class of dreams is that from which fortunes are usually divined.

Third.—Dreams in accordance with daily thoughts and events past or present. These are not real dreams of fancy, but merely the thoughts of our waking hours continued in sleep.

Fourth.—Dreams of impossibilities. These originate from a wearied mind or body and are useless for divination.

Fifth.—This class contains miscellaneous dreams, such as receiving gifts, outwitting opponents, or being guilty of "sharp practices."

There are various spells, charms and other means to avert the evil influences of unlucky dreams. One of these is to write certain Chinese characters on a piece of paper and paste it on the ceiling of a sleeping room; *Shu ya jin*, the god of night, (the Morpheus of Japan) is herein addressed.

The Tapir is said to "eat dreams." If

and Japanese beliefs are alike, though the latter people, true to their national character, have evinced a much greater talent for classification than their older rivals. Amongst good portents, in Chinese belief, are dreams of mounting upwards to the skies, meeting genii, or persons celebrated for their positions or acquirements, and of being present at convivial parties. To dream that one sees bats, turtles or tortoises, or that one is wounded by robbers (provided blood be not drawn) is also of good augury. These are also portents of good fortune to the Japanese; but while the latter consider that to dream of wearing new clothes or of having ulcers on the face is a sign of prosperity, these are both taken to augur impending ill fortune in China.* Of evil auguries common to the two countries are dreams of eating fruit, of breaking mirrors, or of seeing ants crawling over the house matting; to dream of the "sun or moon shedding tears of blood" is a sign of the approaching death of a parent; while to dream of having one's teeth pulled out implies impending unfriendliness on the part of relatives, and to dream of eating pears is an emblem of family broils. In both countries bad dreams should not be talked about at once—in China, until the morning meal has been taken, and in Japan until the mouth has been rinsed with

sketched on screens, or on the paper wrapper of the pillows, or used as a design in the patterns of the bed quilts, dreams will be warded off. Those who awake in a state of fright after horrible dreams are to call out, "Tapir come eat, Tapir come eat."

The following are of good portent to dream of. Those mentioned in the text are not included.

A summer scene with green Wistaria.—In the first dream of the new year to see a hawk (or falcon) or to see egg plant (*Nasubi*.)—To dream of fine weather succeeding a storm.—Placing large stones in a garden.—Climbing cliffs.—To be buried in the earth, dead or alive.—Of planting trees.—Digging drains.—Of land slips.—Of being in a cave.—Trees growing from the mats of a room.—Crossing the sea.—Chewing unboiled rice.—Having one's hair dressed.—Praying at a Shrine.—The hair growing white.—Seeing *no bori* (flags on bamboo poles.)—Sitting in an elevated room.—One's own body giving forth radiance.—To have side-arms at hand (swords &c.)—Removing to a newly-built house.—Wearing a hat of hemp *mino gasa* or *kasa*.—Women wearing a sword.—Wearing a *K'amori* (head dress).—Cleaning out a well.—Of rice bags.—Of spitting out gold and silver.—Seeing a looking-glass.—Of sweeping away cobwebs.—A ship in full sail.—Riding in carriages.—Travelling on a wide road.—Crossing a bridge.—Drinking milk.—Of a funeral.—Of archery (targets, bows and arrows.)—Collecting wild flowers.—Rice raining from the skies.—Drinking water from a valley.—Of *Tori i* (perches at Shintô shrines.)—Of rainy weather.—Receiving a present of a fan.—Being in prison.—Scattering seed.—Climbing hills.—Gathering dragon flies.—Being stung by a centipede.—Horsemanship.—Cats and rats.—Bathing.

The following are unlucky subjects to dream of :—

Frosty weather.—Black lowering clouds.—Mulberry trees broken.—Eating persimmons.—Giving a friend a sword.—The hair falling out.—Perspiring violently.—Catching cold, or coughing.—Eating wheat flour jelly (*ame*.)—Playing on *tsusumi* (small drum).—Meeting a crowd of people.—Using a walking stick.

Females who dream of swallowing the sun or moon bring forth children who become remarkable characters in history. The mother of Nichi ren sho nin dreamed she swallowed the sun, hence the boy's name.—The mother of Hideyoshi, when enceinte, had a similar dream, from which the child was named Hideyoshi maro.

To dream of the Ni-ô-son or of folding up screens is a sign of old age.—Dreaming of running water is an emblem of family happiness, (peace between husband and wife.)—If the outer shutters are split, it is an indication that the servants are faithless and will desert the dreamer's service.—To dream of getting wet from a sudden shower of rain, foretells an invitation to a feast.

* Amongst the Japanese, in order to produce dreams of an absent friend or lover, it is recommended to turn the sleeves of the bed-quilt to the foot of the bed.

water and ejected facing the East, an incantation being at the same time ejaculated. To dream of a bear is in China a sign that the dreamer will have a son; of a snake that he or she will have a daughter; while the appearance in a dream of a white mouse indicates the presence of treasure at the place where the animal is seen. Yet we must not be too hard on our Eastern friends. A half superstitious belief in the prophetic nature of dreams lingers throughout Europe, and a few decades will doubtless find China and Japan as generally incredulous of its existing beliefs in such matters as we assume to be ourselves.

V.—CHARMS, SPELLS, AMULETS AND DIVINATIONS.

The subjects to be dealt with under the above heading afford an *embarras de richesses*. Next to the belief in the prophetic nature of dreams none probably is more widespread than that in charms and kindred matters. The ancient British Druids attempted to cure the generality of diseases by charms and incantations,[*] and the so-called Doctors of modern China follow a similar custom hallowed by a still greater antiquity. But in addition to these, the universal belief in the influence of demons and evil spirits upon the every-day life of mortals has led to the devising of such numerous preservatives that the makers and vendors of such wares find constant employment. I propose to deal in the first instance with charms involving a certain amount of preparation, classing articles worn about the person under the head of amulets.

The superstitious regard paid to mirrors as regards their preservative qualities has been noticed in a previous chapter. This probably arises from the fact that in China they are regarded as all-efficacious household charms against the attacks of evil spirits. Nor are magic mirrors, similar in their use to the ink mirrors employed by modern Egyptian necromancers, unknown to the Chinese. At Canton, only a year or two since, a native was exhibiting for the small sum of 30 cash (about 2¼d.) a jewel stated to possess magical qualities. In it the curious spectator saw various figures such as a beggar, a mandarin, a woman, &c., and was assured that his or her own future condition would be the same as that of the counterfeit thus seen. There exists a belief in many parts of the Empire that the pointed roof or corner of a house's gable end may exert an unpleasant influence upon the dwelling in nearest proximity. To counteract this therefore a concave brass mirror—those of glass are still *articles de luxe* in most districts—set in a wooden frame, is arranged on the wall or roof of the threatened building so as to catch and reflect back the evil influences in question. I can find no trace of any similar practice in Western countries. Small brass mirrors hung near a bed are also all-efficacious to ward off evil influences.

[*] *Popular Antiquities*, Vol. III. p. 268.

It is possible, that, though everybody knows how fire-crackers are used by the Chinese to frighten off evil spirits, all readers are not aware that they are charms pure and simple; the original intention of their manufacture being to imitate the crackling of burning bamboos which were supposed to frighten away a race of malignant demons called Shan siao—"beings in human shape, a foot or so in height, and by nature very fearless," or according to another account a bird with a nest as big as a five bushel measure.* Mr. W. F. Mayers, in his interesting article on gunpowder and firearms in China, in the Journal of the N. C. B. R. A. S. for 1869-70, ingeniously suggests that these demons are but the embodiment of the supernatural agency visible in the attacks of fever and ague to which the inhabitants of the swampy regions of Western China were, and still are, liable. I quote his remarks: "The Chinese themselves do not appear to have pursued any investigation respecting the origin or meaning of the term *Shan siao*, but, guided by the date of its appearance in literature and its foreign garb, we may with some confidence, ascribe the belief in this demon to an Indian parentage. As regards the myth itself, it may be permitted to hazard the speculation that fever and ague, lurking as it did and still does in the swampy regions of Western China, may, by a very familiar process, have become embodied in the conception of a supernatural agency, and that the fires which native wisdom or foreign counsel might suggest as a prophylactic device may have been invested with magical attributes, either by teachers who thought it best to fortify sanitary precautions with a cloak of fetishism, or else by the inherited tradition of succeeding ages. However this may be, the idea of exorcism, dating as far back as the sixth century, has remained inseparably connected with the use of fire-crackers down to the present day." And in a note on the same page the writer adds that subsequently to an execution taking place at Canton in 1868 in a public square, the inhabitants of the locality were not satisfied until they had exorcised the ghost of the departed criminal by a protracted discharge of crackers. It is not difficult to trace a similar motive in the custom which obtains of honouring the departure of a popular resident in any place, in a similar manner. The crackers are to frighten away all demons from the traveller. Such a compliment is frequently paid to foreigners by their Chinese acquaintances in Hongkong. It may, I think, be taken as certain that crackers are charms pure and simple to the Chinese, their use as mere noise-producing fireworks being secondary to the idea of exorcism.

Charms of another sort are sometimes used by the Chinese. It is only three years since that H. E. Li Hung Chang, who is at this moment premier of China, *fired cannon* at the Peiho to make it cease inundating the surrounding country.† The Eagre or bore of the Tsien Tang river, which flows from the boundaries of Kiang-si, Fuhkien and Chih-keang to Hang-chow Bay, and takes its name "money-dyke" from the amount expended on its embankments,‡ has been treated with "charms" on several occasions, but as Chinese annals tell us, with

---

* Journal of the N. C. B. Royal Asiatic Society, 1869-70, p. 78.
† *China Mail*, Sept. 19, 1872.
‡ Journal N. C. B. R. A. S. 1853-54, pp. 34 *et seq.*

very indifferent success. Prince Wu Shu (A.D. 930) made five hundred "daring archers" let fly six arrows apiece at the dreaded tidal wave as it came rolling onwards, and then after praying to Wu Tsz-si, the tutelary deity of the stream, put the key of the dyke water gate into an envelope, and threw it into the river. Forthwith the waters retired; but as they would have retired in the ordinary course of events, even the Chinese did not consider the experiment a remarkable success. In 1131 the Emperor Kan Tsung sunk ten iron plates, each weighing over 130 lbs., in the river by way of charming the mischievous spirits of the waters, but charms and embankments were alike carried off by the resistless power of the tide. Experience however was not availed of in a case where superstition had firm hold, and time and time again was a similar experiment tried—with, I need hardly say, similar success. Such practices, however, have not been quite unknown amongst ourselves, and even at the present day there are many springs in rural Britain supposed to be guarded by spirits who require charming in a very similar way. The crooked pins cast into St. Winifred's well in North Wales, the fourpenny pieces cast into that of Gwern Degla, the rags and clothes thrown into these of Strathfillan and Kenethmont in Scotland, and Benton (near Newcastle-upon-Tyne), and the common offering of three stones as a tribute to the spirit of the stream in Unst (Shetland), are, like the nosegays thrown into wells and fountains in honour of their presiding nymphs at the Roman *fontinalia*, or the cakes of bread-corn similarly offered of old to Juno in Laconia, evidences of a belief not at all unlike that which prompts Chinese acts of a similar nature.

The anti-demoniacal power ascribed to the wood and leafy branches of certain trees in our own folklore is matched by a similar Chinese belief. The elder, the rowan, the yew, and the mountain ash of rural England, or the palasa (a species of mimosa) of India, are represented, in the Middle Kingdom, by the bamboo, peach and willow, which are regarded as peculiarly powerful over goblins and imps. The dry Bamboo is supposed to attract devils. On the other hand a rod of green bamboo is carried at funerals by nearly-related mourners for a contrary purpose. It is called the "dog-driving rod," and is supposed to be efficacious in driving away evil spirits who might stop the way of the departed. The willow is used both to drive away and to raise spirits, but in the former case a twig only must be used. The plum tree is also regarded as possessing mysterious virtues in the same direction, but is not thought equal to the willow. Two other plants are also supposed to be efficacious against evil spirits, and one of them the Fo yeung lak (火映莉) is at Canton hung over door-ways to prevent them from entering houses. We too, formerly put up holly at Christmas with a similar object, though it has now become a mere decoration, and there was a pretty Druidical superstition that the Sylvan spirits would take refuge in the evergreen branches from the chill winds and snows proper to the season.* It would be interesting to trace the superstitions connected with trees somewhat further, but I have not sufficient authorities at command.

Of the charms affixed to buildings, etc., the Chinese have a fair variety.

* *Lancashire Folk-lore*, p. 256.

The all-potent horseshoe is indeed not found nailed against doors and gables; but, oddly enough, a horse's hoof hung up in a house* has the same preservative virtues in native eyes. Chinese reverence for the dead has prevented the adoption of so horrible a charm as that known in France, Germany, Spain, and Ireland as "the hand of Glory" or dead man's hand, consisting actually of the dried hand of an executed criminal. But a nail that has been used in fastening up a coffin is a sovereign charm. This is sometimes beaten out into a rod or wire, and, encased in silver, worn as a ring round the ancles or wrists. The cat here makes her appearance, a clay image of poor pussy—with a bob-tail of course, after the Chinese model,—being frequently placed on the apex of a roof to ward off unpropitious influences. The conspicuous position thus accorded to the cat as a warder-off of evil fortune seems oddly paralleled, though not imitated, by the place accorded to the same animal in popular European folk-lore. I have already mentioned its evil repute amongst the Chinese as a harbinger of ill luck, and this agrees closely with the usual Western estimate, witches and cats being constantly associated, the former indeed being supposed to take upon themselves the shape of the latter at will. The old legend that the chariot of the Goddess Freya was drawn by cats, and that Holda was attended by maidens riding on cats, is referred by Mr. Kelly to a widespread belief in their weatherwise powers. In China the cat is supposed to be in league with the spirits of darkness, and as this includes meteorological prescience, it is propitiated accordingly, the cat's image becoming a popular "charm."

So too those nondescript animals which most people agree to call lions, and which may be seen keeping guard in such disconsolate attitudes on the roofs of most native buildings of importance, are mere charms. The Chinaman in fact, from his cradle upwards, seems to regard himself as ever environed by diabolical agencies, to combat which an all-pervading system of charms and amulets is a prime necessity. While we laugh at this superstition, it is perhaps only a too vivid realisation of the fact of the devil "going about like a roaring lion." It may be interesting to note here that our own custom of depositing coins, papers, &c., in the foundation stones of new buildings is matched by a similar custom in China. I am unable to trace the superstitious origin of the practice in our own case, but the Chinese place coins under the door-sill and under the kitchen fireplace, when building, simply for luck. In some cases, following out the usual notion of contrariety, these and other charms are attached to the ridge pole of the building.

"Cash-swords," a very common form of charm, are thus described: "What is commonly called a *Cash-sword* is considered very efficacious in keeping away evil spirits. It is often hung up on the front and the outside of the bridal bed-curtain, in a position parallel to the horizon. About the time of a woman's confinement, a cash-sword is sometimes taken and hung inside of the curtain. This sword is usually about two feet long, and is constructed out of three kinds of things, each of which is regarded as a preventive of evil spirits: 1st. Two iron rods, about two feet long, constitute the foundation of the

* *Chinese Repository*, Vol. VII., p. 393.

sword. 2d. About one hundred cash, either ancient or modern (if ancient, or if all of the same emperor's reign, so much the better), are ingeniously fastened on these rods, concealing them from view. The rods are placed in the centre, and the coins are tied on the outside in two rows. 3d. Red cords or wires are used in tying on the cash. These three kinds, joined together in the shape of a sword, make a really formidable weapon, of which the maliciously-disposed spirits are exceedingly afraid!"*

Another charm of extensive use amongst Chinese women is a small solid silver or golden triangle, having two little swords suspended from the outer angles and a trident from the centre of the base; on the triangle itself lucky characters are engraved. This shape appears to be a favorite one, as women always fold their written charms in a similar manner, and sew them up in pieces of cloth of a triangular pattern.

The idea of an evil eye is no less common amongst the native population out here than it was and still is in Europe; and this belief, implicitly accepted as regards their own countrymen, is intensified as regards foreigners, owing to the outrageous stories circulated about us during recent excitements. I have often been amused in the North at the request not to stare at any child whose interesting appearance might have attracted my attention. In writing letters the Chinese invoke the person addressed, to cast a glance on the epistle "with the clear part of his eye" (or, as we should say, *white* of the eye) that is, take a favourable view of the matter talked of. A pregnant woman or a man whose wife is pregnant, is called "four eyed," and children are guarded against being looked at by either, as it is thought the sight would be unlucky to the children and would cause sickness to attack them. The superstition as to the powers of an "evil eye" may almost be deemed fundamental to humanity, as I have yet to read of a people amongst whom it does not find some degree of credence.

One of the commonest diagrams to be met with throughout China is the mystic *svastika* or "Thor's Hammer" 卐 (pronounced *wan* in Chinese and given as the archaic form of 萬). It is all-pervading, meeting the eye in all sorts of places, on the wrappers of medicines and sweetmeats, the stomachs or chests of idols, and the flanks of animals, upon dead walls, coins, etc. Dr. Eitel gives a most interesting account of this symbol in the 3rd volume of *Notes and Queries on China and Japan*.† It is ordinarily accepted as "the accumulation of lucky signs possessing ten thousand virtues, being one of the 65 mystic figures‡ which are believed to be traceable in every one of the famous foot-prints of Buddha. This of course stamps its Buddhistic origin so far as the Chinese are concerned. Apropos of this symbol, known by us as the *fylfot*, a recent review of Mr. Waring's *Ceramic Art in Remote Ages* says:—
"Another form of the cross which Mr. Waring has collected very completely is the fylfot. By some this is thought to be only a sort of Greek fret or meander

---

* *Social Life of the Chinese*, Vol. II., p. 313.
† *Notes and Queries on China and Japan*, Vol. III., p. 98.

‡ Mr. Alabaster, in his work on Siamese Buddhism, "The Wheel of the Law," gives the number of diagrams as 108.

pattern; but the evidence of its having been a symbol in past times of mystic significance is too strong to allow of its being reduced to a mere ornament. It has been identified with the Hammer of Thor, the Zeus or Thunderer of the Scandinavians. With the Buddhists this cross had the very opposite signification from that of the *tau* of the Egyptians or the cross of the Christians. General Cunningham is quoted, who says :—' The atheistical Swastikas received their name from their peculiar symbol, the *Swastika*, or Mystic Cross, which was typical of their belief in Swasti. This term is a compound of ' su ' *well*, ' asti,' *it is*, meaning ' it is well;' or, as Wilson expresses it, ' so be it,' and implying complete resignation under all circumstances.' . . . . .

To Mr. Waring's collection of facts regarding the Swastika, or fylfot, it may be added that a Hindoo woman, when she cleans out her simple cottage, and washes over the earthen floor with a thin coating of mud and cow-dung—the latter having, as coming from the cow, which is sacred, a highly purifying virtue—she usually forms the figure of a Swastika on the door-step. In the woman's mind it is supposed to be an efficacious charm to keep away evil from the house. Along with the fylfot we have the very similar figure of the *three* legs which we associate with the Isle of Man. Mr. Waring's book gives us many examples of this symbol. In some cases they are legs, but oftener they are merely three obtuse angles, or curves. This is also found in many parts of the world, as well as some examples which are given with five or six limbs. In such cases it is suggestive of a wheel; and there are a number of Buddhist symbols not unlike to these, which are understood to represent the ' Wheel of the Law,' or the Wheel of Buddha. It may be stated that a three-limbed figure of this kind is much used in the Punjaub, and other parts of India, by the Mohajin log—the banking or moneyed class—as a charm; they place it in their houses, and generally over the door." But Dr. Eitel makes a yet more interesting contribution to the subject in pointing out that Scandinavians, Danes, Germans and Englishmen still attach superstitious importance to this magic charm of their heathen forefathers, and of the Chinese Buddhists of to-day. To the present time the hammer of Thor is used amongst the German peasantry, and in Ireland, as a magical sign to dispel thunder.* The same symbol was frequently cast on bells during the Middle Ages, and many of them still bear this mark. Dr. E. mentions those of Appleby and Scotherne, Waldingham, Bishop's Norton and West Barkwith in Lincolnshire, Hathersage in Derbyshire, Maxborough in Yorkshire, and many more. That this symbol should thus be common to Buddhistic and Scandinavian mythology argues a common fount in ages long gone by; before the Aryan races had commenced their Westward wanderings or the Shang dynasty had ceased to reign in China—coeval in fact with Cadmus, the reputed father of Western letters.

The use of the *Pa-kwa* or "Eight diagrams"—a collection of strokes arranged in hexagonal form and familiar to the merest tyro in Chinese studies —as a charm to ward off evil influences, is universal. It is made of all sizes and shapes, from large ones on boards one or two feet square, down to tiny

* *Curious Myths of the Middle Ages*, Art. " Thor's Hammer."

medals for personal wear not larger than a sixpence. In the centre is the diagram of the Yang and Yin (male and female principle), or sometimes a concave metal or glass mirror. Coarsely executed boards of this description are placed perpendicularly on the highest part of the roof. More neatly carved specimens are hung up in rooms. Go where one will, the inevitable *pa kwa*, carved, painted or written, is almost sure to ornament some portion of the premises. On some houses again will be seen "three arrows placed in an earthen tube, and laid on the side of the roof, the tube pointing towards some distant object—the arrows being fastened in their places by clay." Sometimes the representation of a lad sitting on a three-legged nondescript animal, with a bow in his hands, as if on the act of shooting an arrow, takes the place of or accompanies the other objects described.*

Stone slabs or pillars erected near the entrances of alleys leading into a main street, are supposed to ward off the evil influences proceeding from them. Mr. Doolittle states that in Foochow every family on the first day of the Chinese month nails up a few leaves of the sweet flag *(acorus gramincus)* and artemesia on each side of the front doorway. They are held to represent swords, and so scare away evil spirits! Other charms, not personal, in Chinese use, are red cloth worn in the pockets, or red silk braided into the hair of children; a knife that has been used to kill a fellow-creature; the Chinese Classics placed under the pillow or kept near the owner; knife-cash cast for the purpose and attached to the ridgepole; pieces of old fishing nets, of which demons are said to be especially afraid as they suppose them to be used by the priests to catch spirits; and gourd shells, which it is supposed will attract to their interior such diseases as small-pox, measles, &c., which might otherwise attack children. Images or drawings of tigers, lizards, snakes, centipedes &c.—the list is almost inexhaustible—have similar virtues, more especially guarding children from colic and other infantile diseases.

Most people are acquainted with the cant expression about "taking a hair of the dog that bit you," now-a-days applied by those, who have drank too much overnight, to the morning glass supposed to re-steady the shaken nerves, but originating in a superstition common to both Europe and China. The idea on which it is based is that of the sympathy which a part of the body has with the whole. Thus a dog's virus being powerless on its own body, a person will by swallowing one of its hairs enjoy the immunity possessed by the animal it came from. In Devonshire we find the idea oddly reversed, as, when a child suffers from hooping cough, a hair from its head is put between slices of bread and butter and given to a dog, who thereupon, it is believed, gets the cough instead of the child.† In the same country it is supposed that you can give a

---

* *Social Life of the Chinese*, Vol. 2, p. 311.

† Not long ago a native said to me, "Would you like A to hate B?" speaking of a bad man who had a very evil influence over a good honest man. Without thinking, I replied, "Yes; it would be the best thing that ever happened." He only answered me by a gesture of the hand, which literally means, "Leave it to me." The next day he secured a bit of the bad man's hair, and sewed it into the coat of the good man. Strange enough, as chance fell out, that day an event happened which opened the eyes of the latter to his friend's character, and they parted company. Of

neighbour ague, by burying a dead man's hair under his threshold.* The fact of a dog's hair possessing mystic powers, in Chinese Hakka† belief, is illustrated by the following incident related to me by a distinguished sinologue in this Colony.

While on his missionary tours in the Canton province he was usually accompanied by a powerful dog, at which, in some of the villages he passed through, the children were somewhat frightened and once or twice very slightly bitten. In such a case the mother would run after him and beg for a hair from the dog's tail, as a charm against the evil one. The hair thus obtained would be put to the part bitten in the belief that the spirit which the fright suffered by the child had caused to pass into his person, would thereby be attracted from it.

My informant used sometimes, jokingly, to say to the applicant, "Oh! take a hair from the dog yourself," but not liking his looks, this offer was usually declined, and the alternative suggested brings into notice another curiously wide-spread superstition. He was asked *to spit in her hand*, as a charm against evil. Now the virtues claimed for this not very cleanly proceeding by the Chinese found a thorough belief amongst the ancients, which survives to this day amongst the lower classes in England. Brand gives a most interesting chapter on this subject.‡ The Roman custom of lustrating an infant by spittle on the day of its being named, that of the Mandingoes who spit thrice in the child's face on the same occasion, and the custom of fishwomen at home who still "spit upon their handsel," or the first money they take in the day, all point to the same belief as that entertained by the Hakkas. There is still a rural English belief that spitting three times in a person's face is a charm against the evil eye. The Hebrew belief in the mystic properties of saliva is said to be of considerable antiquity, and we find our Saviour on two occasions (St. John ix. 6 and Mark vii. 33) using it in curing the blind.

"Characts," or written charms, are as common in China as in Europe. We settle the origin of our own former confidence in their efficacy by a somewhat off-hand reference to the Jewish phylactery—a derivation I am inclined to doubt —but we have nothing that I know of to guide us in finding the *root* of the Chinese superstition. However that may be, the fact that written charms have ever been deemed efficacious, wherever the art of writing is known, is curious. Not a very long time ago the still warm body of a deceased male child was picked up in the streets of Hongkong, having affixed to its cap one of these charms, which had evidently been sold to the parents by one of the itinerant fortunetellers who infest the city. It was kindly placed at my disposal by the Coroner, and a facsimile of it is given on the opposite page.

course nothing would persuade the native that it was not the effect of his charm.
—*The Inner Life of Syria*, by Isabel Burton.

* In France, an old woman told me to take a small piece of hair exactly at the top of my head and twist round a little slip of wood tightly, to cure a relaxed uvula, or sore throat.—Correspondent, *Notes and Queries*.

† The Hakkas are a separate, and it is believed older, race than the Cantonese. They speak a different dialect.

‡ *Popular Antiquities*, Vol. III, p. 259.

A FORTUNE-TELLER'S CHARM.

天德 傷 食 玉堂 財 進神 甲午 癸卯才 壬申 傷刻印 貳月十七日午時左

殺貴人 殺印 名培 垣

初三 十三 廿三 卅三 四三 五三

甲辰 乙巳 丙午 丁未 戊申 己酉

剃頭宜三月十六巳時。
週歲方可種聖痘。
立命在申。
小限同垣。宜土邊乃大吉。
花城隍取名字
厚。惟宜契金
神他日定然福
進神玉堂衆吉
午時出世常貴
此八造秀妙得

It is almost untranslateable, but if you bear in mind that the Chinese words refer to horary or astrological terms, the following will give you some idea of what it meant. The paper refers to an infant born in the *yam shan* year (1872), 2nd moon, 17th day, at noon; the character for "left" appended to the date signifies that the child is a male, that for right signifying a female.

"Being born in the *yam shan* year, *kwai mou* month and *kap ng* hour, the child is subject to the combined influence of these dates. Under *yam shan* it will be adverse to the influence of *koon* (officials) [that is an indication of evil], but will find powerful friends. He will have brothers who will impoverish him. According to the portents under the character *kwai mou*, he will always have plenty to eat and great wealth. Under *Sun mi* he will meet with counter influences from an evil spirit. *Kap ng* indicates that he will meet with good influences indicating wealth and powerful friends, but these good influences will be counteracted by an evil spirit.

"For 3 years, the first epoch under prediction, his fate is good. Thence to the age of 13, the first five years will be bad, the second five good; from 14 to 25 the first five years will be bad, the second very bad; from 26 to 33, five years will be bad, the latter five very good; thence to 43, good and very good fortune will be his fate. For five years after this his fate will be good, continuing till his death, which will happen before he is 53.

"The life of this child indicates purity and prosperity. His good fortune lies in being born at the hour of noon, as this indicates powerful friends and other good influences. His future life will be one of bliss, but he ought to adopt the Kum-fa goddess, in the municipal temple, as his spiritual mother. In selecting a name for him some character should be chosen having *To*, earth, as a component part. It will then be lucky. The date fixed for shaving the child should be the 18th day of the 3rd moon from 9 to 10 a.m. The child should be a year old before he is vaccinated."

So much for this written charm;—sad rubbish no doubt, but not much worse than the whining predictions of gypsy crones in enlightened Europe, and harmful chiefly in the widespread belief attached to its value.

The charm here given was written on red paper, that colour being supposed to be peculiarly obnoxious to evil spirits. Hence the red cloth and silken twist already noted. But charms on yellow paper are quite as numerous. Yellow is the Imperial colour, one of the five recognized in the Chinese cosmogony, and a superstitious value attaches to its use. "Sometimes a picture of an idol is printed or written upon this paper, or some Chinese characters, or various scrolls, are drawn on the paper with red or black ink. It is then pasted up over a door or on a bed-curtain, or it is worn in the hair, or put into a red bag and suspended from a button-hole, or it is burnt, and the ashes are mingled with tea or hot water, and drank as a specific against bad influences or spirits. An incredible number of these charms are used in the various ways indicated. Many houses have eight or ten or more on the front side or under the eaves. Immense numbers are burnt in idolatrous or superstitious ceremonies."* Similar

* *Social Life of the Chinese*, Vol. II. p. 308.

charms are hung upon bed-curtains, placed upon the ridge poles of houses, and hung over door-ways. The veneration entertained for the written character in China is doubtless partially owing to the superstitious belief in the protective nature of written charms. The Biblical, or at all events Talmudical, authority for the use of Phylacteries seems to have indirectly produced a somewhat similar effect amongst the Hebrews. Brand gives numerous instances of the belief in written charms in England, and a gypsy charact, sold within the last few years, has come under the present writer's personal observation. In this case, as in all others, it may be truly said, that the more we enquire the less do we find to be the divergence between Chinese and Western beliefs and superstitions.

But amulets and charms worn about the person are, perhaps, even greater objects of importance in Chinese estimation than household or other charms. Retaining as we do the words, now applied to harmless trinkets worn on the watch-chain,* we are apt to forget the deep significance attached to them by our forefathers, and to somewhat unduly ignore the influence which a belief in their virtues once exercised over our own ancestors, and still exercises over people like the Chinese. I may here note that small trinkets, believed to be veritable amulets, are worn by the well-to-do Chinese just as among ourselves. The most popular form of charm is, both in China and England, a piece of money. Most boys have treasured a "lucky fourpenny" with a hole in it, and most Chinese babies have been the unconscious owners of "lucky cash" attached to them by a red string and bearing certain lucky characters inscribed on them. The cash chosen for this purpose are, as a rule, ancient. The older the cash the greater its virtue. Sometimes coins of this sort are tied on the wrists of a new-born child and worn by it for a considerable time. Similarly a number of cash belonging to the reigns of different Emperors are placed under the bed of a newly-married couple. Collectors of old coins frequently come across curious specimens of the numismatic art produced for this purpose, metals generally in China being favourite substances for amulets. One of the commonest amulets given to an only son is a small silver lock. The father collects a number of cash from the heads of a large number—strictly speaking a hundred—different families, and having exchanged them for silver has the latter converted into a native padlock which is used to fasten a silver chain or ring on the boy's neck.† This it is supposed will be respected by evil spirits, and will therefore contribute to the boy's longevity. Another popular amulet is made in the shape of a flattish silver hook with some fortunate inscription thereon. But most common of all are the little bells worn by the Chinese child of every degree in the Southernmost provinces and, more sparingly, used in the North also. The origin

---

* Louis Napoleon in his will emphasizes the solemn declaration: "With regard to my son, let him keep as a talisman the seal I used to wear attached to my watch." This piece of fetishism would appear to have formed yet another link between the imperial exile that has passed from our midst, and those Latin races whose cause he affected to represent, whose superstition he certainly shared.—*Chambers' Journal.*

† *Social Life of the Chinese*, Vol. II. p. 314.

of the custom as regards Canton has been already given. But a belief in the occult qualities of bells is so wide-spread* that considerable doubt may reasonably exist whether, even if the legend be true, the Cantonese did not merely amplify an existing practice by way of appeasing the Demon of the bell. It is at all events strange that our own ancestors should have credited bells with possessing occult powers to aid mankind in their combat with the spirits of darkness, while the Chinese propitiate the same enemies by wearing models of bells upon their clothes. But a yet more odd coincidence is found in the sixty-six bells attached to the Ephod of the Jewish High priest when engaged in sacerdotal ministration.† At the present day we give bells to babies mounted on a piece of coral—itself a celebrated charm since the days of Pliny, by whom it is noted as an amulet against fascination and able to preserve and fasten the teeth. Few substances, by the way, except metal are used by the Chinese as amulets, jade being almost the only exception.‡ It would be interesting to ascertain whether the ear-ring was ever regarded in China, as by the Semitic races, as a sort of amulet or charm.

Divination is in China as popular as, and probably more respectable than, it was amongst the Israelites in the days of the witch of Endor, and it is not perhaps going too far to say that there is not a single means resorted to in the West by way of lifting the impenetrable veil which hides the future from curious mankind which is not known to and practised by the Chinese. From "Pinking the Bible" to using the Planchette, from tossing for odd and even to invoking spirits to actually speak through crafty media, the whole range of Western

---

* A correspondent of the Indian *Pioneer* says that, among the articles taken as fines from the Duflas are certain gongs supposed to be very ancient, and which they appear to regard with the greatest reverence. For the edification of readers curious in such matters, we may observe that gongs, or bells, are also among the holy paraphernalia, or fetishes, of the Neilgherry Todas. A Duflla Chief would sooner part with half his kingdom than with his gong.

† Kitto's *Cyclopædia of Bib. Lit.*, Art. *Bell*.

‡ While these pages are passing through the press I come across the following paragraph in the Paris correspondence of a leading London Journal. The rumour it gives may be entirely untrue, but I quote it as a specimen of ordinary newspaper gossip in 1875 on the subject under notice:—"It is now known that the Napoleonic talisman is safe; and, so long as that talisman remains in the Bonapartist family, the tradition is that, however much the eagle's wings may be clipped, the imperial bird will soar at last. On the afternoon of September 4, 1870, as the Empress Eugenie was flying from her apartments to the dentist's cab which was to take her out of Paris, she pointed to several large boxes containing important papers, and to a small but extremely heavy metal casket, and said to M. Thelen, one of the few faithful servants that remained with her to the last—'Save those papers, but above all save that casket, and preserve it as you would your own soul.' In that mysterious casket, doubly and trebly locked, the Napoleonic talisman lay. M. Thelen had the boxes and casket thus confided to him transferred with all possible speed to the house of his sister in one of the quietest suburbs of Paris. But the September 4 Government soon got wind of the affair, and their emissaries were not long before making a descent at the house of M. Thelen's sister. They found and carried off the papers, but the casket containing the talisman escaped them. It had been concealed in a hole in the wall behind a small map representing the seat of war. In due time the talisman was conveyed to Chiselhurst, where it now is; and so long as it remains in the keeping of the Imperial family, it will be safe to bet on the restoration of Napoleon IV. As the curious reader would, perhaps, like to know in what the talisman consists, I may inform him that it is a large sapphire which Napoleon I. cribbed from the crown of Charlemagne when he took the indecent liberty of having that monarch's coffin opened up at Aix-la-Chapelle."

CHARMS, SPELLS, AMULETS AND DIVINATIONS.

superstition in this regard is as familiar to the average Chinaman as to the most enthusiastic spiritualist at home. The coincidences of practice and belief are indeed so startling that many will doubtless see in them a sort of evidence either for their truthfulness, or for a common origin of evil. Divination by the *ka pui* has been already noted, together with that by bamboo slips. Cash and many other objects are similarly used, the mode of procedure in no way differing from our own. Such modes of consulting the gods are, however, every-day matters. It is when we come to the consulting of media, the use of a forked stick, writing on sand, and similar matters that the Chinese practice becomes singular in its resemblance to superstitions openly avowed at home. I would here remark that I am no spiritualist. But how, without any apparent connection with each other, such beliefs should at once be found in full force in the farthest East and the extreme West is puzzling. Is our Western spiritualism derived from China?

It is only within the last ten years that the attention of English readers has been markedly drawn to this strange agreement of Chinese with Western belief and practice—in the first instance,* by the Rev. J. Doolittle, in a series of papers contributed originally to the *China Mail* and subsequently published in book form in 1867; and in the same and following years, more exhaustively, in *Notes and Queries on China and Japan*, by the Rev. E. J. Eitel, PH.D., whose thorough and scholarly papers on Chinese matters render him a high authority. Readers of that now defunct periodical will doubtless, in consideration of the papers in question being out of print and unknown to the majority of the British public, pardon my here transferring Dr. Eitel's remarks almost verbatim; the more so as any original account I could give would be but a mere variation in language:—

"A certain form of spirit-rapping is practised among the officials and literary classes of China. A spirit is sometimes made to appear, to communicate by writing revelations about the future, and questions are answered as regards the lucky or unlucky result of intended transactions, about success at impending examinations, about progeny to be expected, and so forth. The pencil to be used by the spirit must be made from the twig of a peach-tree. But this twig should be cut off a branch pointing towards the East, and before cutting the twig the following magic formula consisting of four lines (with four syllables each) has to be pronounced: 'Magic pencil most efficacious, daily possessing subtle strength, now I take thee, to reveal clearly everything.'† After the recitation of this formula, a compound character is to be carved into the back of the tree. This

---

* I speak in the text of writers in the English language. But Du Halde gives some interesting details in his well-known work. Colonel Yule, in his *Marco Polo*, Vol. I., p. 290, draws attention to this fact in a note upon the Taosse (Taoists), whom he defines as "worshippers of the mystic cross *Swasti*. Apparently they had at their command the whole encyclopædia of modern spiritualism. Du Halde mentions amongst their sorceries the act of producing by their invocations the figures of the Laotseu and their divinities in the air, and of *making a pencil to write answers to questions without anybody touching it*." This is evidently a Chinese version of Mr. Daniel Home's alleged powers, and the coincidence is more than strange.

† 機筆靈靈日有精神
我今取爾用事指明.

character is composed of two radicals, of which the upper one signifies water from clouds; the lower one means demon, which indicates that the spirit to be conjured up resides in the clouds. The other characters* 'the mysteries of Heaven wondrously mastered' refer to the revelations which the pencil is expected to communicate under the direction of the spirit. When this compound character has been cut into the bark of the peach-tree, a twig from one of its eastern branches, which moreover must have a little curvature at its end in the form of a hook, is cut off and fitted into a small piece of wood of about six inches length, which is intended for being laid on the palms of the medium acting at the ceremony. Every one who intends to witness it, has to purify himself by fasting and ablutions and to dress in perfectly clean clothes. In the hall where the ceremony is to take place two long tables are placed together. On the upper table sacrifices are placed, consisting of wine, fruit and and confectionery, while the other table is to be covered with fine red sand, which should be rolled even and smooth by a small bamboo-roller, so that characters can be traced in the sand without difficulty. All these preparations should be finished before night-fall, when a petition to the Great Royal Bodhisattwa† is to be written on a card, informing this Deity that sacrifices are prepared, and requesting that one of the great spirits wandering through the clouds‡ should be sent to the house of the petitioner whose name and address is mentioned minutely to prevent any mistake. This card, together with a quantity of gold paper, is conveyed to the temple of the abovementioned Deity, and burnt before the idol's shrine. On returning to his own house the petitioner writes his address, as given on that card, on a slip of paper which he pastes on one of the door-posts.

"Later in the evening two or three of the company assembled go to the door, burn there some gold paper and make then an indefinite number of bows and prostrations, receiving as it were the spirit on entering the house. Having conducted him into the hall, an arm-chair is moved to the table whilst incense and candles are lighted. At the same time the medium approaches, the handle of the magic pencil resting on the palms of both hands, but so that the end of the twig touches the surface of the table strewn with sand. He places his out-spread hands near the head of the table and addressing the spirit with becoming reverence says: 'Great spirit, if you have arrived, be pleased to write the character "arrived" on this table.' Immediately the magic pencil begins to move and the required character appears legibly written in the sand, whereupon all assembled request the spirit to sit on the large arm-chair, whilst the Deity, that is supposed to have conducted him thither, is likewise politely asked to sit down on another chair. The whole company now bow and prostrate themselves before the seats of both spirits, and some pour out wine and burn gold paper. Then the medium approaches again with the magic pencil on the palms of his hands, whilst all assembled say with one voice: 'Great spirit, what was your august surname, what your honourable name, what offices were you invested with, and under which dynasty did you live on earth?' Immediately

*妙奪天機・   †(大王菩薩・)   ‡(雲遊大仙・)

CHARMS, SPELLS, AMULETS AND DIVINATIONS. 59

the magic pencil is seen moving and answers to these questions appear written in the sand. After this every one of the assembled may put a question one after the other, but each question is to be written on a slip of paper and burnt together with some gold paper. As soon as each paper is fairly consumed by the fire, the magic pencil writes down the answer to it, generally in poetical form, and each sentence is followed by the character* 'I have done,' whereupon the pencil ceases to move. Then all assembled try to read the characters aloud. If they fail to decipher them, the pencil moves again and writes the same sentence more distinctly, until it is intelligible. As soon as one of the assembly succeeds in deciphering a sentence, the magic pencil moves again and writes on the sand the two characters† 'that's it.' When a sentence is finished in this way, the sand on the table has to be smoothed again with a bamboo-roller, and whilst this is being done the whole company address flattering speeches to the spirit, praising his poetical talents, to which the magic pencil replies by writing on the table the characters‡ 'it's ridiculous.' If any one present behaves improperly, displaying a want of reverence, the spirit writes down some sentences containing a sharp rebuke. The motions of the pencil are quite extraordinary and apparently not produced by the medium on whose open palms the handle of the pencil rests, and who merely follows the spontaneous movements of the magic pencil. In this way conversation is kept up without flagging until midnight (when the male principle begins to be active). Then the spirit breaks off the conversation and addressing the whole company writes on the table: 'Gentlemen, I am much obliged for your liberal presents, but now I must beg leave to depart.'§ To this all persons present reply saying: 'Please, great spirit, stop a little longer,' but the spirit jots down as if in a great hurry the two characters‖ 'excuse me, I am off.' Then all assembled say, 'If there was any want of respect or attention, great spirit, we beseech thee forgive us this sin.' All walk then to the house-door burning gold-paper, and there take leave of the spirit with many bows and prostrations.

"I proceed now to point out another form of spiritualism by which more especially the lower classes of Chinese society allow themselves to be blinded. There are somnambules in China,¶ and no matter whether they be real clairvoyants under the influence of animal magnetism, or merely clever impostors, they are at least in the South of China everywhere to be found, enjoying the entire confidence of the mass of the people, and holding a position very much like that of the witch at Endor who conjured up Samuel before Saul, or like those priests in the temple of Pluto and Cora at Acharaca, who used to prescribe to their patients the remedies revealed to them in their dreams; in some respects also like those oracles which were obtained at the lake Aornos, and in which those consulted called up the spirits of the dead (see Smith, *Dict. of Antiquities*, on Oracles). The fact is that, at least as far as I am aware,

* 成. † 是也. ‡ 見笑. ‖ 請去.
§ 蒙諸君厚禮我今要請別而去. ¶ 隗迷魂法者).

somnambulism in China is generally made subservient to necromancy. The Chinese mind is so deeply impressed with the stability of family ties, that even death is not considered as separating a man or woman from their respective families, and it is, therefore, the common belief of the people that the ancestors of each family, though living in Hades, are continually watching the interests and welfare of all their descendants that live on earth. Consequently if a family be in great distress on account of the severe illness of some one of its members, or in doubt with regard to the advisability of an intended marriage, or anxious to know if a certain site chosen for a tomb would ensure rest and peace to the soul of a deceased relative,—on each of these subjects the Chinese feel a craving desire to consult the spirits of their ancestors. Now as the Chinese well know that it is not so easy to influence those spirits and to induce them to submit to consultations and cross-examinations, there is a class of people, chiefly women, who make it their profession to conjure up spirits from the dead, and to act as the mediums in the consultations to be held with them. These women are called *shang-p'o* in Canton city, whilst in other parts of the province they are usually known by the name of *sin-p'o*.* If there be any family in trouble or anxiety for some one or other of the reasons mentioned above, a somnambule is sent for. No preparations are required, no sacrifices are to be offered, except that some incense sticks are lighted and put into that niche dedicated to the spirit of the hearth,† which may be seen in every Chinese house in the wall over the cooking range. When the somnambule arrives at the house, she is received by the female portion of its inmates and conducted to some quiet back room. No man is allowed to be present, especially no scholar, and great care is to be taken, that no copy of the Chinese classics, among which the 'great learning'‡ is most dreaded by the somnambules, should be left lying about in the room. If any of these precautions are neglected the somnambule will declare it impossible to hold any conversation with the spirits. When all is ready she ascertains first the nature of the difficulty under which the family labours, and the name and sex of the ancestor whose spirit is to be conjured up. As soon as she has learned these particulars she seats herself on a low stool and crouches down on it, so that her head rests on her knees. Then she utters in a low and measured tone the following incantation:—

> 'Ye sisters three—ye ladies four,
> 'O! lead me now to Hades' door!
> 'What would ye do in Hades? Speak!
> 'My kindred only would I seek—
> 'My kindred seek, one word to say.
> 'Then quickly lead me back, I humbly pray.'

"This incantation she repeats three times, and soon after she has spoken it for the third time a sudden change seems to come over her body. Her arms drop down, her limbs are one after the other seized by a sort of torpor, convulsions shake her all over, and cold sweat covers her face and temples. At last

*(仙婆). †(司命灶君). ‡(大學).

she seems fast asleep and now questions may be put to her. 'What do you see?' she may be asked. 'I see nothing,' is the answer, 'it is all dark and chilly.' After a while she is again asked, 'what do you see now?' 'Now,' she replies, 'now it is lighter; yes, at a distance I see pagodas and towers and palaces and houses.' 'Do you see any human being?' 'No, I cannot see distinctly; yes, now I see them, there are men and women with pale sallow complexions, and one approaches me, speaks to me!' 'How is that person dressed?' Then the somnambule describes the dress and the whole appearance of that person, and her description coincides exactly with all that her employers can remember with regard to the peculiarities in dress and general appearance of the deceased relative whose spirit is being conjured up. The identity of the person required being thus established, questions may now be put as to the particular difficulties on account of which the family want to consult the spirit of their ancestor. This spirit, however, is not made to appear, but the somnambule pretending to see it and to be in conversation with it, acts as interpreter, and answers all questions in the name of that spirit and with an unnatural shrill voice. When the curiosity of the audience has been thus satisfied they try to awake the somnambule by shouting her name three times into her ears. Soon her body begins to tremble, one limb after another seems to shake off its torpor, the woman raises herself up, and goes through all the pantomime of a person suddenly roused from a heavy sleep, expressing most dramatically an immense surprise at finding herself in such a place and in such circumstances. Then the somnambule speedily falls into her professional swagger, asks for her wages, which, according to the means of her employers, vary from five cents to five taels or more, and departs chuckling, I imagine, over the credulity of her deluded victims.

"In conclusion I may remark that the deity to which the above given incantation is addressed, is supposed to be that popular deity which is commonly called 'the seven sisters.'* By some it is considered identical with the spirit of the Wega in Lyra,† by others it is identified with the spirit of the Pleiades;‡ and this latter explanation I consider to be most plausible, because the Pleiades are in Chinese colloquial called 'the star of the seven ladies.'§"

Another mode of divination employed is by means of a small image carved out of willow wood (See *supra* for qualities attributed to this wood). The medium is in this case also a woman. A recent writer thus describes the *modus operandi*: "The image is first exposed to the dew for forty-nine nights, when after the performance of certain ceremonies it is believed to have the power of speaking. The image is laid upon the stomach of the woman to whom it belongs, and she by means of it pretends to be the medium of communication between the dead and the living. She sometimes sends the image into the world of spirits to find the person about whom intelligence is sought; it then changes into an elf or sprite, and ostensibly departs on its errand. The spirit of the person enters the image, and gives the information sought after by the surviving

* (七姊).　† (織女星).　‡ (昴星).　§ (七姑星).

relatives. The woman is supposed not to utter a word, the message seeming to proceed from the image. The questions are addressed to the medium, the replies appear to come from her stomach; there is probably a kind of ventriloquism employed, and the fact that the voice appears to proceed from the stomach undoubtedly assists the delusion; any way, there are scores and scores of these mediums implicitly believed in, and widows who desire to communicate with their deceased husbands, or people who desire any information about a future state, invariably resort to their aid." In Kwang-hsi again there are wizards who use a magic water called *ku-tu*.* They take this medicine and smear it on a grain of rice, which they throw away. The natives gravely believe that if any one is unfortunate enough to touch this grain of rice, he at once grows ill; his stomach swells, and continues to do so for a month or so until he at length bursts and out gush, not bowels, but unboiled rice. If the *ku tu* is smeared on straw, the stomach of the person touching it, in like manner, becomes full of straw!

Mesmerism also has its Chinese votaries. A practice somewhat similar to our mesmerism and used to gain money by exhibitions on the 5th of the 8th moon, is very common in Canton. The performer reads with the person operated on certain incantations, *chou*,† whereupon the patient falls into a mesmeric sleep. During this sleep, he is able, though never taught the exercise, to go through all sorts of tricks of fence—the native explanation being that the patients' soul having departed from the body, the spirit of a deceased fencing-master occupies the empty tenement.

Divination by Virgilian, Homeric or Biblical Lots, in which the book being opened at random the sense of the words covered by the thumb is held to be prophetic, finds an exact counterpart in a Chinese practice. The classical works (an odd coincidence, as the two most celebrated of Western classics give their names to the *Sortes Homericæ* and *Sortes Virgilianæ*)‡ are chiefly availed of for this purpose; but the Chinese pay more attention to the lucky or unlucky meaning of the particular characters touched than to the sense of the sentence in which they occur. Any one even but slightly acquainted with the written character of the language will easily conceive the vast field it presents for such purposes. Thus *nu*,§ a woman, enters into the composition of a large member of characters having an evil signification, and its presence in the word touched is therefore unlucky. The literary section of the community rather discourage frivolous appeals to such divinations, but are not above being guided by them in affairs which they deem important.

I have already referred to the omens deduced from bamboo slips selected or shaken out at random from a bamboo box. Fortune-tellers and joss-house

* 蠱毒   † 咒.

‡ Gibbon (*Decline and Fall of the Roman Empire*) says: " This mode of divination by accepting as an omen the first sacred words which in particular circumstances should be presented to the eye or ear was derived from the Pagans, and the Psalter or Bible was substituted for the poems of Homer or Virgil. From the fourth to the fourteenth century these *sortes sanctorum*, as they are styled, were repeatedly condemned by the decrees of councils, and repeatedly practised by Kings, Bishops and Saints."

§ 女.

keepers divine future events for their credulous clients in a somewhat similar way. A number of papers are prepared, marked with characters the same as those on the bamboo slips, but also having short sentences added indicative of good or ill luck. A slip being thrown out, the paper containing its character is referred to, and the sentence inscribed on it is accepted as the answer. Street fortune-tellers frequently train birds to select one or more from a heap of papers, each marked with a single ominous character. The fortune-teller then proceeds to explain the prophetic meaning hidden in the character thus chosen. Or, if he does not possess a trained bird, the client himself picks out a paper for similar interpretation. A very popular form of domestic divination is that already noted as availed of at the new year—going out into the street and accepting the first words heard as an omen.

Chiromancy or Divination by Palmistry has its votaries in China as in Europe, the predictions of our English gypsies being arrived at in very nearly the same way. The lines in the palm of the hand known as the "line of life or longevity," "line of fortune," "line of the stomach," bear similar names in the vocabulary of native chiromancers, the same line both in China and England being referred to as that of longevity. A native account says: "The lines indicate whether a man be spendthrift or the reverse; whether he will be lucky, wealthy, and prosperous, or attain high position; whether he will have children, their sex, and whether or not they will survive; and finally whether he will have more than one wife." The skin peeling from the palm of the hand (a common occurrence when a person unused to manual labour performs work which abrades or blisters the palms) is looked upon as an unlucky omen. The evil omen attached to white specks on the finger nails has been already noticed; but there does not appear to exist any practice of divination by this means such as was formerly practised in England under the name of Onychomancy or Onymancy.*
Physiognomy is however much believed in by the Chinese, and auguries from the countenance—a form of divination which we all more or less unconsciously adopt, as witness such phrases as "he looks born to be hanged" &c.—are frequently drawn and believed in. The Chinese have a quaint way of dividing off the facial ages. At 30 years a man is said to have arrived at the epoch of the eyebrows; at 36 at that of the eyes, and so on, at the epoch of the nose, lips, cheek, bone, chin, &c.

Finally the "Divination by a green ivie leaf" recorded by an old writer,† in which the health or sickness for the coming twelve months of the party practising it is divined by the green or black appearance of a leaf immersed in water for six days, is faintly paralleled by the ominous virtues attributed by the Chinese to the leaves of the juniper tree and pumelo plant. No doubt a fuller investigation than the present writer is able to institute would elucidate other points of agreement in this class of superstitions. But enough has been given to shew that the Chinese mind has for ages been subject to the same influences as obtain amongst ourselves, though happily in our case (with the exception of spiritualism) now only surviving amongst the lowest classes of the community.

* *Pop. Antiquities*, Vol. III., p. 350. † *Ibid.*, Vol. III., 357.

VI.—SUPERSTITIONS AS TO VARIOUS SUBJECTS.

There are in China a large number of generally believed Superstitions which it is difficult to class under any of the foregoing heads. The mysterious properties ascribed to the hare are peculiarly interesting. A prejudice against eating its flesh is coeval with Chinese history. In the Erh-ya* we find it stated that the people of Yo-yang "considered the hare to be a telluric genius so that nobody dared to hunt it," and throughout China it has always been looked upon (especially the red variety) as a divine animal.† Albino hares are regarded as omens of good, and their appearance a mark of heavenly approval. In Dr. Eitel's *Handbook of Chinese Buddhism, Art.* SAKCHI, we read, that an unselfish hare who threw itself into the fire, to offer its flesh as food for others, was transferred by Indra to the centre of the Moon.‡ The superstition concerning hares is common to China and India. Nor, though it does not take precisely the same form, is a belief in the portentous attributes of this animal wanting at home. For a hare to cross a man's path early in the morning is an ill omen throughout Europe. And a Highlander of the 42nd Regiment, in his printed memoirs, notices the same harbinger of evil as having crossed his own path on a day of personal disaster in Spain.§ It is noteworthy that the Goddess Freya is represented as attended by hares, who act as train and light-bearers. The hare moreover is reputed to be the commonest disguise of a witch in all the Northern Countries of Europe.‖

Equally as widespread as the foregoing superstition is a common belief, that drowned bodies may be discovered by throwing into the water certain objects which, it is asserted, will stop over the exact spot where the corpse may lie. The American Indians use a chip of cedar wood. In England a loaf of bread loaded with quicksilver is used, while in Ireland similar use is made of a wisp of straw, bound round with a strip of parchment on which some cabalistic words have been written by the parish priest. In Java and in some parts of China a living goat (a sheep, I believe, will do as well) is cast into the water, and its dead body will, as is believed, indicate the resting place of the drowned man. As regards running streams it is easy to account for this common superstition by natural facts, but the varied forms it assumes are interesting. Another Chinese superstition relates to the use of salt, which is thrown into the water when any one has been rescued from drowning. A few months since a correspondent wrote to a Shanghai newspaper as follows:—"Yesterday afternoon

---

* 爾雅.
† *N. & Q. C. & J.*, Vol. II., p. 69.
‡ *Handbook of Chinese Buddhism*, p. 107.
§ *Predictions Realised*, p. 87.
‖ *Folk-lore of the Northern Counties*, p. 166 *et seq.*

a youngster of the Chinese nationality fell into the water off a pontoon. So his relatives set to work to fish him out, which humane act being accomplished, was followed by two old women very properly pulling his ears for trying to drown himself, and giving them trouble, while another old woman threw salt into the water at the spot he had fallen in. Can any of your readers inform me what the salt-throwing meant, and whether it is a custom on such occasions to do so?" The query remained unanswered. Nor has subsequent enquiry enabled me to throw any light upon the subject. "It's a local custom," was the only answer I could get. But a reference to Brand gives us some very interesting facts in connection with the use of salt for the purposes of lustration.* Flinging salt over the left shoulder to avert threatened calamity is a well-known custom. The Greeks and Romans used it in their lustrations, and Jews and Pagans alike used it in their sacrifices *as a propitiation*. The Romans especially designed it as a propitiatory offering to avert the vengeance of Stygian or infernal Gods—an exact parallel to the Chinese custom. In the Isle of Man, a gift of salt is an essential element in numerous transactions. The Scotch used to, and perhaps still, put salt in the first milk taken from a cow after calving. That the Chinese should credit salt with propitiatory virtues also is therefore curious. Another item of our own household folk-lore, concerning the last piece of any edible left on a dish, is purely Chinese. While our goodwives give it the name of the "bachelor's bit," the Chinese call it the "poison piece,"—not because it is in itself poisonous, but because he who takes it may fare as badly as if he had been veritably poisoned. The Chinese think it unlucky to have the spout of a kettle, standing on the fire, turned outwards;—a belief I can only match by our superstition that it forebodes ill to cross two knives on the dinner table, being unable to trace the origin of either superstition.

I can hardly avoid in this place a notice of the singular geomantic superstitions known as *Fêng-shui*, regarding which Dr. Eitel has written so excellent a brochure. That learned writer answers the question "what is Fêng-shui?" in the following words: "Fêng-shui [the words themselves signify wind and water] is, as I take it, but another name for natural science. . . . It is simply the blind gropings of the Chinese mind after a system of natural science, which gropings, untutored by practical observation of nature, and trusting almost exclusively in the truth of alleged ancient tradition, and in the force of abstract reasoning, naturally left the Chinese mind completely in the dark." No more accurate definition for scientific purposes could be given, and to those who feel an interest in the subject I cannot do better than recommend the perusal of his work. But for present purposes, in which the practical rather than the theoretical side of popular belief is necessarily dealt with, the reply must be framed somewhat differently. Fêng-shui, then, is a system of geomancy which determines the good or ill luck of localities as regards their occupation for purposes of building, cultivation, burial, etc., etc. By way of illustrating

---

* *Pop. Antiquities*, Vol. III., p. 160 *et. seq.*

this interpretation the following paragraph from a Shanghai newspaper, written of course simply for "news" purposes, is apposite:—"The general excitement caused in Hangchow, in common, apparently, with the rest of the province, was some weeks ago intensified by a development of the well-known superstition of *Fêng-shui*. A number of people having died in a certain part of the town, enquiries began to be made as to the cause of a mortality somewhat specially localised. But instead of looking, as Westerns almost instinctively would, to the physical conditions and environments of the district, the good folks of Hangchow called in the learning of the geomancers to explain the cause of the 'evil influence.' These worthies were not long in pointing to a range of buildings belonging to one of the American Missions, that stood on a hill overlooking the district where the abnormal mortality had prevailed. These buildings, though not high in themselves, were yet elevated by their site above all the surrounding buildings, and thus they interrupted the benign influences of the *Fêng-shui*. The question then came to be, how the evil was to be remedied. The traditional mode of procedure would have been to organise a mob, raise a disturbance, and during its continuance contrive to pull down or burn the obnoxious premises. But, on the one hand, past experience of foreigners has convinced the authorities that this way of dealing with foreign property is sure to entail serious consequences; while, on the other, the satisfactory results of diplomatic action as illustrated at Peking has gradually inclined them to the *suaviter-in-modo* policy. Accordingly a number of the gentry were commissioned to proceed to Ningpo and put themselves in communication with the United States Consul on the subject. Arrived in Ningpo they drew up a petition to that gentleman, setting forth the fears and anxieties which were excited among the common people of Hangchow, by the disturbance of the *Feng-shui* occasioned by the mission premises in question, and setting forth the willingness of the authorities to grant them a site and erect buildings on some other site to be agreed on between them and the missionaries, or to pay the missionaries a money equivalent for the surrender of their property. The missionaries, on being communicated with by Dr. Lord, signified their preference of the proposal to grant them an equally eligible site and erect suitable buildings elsewhere, in exchange for their existing property, and this arrangement is now in course of being carried out." No better instance of the difficulties which Fêng-shui presents to foreign missionary and commercial enterprise could be adduced.

A superstitious belief in the value of human blood and portions of the body as medicinal aids seems to be common to the ignorant classes of many nations. Just two years ago, a number of lepers were reported to have made their appearance at Whampoa and its vicinity, attacking and killing healthy men, that they might drink the blood and eat the intestines of those killed, which, lepers are under the firm belief, will cure them of their loathsome disease. The native residents at Whampoa became very apprehensive about this, and exercised very great caution in their trips into the surrounding country in obedience to the time-honoured custom of worshipping at the tombs. A Chinaman, who was employed on board one of the river steamers, caught the disease, and, as was currently stated at the time, resorted to the *modus operandi* stated above. Female lepers, by the way, believe that they will become free from the disease if they communicate it to men willing to live with them, and as some are always to be found sufficiently dead to ordinary feeling to do so, leprosy has by this means been spread more than it would otherwise be.

The idea of cannibalism for other purposes is by no means unfamiliar to the Cantonese. When the rebels, called "patriots" by the half-informed enthusiasts of those days, held possession of the Blenheim Reach Fort, they used to drink the blood and eat the hearts of the Imps, (*i.e.* foreigners) whom they made prisoners. Colonel Yule, in his exhaustive work on Marco Polo (Vol. I., p. 275), devotes a lengthy note to the subject of Chinese and Tibetan cannibalism. The Arab travellers of the 9th century relate that, "In China it occurs sometimes that the governor of a province revolts from his duty to the emperor. In such a case he is slaughtered and eaten. In fact the Chinese eat the flesh of all men who are executed by the sword." Dr. Rennie states (and I can myself confirm the assertion) that after an execution at Peking certain large pith-balls are steeped in the blood of the defunct criminal, and under the name of "blood-bread" are sold as a medicine for consumption. It is only to the blood of decapitated criminals that any such healing power is attributed. "It is asserted that the executioners of Mr. de Chappedelaine, a Romish missionary murdered in Yunnan in 1862, were seen to eat the heart of their victim, and Mr. Cooper, the well-known traveller, was told by a Bishop of the same mission, that he had seen men in Yunnan eating the heart and brains of a celebrated robber, who had been executed." In all these cases the idea underlying this horrible act is, that by eating a portion of the victim, especially the heart, one acquires the valour with which he was endowed.

Nor do the Chinese stand alone in their silly stories respecting the use of the children's eyes and blood for photographic purposes. I note that a recent report of the Smyrna mission alludes to a superstition amongst the Greek Christians of the Levant curiously similar. They hold that the Jewish ritual enjoins the shedding of blood at the feast of the Passover, and that the Jews annually inveigle a Christian child into their toils, fatten it up, and then open its arteries to utilize the blood.* This blood, it is believed, is kneaded into the unleavened bread by the priests, who afterwards distribute this

* Alexander, if we may credit the account given by Quintus Curtius, was terrified by blood flowing from inside his soldiers' bread during the siege of Tyre in 332 B.C. His seer, Aristanda, foresaw in this crimson efflux of the vital stream out of the commissariat a happy issue for the Macedonian; and the warriors thus never took Tyre. From the year 1004, the alarming spectacle of the bleeding host and bread, as well as the bewitched bloody milk, several times in each century, gave simple folk a scare. But the victims of superstition have the bump of casualty remarkably developed, and, in 1410, thirty-eight Jews were burnt to ashes because they had tortured the consecrated host until it bled.—*Chambers' Journal.*

devilish confectionery to their congregations, for a small pecuniary consideration.*

But the superstitions regarding the uses of human blood or flesh are not confined to the instances above given. It used to be believed at Canton, and perhaps now is, that the blood of an unborn infant was all effective for magical purposes.† It is used as a charm against husbands by a sect called 迷夫教, a set of young unmarried women, comprising a sisterhood who are sworn never to marry. If forced by their parents to do so, they then employ this charm to destroy their husbands in order to remain single, and be faithful to the oaths of the sisterhood. A case is on record in which a Fokienese availed himself of this drug to influence a woman for improper purposes, and her subsequent death in child-birth was regarded as the natural result of her yielding to the horrible charm.

More wide-spread is a belief in the restorative qualities of human flesh and blood to the sick. Parents suffering from long-standing or dangerous diseases are frequently offered a decoction of medicine in which is mixed a piece of the flesh of one of their children. It is considered an act of great filial piety to cut a slice off one's calf to mix it with medicine for a parent. The practice is still followed even to the present day. Honourable mention is often made in the *Peking Gazette* of such cases. It has of late been written down by the native press, particularly by the *Chinese Mail*. A recent issue of the Shanghai *Courier and Gazette* (November 1875) contained the following paragraph amongst it local items:—"Two model sons are now living at Soochow, whose mother was one day taken alarmingly ill. They were very poor; but medical assistance was urgently necessary, and so the elder brother went to implore the assistance of a celebrated doctor. He was only able, of course, to offer the great man a small fee; and the great man loftily refused to come. The poor lad threw himself on the ground before him and bumped his head till it ached, but the doctor was quite immoveable. So he went home and told his younger brother how unsuccessful he had been. The unfortunate woman

---

* The object of the ceremony is, according to the myth, to cleanse the Jewish race in general, and the participators of the rite in particular, from the guilt of Calvary. It does not appear that the Chinese Jews have any legend of similar import.

† A correspondent of *Notes and Queries* writes: "Wife-beating, to the effusion of blood, may be a novel method of securing luck in herring-fishery, but to draw blood is practised in some of the fishing villages on the north-east coast of Scotland, under the belief that success follows the act. The act must be performed on New Year's day, and the fortune is his only who is the first to shed blood. If the morning of the New Year is such as to allow the boats of the village to put to sea, there is quite a struggle as to which boat will reach the ground first, so as to gain the coveted prize, the first to shed blood of the year. If the weather is unfavorable for fishing, those in possession of guns—and a great many of the fishermen's houses possess one—are out, gun in hand, along the shore, before daybreak, in search of some bird or wild animal, no matter how small, that they may draw blood, and thus make sure of one year's good fortune."

Mr. Latouche in his *Travels in Portugal* (1875) narrates a story illustrative of the national belief in the wehr wolf (lobishomem), in which a Portuguese "wise woman" is reported as saying that "if a *lobis homem* can murder and drink the blood of a newly born child, the enchantment ceases and she is a lobis-homem no longer."

was dying; what was to be done? At length the young boy hit upon an expedient. He cut a great piece of flesh out of his left arm, boiled it down to a broth, and gave it his mother to drink. It is said that she recovered." In May 1874, a memorial in the *Peking Gazette* records how the Deputy Governor of Honan petitioned in reference to a dutiful daughter who cut a piece of flesh from her arm, in order to cure her father of his sickness. "In the present Holy Dynasty, filial piety rules the Empire, and this doctrine originates in the female sex. In the district of Chinyang there lived a daughter remarkable for her filial piety, whose name after her marriage, was Mrs. Wang. In the fifth year of the reign of the Emperor Hëen-fung, this young lady's father became dangerously ill, and his filial daughter, lighting incense sticks, announced (to the gods) her desire to sacrifice her own body for her father's sake. After this announcement, her father's illness increasing, and his physicians being unable to cure him, this filial daughter secretly cut off a piece of flesh from her arm, and putting it into the medicine prescribed, gave it to her father who, on eating it, immediately recovered. Some time afterwards the daughter's female attendants, perceiving the mark on her arm, questioned her as to the cause and learned from her the facts already stated. There was not a single individual of all those who heard the narrative who was not struck with amazement." The young lady in question was shortly afterwards married, but her father dying some ten years afterwards she "pined away and died for grief." The petition from which the above quotation is made prays the Emperor to order that a Triumphal Arch be erected to her memory, as was usual in cases when extreme filial piety had been displayed, and the petition was of course granted.

A common saying that "a selfish child will be cut while being shaved" embodies an idea not altogether unfamiliar to ourselves. But another Chinese superstition, which certainly existed in full force at one time, though I have failed to get any positive confirmation of its existence at the present day, obliges us to seek its parallel amongst other than Aryan races. A belief in weather conjuring by means of "rain stones" seems to have been introduced into China from Mongolia, and though it never took extensive root it attracted sufficient attention to induce the Emperor Shih-tsung in 1724-25, to issue an edict on the subject. It is addressed to the Mongolian Banner Corps, and says: "If I offering prayer in sincerity have yet room to fear it may please Heaven to have *my* prayer unanswered, it is truly intolerable that mere common people wishing for rain should at their own caprice set up altars of earth, and bring together a rabble of Hoshang and Taossŭ to conjure the spirits to gratify their wishes." Colonel Yule, in his *Marco Polo*, from which (I. p. 273) I take this reference, gives some long and interesting notes on the subject. Rain stones are used by the Samoans in the Pacific, and if my memory does not deceive me, by some of the North American Indian tribes also.

A popular belief exists in Central China that the practice of gymnastics, if carried out with sufficient faithfulness, will enable the student to avoid the common lot, and pass bodily into a future state "ascending to heaven with his fleshly body." That such a belief exists is not unlikely, and it is probably a vulgar superstition based on the more reasonable opinion that such exercises tend to extreme longevity. Another queer superstition (the adjective is not classical but expressive) relates to bridges. I have already adverted to the care taken as regards houses by placing on them charms, &c., to avert possible evil. But bridges, for some mysterious reason, have occult virtues and defects of their own. A native account says, "If bridges are not placed in proper positions such as the laws of geomancy indicate they may endanger the lives of thousands by bringing about a visitation of small-pox or sore eyes (!). They materially affect the prosperity of the neighbourhood. There is a legend that during the building of the stone bridge situated near the small eastern gate of Shanghai (陸家百僑 the 'Loh-family bridge,') some difficulty was found in laying the foundations. The builder thereupon vowed to Heaven the lives of two thousand children if the stones could be placed properly. The Goddess addressed, however, intimated that she would not require all their lives, but that the number in question would be attacked by small pox. This took place, and about half of those attacked died." Stories like this circulated amongst coolies and compradores are a fair specimen of popular legendry in this connection. But why bridges should especially require such sacrifices it is difficult to say.

Amongst what may be termed domestic superstitions is one that, if a person be afflicted with a swelling, touching it three times with the hem of a woman's garment is efficacious as a cure. If, when one is boiling a pot full of liquid, a straw be tied round the neck of the pot, it is believed that the contents will never boil over or get burned. Another piece of cook's folk-lore relates to eggs. As everybody knows an egg suddenly plunged into boiling water will most likely break. But the Chinese cook averts this occurrence by previously describing a circle with the egg round the rim of the pot, which he believes is an infallible protection against any fracture of the shell. The Japanese, by the way, draw auguries from the noise made by boiling. Over a bright fire, a rice boiler is said to vibrate with such violence at times as to give forth a loud humming noise. If this begins faintly and grows afterwards stronger, it is said to indicate good luck; if loudly, the reverse is predicted, but in such cases it should at once be stopped by enveloping it in the under-clothing of a female (a virgin, if possible.)

A curious antidote against sickness is very commonly applied by parents at Canton to their infant children on the fifth day of the fifth month. This consists in staining their foreheads and navels with cinnebar or vermilion, leaves of the sago palm and garlic bulbs being at the same time suspended over the entrance doors to prevent the intrusion of evil spirits. A medicated cake prepared at *noon* of the day in question, and known as "the noon day tea" (午時茶) is also in much repute for the cure of diseases, as is also a sort of congee boiled at the same hour with five kinds of pease.

The all-pervading *yang* and *yin* principle so naturally influences the whole arcana of Chinese belief that it is not surprising to find it applied to the care of such useful contributors to the national industries as silkworms. These are said to belong to the *yang* or male influence and to be under the protection of a special constellation. Anything male, such as men, sunlight, &c., is congenial to them, and anything female deleterious. Hence pregnant women (development of the *yin* principle) are not allowed to approach them ; and even the presence of a new-born child in too close proximity is thought to be deleterious.

Finally, I may note that a curious superstition obtains regarding murderers. It is believed that if the corpse of the murdered man lies with its fists closed, it is a sign that the murderer will soon be captured. If, on the contrary, the hands are extended, the omen foretells that he will for at least some time make good his escape. It is strange, by the way, that so widespread a belief as that relating to the bleeding of a corpse when touched by its murderer has not some analogy in China. At least I have failed to find any, though a not quite dissimilar superstitious idea is prevalent, that if a man has died a violent death—either by process of the law, or by the act of a murderer—and the dead man is dissatisfied, blood will come out of his mouth, eyes and nostrils on the appearance of a close relative.

VII.—GHOSTS, APPARITIONS, AND SUPERNATURAL BEINGS.*

No one who has thus far followed my imperfect efforts to convey an idea of the popular beliefs of the Chinese will be surprised to find that ghosts and apparitions occupy an even greater place in their superstitious lore than is the case with ourselves. In the words of a native friend, "China is full of ghosts." There is scarcely a popular play in which a ghost does not play a conspicuous part in aiding to right the wronged or to punish the guilty. The person to whom he appears on such occasions generally counterfeits either sleep or insensibility; but now and then while wakeful and active the actor (especially if he be the ruffian of the piece) is scared out of his senses by the apparition in the most approved melodramic style. Many popular stories turn also on the appearance of supposed ghosts, who turn out to be quite *bona fide* citizens in the flesh, and simply enforce the moral that conscience makes a coward of the wrongdoer. A story of this sort runs to the following effect, and narrates an incident stated by Mr. C. T. Gardner to have happened only some five years ago at Chinkeang. There were two partners, named Chang and Li, on one occasion returning by way of the canal from Yangchow, where they had been collecting debts. Chang saw Li standing on the edge of the boat, and the crime of pushing him into the water, and thus becoming sole possessor of the money, suggested itself. Chang, therefore, pushed Li into the canal. Next year, at the time the murder was committed, Chang fell very ill, and the ghost of Li appeared to him in a threatening form, and told him that unless he paid over the sum properly belonging to the dead man's family, he would die. Chang promised to do so, and got well, but his health being restored he broke his promise, and still kept the money. Again, the following year, at the same time, Li's ghost again appeared, looking still angrier. Again Chang was induced to make the promise, and this time he kept it. However, his health seemed permanently to suffer, everything went wrong, business fell off, and he determined to try and change his luck by migrating to other parts; he consequently went to Honan. What was his astonishment when he again saw Li, not now in the middle of the night by the side of the bed where he lay sick, but in broad daylight, and in the street. His terror was extreme, he rushed forward, and made a ko-tow, and said, "I have already done as you ordered me, why do you still haunt me?" To which Li replied, "I am no ghost; what do you mean?" Then Chang told him how he had twice appeared, and how his share of the money had been paid to his family. Li then said, "So, it was not an accident my falling into the river? I had neglected to pay due respect to the spirit of my father, and when I tumbled in the river, and was nearly drowned, I thought it a punishment for my impiety."

"The spirits of the dead," remarks Mr. Chalmers, "were perhaps known at first only as objects of superstitious fear under the name Kwei 鬼 *ghosts*. The top of this character is supposed to represent a human skull. It had from the first an unpleasant association, and hence it is seldom used in speaking respectfully of the dead. In the poetry it occurs only twice, once as our modern Ghost, and once as the name of a place—Ghostland.

"An interesting statement is attributed to Confucius in the Book of Rites (§ Tan-kung) that in the time of the Hea, the earliest dynasty, they did not sacrifice to the dead, but simply made for them incomplete implements of bamboo, earthenware without polish, harps unstrung, organs untuned, and bells unhung, which they called 'bright implements' implying that the dead are spirits (shen) and bright. There is something really beautiful in this; and the substitution of 'bright spirits' or 'spiritual intelligences' for 'ghosts' is an euphemism of which we feel the necessity as much as the Chinese; for who likes to speak of his relations as gone to the shades and to the fellowship of ghosts?"

One peculiarity of the Chinese belief respecting ghosts is forcibly recalled by Charles Dickens's description of the Ghost of Christmas Past in his famous "Carol." They are frequently seen in shapeless form, *i.e.* that the head will first be visible and then the feet, then the body, and so on, the various parts appearing and disappearing in swift succession. Another quaint belief is that a ghost has no chin, and to say to a Cantonese "*ni mo ha-pa*"—"You've no chin," is equivalent to saying "You're a Ghost." Furthermore, the conventional white clothing which European superstition bestows on nearly all ghostly visitors is absent from the Chinese idea. A ghost in this country always appears in the dress he was accustomed to wear during life—a very Marley in fact—and conducts himself in a very ordinary way. There is indeed a refreshing absence of the fee-faw-fum element in Chinese ghostology, this eminently practical people taking a most matter-of-fact view of spirit vagaries. They agree with us however in allotting the hours of darkness to such visitors, who, as with ourselves, are compelled to disappear as the cock's crow announces the returning dawn. The candle flame, which with us burns blue as the being from another world intrudes himself, is in China alleged to burn green—an odd reminder of the "green fear" of the Greeks. Most Chinese ghost stories turn upon some end to be accomplished by the supernatural visitor; they retail none of the sprightly friskiness attributed to ghosts in Western lands, and altogether the Chinese specimen presents, as a rule, an edifying illustration of how to do one's work in the quietest and most straightforward manner possible. It must not, however, be imagined that they are endowed by popular belief with benevolent intentions. On the contrary they are supposed to be maliciously inclined, and the very fact that the words for "ghost" and "devil" are the same, and form a portion of the objectionable epithets applied to foreigners (*Kwei-tsze* in mandarin or *Fan-kwai* in Cantonese) demonstrates the popular belief. To see a ghost is almost always regarded as an evil omen, and a Chinaman is quite as easily scared as a European by the unwelcome sight. One thus visited is described by his pitying neighbours as "down in his luck." As a rule, ghosts in China, it is alleged, most often appear either to intimate friends or relations, or to downright enemies. In the former case it is to request the fulfilment of some unaccomplished duty or to aid virtue in distress, in which latter case the ghost gives the weaker but upright party material aid in disposing of his antagonist. As an illustration of the first-named sort of apparition, I quote the following, recently communicated by a resident to the *North China Daily News*, as told him by his teacher to excuse his non-appearance for some few days:—

"It happened thus; three years ago a soldier who lived near our house was ordered to join his regiment, which was about to march against the rebels. As he was going to battle he did not wish to take his money with him, and he called on my uncle and asked him to take charge of $40, the amount of his property, until his return. My uncle accordingly took charge of the money, and the soldier joined his regiment; but he must have been killed in battle, as we have never heard from him since. The day before yesterday, my uncle, who has for some time been suffering from illness, called us to his bedside, and told us that he was about to die. The soldier, he said, had appeared to him and insisted that my uncle should immediately join him in Hades. We asked my uncle whether he had committed any fault with regard to the $40, for which we might make some atonement by punishing him in any way? He replied that the money was all right, and that we should find it in a certain drawer which he pointed out. My uncle died that day, and it was of course impossible, under such circumstances, that I could come to your Excellency's place to study."

Among recent stories of ghosts is one related in a native newspaper of a mandarin who met his death in the late collision between the steamers *Fusing* and *Ocean*. The unfortunate man was a passenger in the former steamer, which was sunk in the catastrophe, over 60 other people being also drowned. According to the story his ghost appeared to his wife, who was living in Soochow, streaming with water from head to foot. He told her that he had unfortunately been drowned and could therefore enjoy no more of her society. He also stated that he had sent by a certain friend of his some money for her use before he took passage in the *Fusing*, and that the friend would arrive shortly. The wife was left in a state of bewilderment, and did not exactly know what to make of it. A day or two afterwards the friend named actually came with the packet of dollars, his arrival being shortly followed by the intelligence of the *Fusing's* disaster.

Another story relates to a young Cantonese, who was made commander of a Chinese man-of-war belonging to the Foochow Arsenal fleet. Shortly after his promotion, he was taken ill and died. He was unmarried, as he was very young —only 23 years of age. When he fell sick, he was living at the house of a very intimate friend, a compradore in one of the foreign firms at Foochow. After his death, the friend frequently saw his ghost, and one night he saw it more distinctly than ever. He was lying in bed half asleep and half awake, when he saw the ghost standing by his bedside weeping. The friend addressed it and said: "Young man, you need not cry, it is your fate; you should be satisfied with it." Thereupon the ghost disappeared, and never shewed itself again to the same party. The ghost appeared however to the men on board the ship he had been commanding, being often seen to pace up and down the deck, as was his wont at night during his lifetime, and sometimes to place itself in the attitude of drilling the men. Though the appearance here narrated seems to have been objectless, the story is quoted as being the type of numberless others which find insertion in the native prints.

The Chinese endow certain sorts of ghosts with peculiarly malevolent powers. Thus those of women who die in childbed, or while pregnant, are peculiarly obnoxious, and those of suicides still more so. The ghosts of those who die natural deaths seldom appear to the survivors; as a rule the fact of a man's ghost appearing implies that he has died by violence.* The commonest type of ghost story to be met with in China is that wherein somebody who has been foully dealt with appeals to those who represent his interests to avenge him. It would of course be more odd if there were no coincidences pointing to the truth of the alleged appearances than if there were not. But I must confess that in China as elsewhere they sometimes leave a *bona fide* impression of the marvellous which can neither be explained nor rejected.

---

* Lady Fanshaw, visiting the head of an Irish sept in his moated baronial grange, was made aware that banshees are not peculiar to Scotland. Awakened at midnight by an awful, unearthly scream, she beheld by the light of the moon a female form at the window of her room, which was too far from the ground for any woman of mortal mold to reach. The creature owned a pretty, pale face, and red, dishevelled hair, and was clad in the garb of old—very old—Ireland. After exhibiting herself some time, the interesting spectre shrieked twice and vanished. When Lady Fanshaw told her host what she had seen he was not at all surprised. "A near relation," said he, "died last night in this castle. We kept our expectation of the event from you lest it should throw a cloud over the cheerful reception which was your due. Now, before such an event happens in the family and castle, the female spectre you saw always becomes visible. She is believed to be the spirit of a woman of inferior rank, whom one of my ancestors married, *and whom he afterward caused to be drowned in the moat, to expiate the dishonor done to our race*."—*All the Year Round*.

When a man has been murdered by another, his ghost will, it is believed, haunt the murderer wherever he goes, and will only be prevented from doing him a mischief by the want of a suitable opportunity. Thus the presence of idols in the same room completely neutralizes the ghost's power, and it is moreover believed that in any case no vital injury can be inflicted on the guilty party until the time of his death, as recorded in the Book of Fate, has arrived. The ghosts of suicides (who are distinguished by wearing red silk handkerchiefs) haunt the places in which they committed the fatal deed and endeavour to persuade others to follow their example; at times, it is believed, even attempting to play executioner by strangling those who reject their advances. Mr Gardner gives the following story as related to him by a Chinese friend:—"A friend of mine, enticed by low rent, took a haunted house, and invited a guest to stay with him. My friend declares he had no dread whatever, and that his guest did not even know that the house was haunted. In the middle of the night he heard a noise as if of struggling proceeding from the guest's bed. He went to see what was the matter, and found his friend choking in his sleep. Thinking this might be accidental, he invited three friends to stay with him, and the phenomenon repeated itself on all three at the same time. Frightened at this, he made enquiries, and found a woman had committed suicide in the guest's chamber, and gave up the house." Another story runs as follows :—"Outside the north gate at Hang-chow there was a house haunted by demons, where no human being dared reside, of which the doors were ever barred and locked. A scholar named Ts'ai bought the house: people all told him he was doing a dangerous thing, but he did not heed them. After the deed of sale had been drawn out, none of his family would enter the house. Ts'ai therefore went by himself, and having opened the doors, lit a candle and sat down. In the middle of the night a woman slowly approached with a red silk handkerchief hanging to her neck, and having saluted him, fastened a rope to the beam of the ceiling, and put her neck in the noose. Ts'ai did not in the least change countenance. The woman again fastened a rope and called on Ts'ai to do as she had done, but he only lifted his leg and put his foot in the noose. The woman said 'You're wrong.' Ts'ai laughed, and said, 'On the contrary, it was you who were wrong a long time ago, or else you would not have come to this pass.' The Ghost cried bitterly, and having again bowed to Ts'ai, departed, and from this time the house was no longer haunted. Ts'ai afterwards distinguished himself as a scholar, and some have identified him with Ts'ai-p̓ing-ho, the Provincial Chancellor." A third tale from the same source illustrates what I have called the practical element in Chinese ghost stories: "At Nanchang, in Kiangsi, were two literary men who used to read in the Polar monastery; one was elderly, the other young; they were united by the bonds of closest friendship. The elder one went to his home, and suddenly died. The younger man did not know of it, and went on with his studies at the monastery in the usual way. One night after he had gone to sleep, he saw his old friend open the bed curtains, come to the bed, and put his hand on his shoulder, saying, 'Brother, it is only ten days since I parted from you, and now a sudden sickness has carried me off. I am a Ghost. I cannot however forget our friendship, and so have come to bid adieu.' The young man was so astounded that he could not speak. The old man reassured him, saying, 'If I had wished to injure you, why should I have told you I was a Ghost; do not fear then. The reason of my visit is that I have a favor to beg of you with regard to the future.' The young man grew a little calmer, and asked 'What can I do?' The Ghost replied, 'I have a mother over 70, and a wife not yet 30; a few piculs of rice are needed for their maintenance. I beg you to have mercy upon me, and supply their wants. That is my first request. I have also an essay which I have written, which has not been printed. I beg of you to get a block cut for it, and print it, so that my name may not utterly die out. This is my second request. Next I owe the stationers some thousands of cash, which I have not paid; kindly settle the claim. This is my third request.' The young scholar assented with a nod. The dead man stood up, and said, 'As you have been kind enough to grant my requests, I will depart.' Saying this he was about to go, when the young scholar, who had observed from what he said that there was a great deal of human feeling in him, and also that his appearance was as usual, lost all fear of the Ghost, and tried to detain him, 'We have been such close friends; will you not stay with me now a little while?' The dead man wept, and came back and sat on the bed, and having conversed about ordinary topics, again stood up, and said, 'I must now go.' He stood up and did not move, his eyes stared, and gradually his features changed. The young scholar got frightened and said, 'Now you have finished what you had to say, you had better go.' But the dead man stood still, and did not depart. The young man shivered in his bed, and a cold perspiration came over him, but still the guest went not, but stood erect by the bedside. The young man got in a still greater fright, and jumped up and ran away. The Ghost ran with him, and the faster the young man ran, the faster ran the Ghost. After a mile or so of this race they came to a wall, over which the young man vaulted, and fell to the ground. The dead man could not get over the wall, so he hung his head over its ledge, and from his mouth fell some saliva which fell on the young man's face as he lay. At daybreak some passers-by gave the young man some ginger, and he awakened from his trance. Meanwhile the family of the dead man sought the corpse, but could not find it, but when they heard the news of the corpse looking over the wall they took the body and buried it."

Although as I have said there is a general absence of "friskiness" in Chinese ghosts, such pranks as those which have attracted attention at home—throwing down crockery, trampling on the floor, &c.—are not unknown. The only difference is that with us, such annoyances seem usually to be purposeless, while in China they are resorted to attract attention to the ghost's demands. Ghosts, say the natives, are much more liable to appear very shortly after death than at any other period. For the first ten days after the spirit has quitted the body a ghost is said to be 回煞 *ui shat* (in Cantonese), returning to its former haunts and attempting to pursue its ordinary avocations. In such cases it is supposed to be accompanied by celestial police termed Yen-lo-hwang, who are responsible that it duly returns to Hades. In order to discover whether such a visit has been paid, the hall in which the body is laid out is strewn with a smooth layer of sand. If it appear clean, or footmarks only are visible, it may be concluded that the deceased is in a state of happiness; but should the marks of chains or dirt be detected, his fate is supposed to be very much the reverse. I may, by the way, note that to constantly dream of deceased relatives is regarded as a sign that the dreamer will soon die.

The superstitions as to deceased husbands visiting their wives are peculiar, but scarcely calculated for popular explanation. A somewhat contemptuous idea seems to prevail amongst the Chinese regarding the intelligence possessed by ordinary ghosts. They are usually spoken of as stupid and easily amenable to the control of those who remain self-possessed. The ghostly hierarchy is well marked off as to its degrees. Thus, on the 17th of the 7th moon, a ceremony called "appeasing the burning mouths," consists in laying out plates filled with cakes and bearing above them invitations to the "Honourable Homeless Ghosts," or those whose relations being too poor to provide for them, leave them to the tender mercies of the general public. Those are the paupers of Ghostland. The writer already quoted, says in his amusing paper:—"Though the invitations are addressed to Ghosts near and far, there seems to be a sort of poor law which practically confines the relief afforded to Ghosts of the parish. Of course, it is only disreputable Ghosts who thus consent to live on charity. These pauper spirits are said to do a great deal of harm, and cause epidemics, but luckily the firing of crackers is a cure for the diseases thus caused, as it drives the hungry Ghosts elsewhere. Besides these low bred and malevolent hobgoblins, there are aristocratic and benevolent spirits, one of whom rules the destiny of each of the Chinese cities. These Ghosts are called Chêng-hwang, and receive their appointments in various manners and for various terms. Thus the Chêng-hwang of Chu-chow in Chê-kiang, is the ghost of a man named Shih, who was formerly magistrate of the place, but who died of grief on being unjustly disgraced. He received his appointment from heaven, and appeared to his successor in office to notify the fact. The Chêng-hwang of Hangchow is the ghost of a censor named Chow, who, being unjustly sentenced to death, memorialized the throne to slay his only son, as he feared he would rebel to avenge his father. Both were executed, and afterwards it being found out that the accusation was false, the Emperor, to make amends, appointed his ghost Chêng-hwang of Hangchow in perpetuity, and having executed his accusers, man and wife, made stone images of them, kneeling and in chains, which he caused to be placed in the Chêng-hwang's temple. The Chêng-hwang of Wu-chang is changed every three to six years, and receives the appointment from the Taoist Patriarch residing at Chang-tien joss-house in Kiangsi, and this is notified to the various Taoist priests."

"The Chinese almanacks describe sixty 'Shin of Offence' or evil ghosts, one of which is abroad on each day of the cycle of sixty. If any one goes out in any particular direction, and afterwards feels heavy-headed or feverish he is supposed to have met this *shin*. He therefore takes some fruit, rice, &c., and politely bows the creature away in the direction where he met the accident. The *shin* are pictured in the almanacks as little naked men. When the demons take possession of a sacrificing witch she talks about happiness and misery. Every time they come she is altogether a *shin* in her eating and drinking and speaking, and every time they go she is altogether a human being. It would be hard to say whether demons are in the witch or the witch in the demons." *

In an old Chinese farce said to date from the Sung Dynasty entitled 王道士收妖 or "How the Taoist priest Wang exorcised the Ghost," Wang goes to a haunted house with all his spiritual apparatus, full robes, mitre, &c., and a gong big enough and noisy enough to frighten the boldest devil. Not a bit however does the ghost quail in the present instance, but seizes the gong, the cap and the robes of the holy man, and vows he will turn the tables. At last the priest goes on his knees, and beseeches the ghost not to exorcise him, as he only came in order to earn a few cash; and had he only known beforehand that his Excellency the ghost was really in the house, he would not have ventured to disturb him. The farce ends by the ghost exorcising the priest.

Ghosts of idols are not unknown to the Chinese. "Ten years ago, when the rebels infested the country and the cities were kept under strict restraint, the people of Canton reported that the idol Kwan-yin's *shin*, her body dressed in white and in her hand a yak's tail, perambulated the city wall protecting the rampart; and at San-shuey the common people reported that the rebels saw the *shin* of the idol Hiun-tan, which is outside the South gate, bodily riding on a black tiger and in his hand a golden whip too awful to be meddled with." *

Another case of god-ghosts visible to the vulgar eye was gravely recorded a few years since in the *Peking Gazette*. When the Mahometans were some time ago besieging the district city of Chang-wei, they suddenly halted, and ran away. The explanation is that when the rebels approached the temple of Ta pi-peh (god of the star Venus) they saw a terrible vision—"gods clad in golden mail and armed with swords and shields, drawn up in battle array, numerous as forest trees, and all along the top of the city wall innumerable red lamps;" and as a general fire of musketry and cannon from the wall was heard, the assailants were scared, and they abandoned their onslaught on the city.

The residence of human ghosts in Hades is supposed to be subject to conditions very like those obtaining amongst mortals. They sally forth on their visits to the world at permitted times and are free so long as they behave themselves. But any infringement of the ghostly laws which regulate their conduct is met by prompt punishment and a seclusion which effectually prohibits their revisiting earthly scenes of pleasure or business. Even when enjoying to the full all the privileges of ghostdom, they are not able at all times to do what they would. Mortals may deter them from appearing by pasting up pictures of

* Chalmers.

Chung-Kwai 鍾葵 the Beelzebub of China, on the walls of their rooms. Talismans written in perfectly unintelligible characters are also in use, and, as already seen, Taoist priests are credited with the possession of curious powers as exorcists. Pictures of Warriors pasted on the doors of houses are efficacious, as are also the pieces of perforated paper so often seen waving from the lintels.

The belief in ghosts does not limit itself to those of mankind only. The spirits of certain animals are also supposed to manifest themselves in a similar way, but this section of the subject will be more fully dealt with under the head of witchcraft and demonology. As an illustration however of animal ghostdom pure and simple, the following story may be cited:—A resident at Canton named Ling was the owner of a monkey belonging to a species known as *yuen*, which is supposed to be peculiarly intelligent and possesses an almost human mind. The natives believe that if one of these monkeys has plenty of water given to it, it will attain an enormous size, larger than that of an average man. The monkey in question had been in Mr. Ling's family for some 40 years, but never having been allowed to drink water, was of small stature. One day Mr. Ling's little son was passing the monkey when it put out its hand and snatched away his cap. The child complained to his father, who thereupon chastised the animal heavily with a whip; upon this the monkey became sulky, refused all food and in a few days died. Shortly afterwards the monkey's ghost began to haunt the house. Food placed on the table vanished mysteriously and many of the curious phenomena attributed to ghostly interference took place. At last a fire broke out in the house unaccountably, and Mr. Ling shifted his residence. But the monkey's ghost still followed him and continued its persecutions. Again he moved house and again the ghost accompanied him, until at length, as a last resource, he took a room in the Temple of the 500 Worthies and finally evaded his persecutor. The monkey ghost did not dare face the gods, and so left him in peace. The party mentioned was but a year ago still residing in the temple.

The foregoing pages, though by no means exhaustive of the subject, will it is thought be sufficient to indicate the agreement of Chinese with Western belief as regards ghosts and apparitions. The line of demarcation between the subjects already treated of, and that of witchcraft and demonology, being somewhat indefinite, those curious in the matter will find additional information in the succeeding chapter under that head.

VIII.—WITCHCRAFT AND DEMONOLOGY.

The subject of Witchcraft and Demonology presents as inexhaustible a field of interesting matter as any other in the wide domain of Chinese Folk-lore. So much however has already appeared on the subject of witchcraft that, were not a full notice of popular Chinese superstitions in this respect an essential portion of the plan I have proposed, I should scarcely venture to deal at length with a matter which has already been handled with considerable ability by other pens. And indeed the following details consist more of a re-arrangement of already accessible information than of much that will be new to students of Chinese social life.

Thirteen hundred years before the birth of Christ, witches and wizards were familiar objects of Chinese superstitious respect. It is probable that they practised their occult arts at a period long anterior even to this, but the direct evidence to that effect is scanty and unreliable. Suffice it to say that the office of "Chief Wizard" was at that date a recognized appointment, and that he and his brethren exerted in those early days a powerful influence over the popular mind. They could "call spirits from the vasty deep," avert pestilence and famine and do all that is pretended on behalf of their modern successors. But scant notices of their doings however are to be found in the ancient records of the Empire. Every now and then it is related how some emperor or celebrated man resorted to the wizard fraternity to discover future events, or the means of avoiding some threatened evil. But it was not until about the third century before the Christian era that such notices were at all common. We then read that wizards existed who could summon familiars and were often consulted by the reigning potentates.

It is especially noteworthy that the hatred of witches and wizards cherished in the West does not seem to exist in China. Those reputed to possess magic powers are regarded with dread, but it is rare to hear of any of them coming to untimely end by mob violence. The more educated literati ridicule the implicit belief placed in their pretensions by the unlettered mob, but take no part in exciting it to violence, and the feeling is abundantly evidenced by the tone adopted in popular novels wherein witchcraft often plays a conspicuous part. Besides those who make a living as professed exorcists, the members of two trades—builders and plasterers—fall under a suspicion of similarly unholy proclivities. Witchcraft has always been deemed a communicable art in China. In the *Supplement to the History of the Genii* we read: "Yang T'ung Yew when a child met a Tauist priest who taught him the art of invocation and gave him a celestial writing of the three August Ones, by which he could command and subject all ghost *shên*, none of them failing to answer him instantly. Yang went down to the ninth depth of the earth to seek for the ghost of a royal concubine amongst the ghost *shên* in that quarter." Indeed the power of summoning demons is a conventional portion of Chinese supernatural tales. Thus, in a recently published translation of a popular novel entitled *The Thunder Peak Pagoda*,* we find the heroine and her servant (both originally serpents) consulting together as to how they shall raise money:—

"'What then can we do?' says the mistress. 'It will be very easy for you, Madam, to find money,' replied the slave girl, 'for you are possessed of supernatural powers, and you have only to make use of some spell this evening, to

* 雷峰塔 *Lûi-fung Tá,* "Thunder-Peak Pagoda," or "The Story of Han-wăn and the White Serpent," Translated from the Chinese by H. C., Interpreter in Her Majesty's Civil Service in China.

enable you to procure whatever sum you may require, and by these means you will prove to him that you are truly of a wealthy family, and that you are the daughter of a high officer.' Pï-chau-niang agreed to what her servant advised, and accordingly that evening, at the third watch, she prepared seven pans of burning charcoal in a circle, and entering therein with a drawn double-edged knife, began walking round and round, muttering incantations; suddenly she uttered a loud cry, and summoned to her presence all the chiefs of the demons from the four corners of the earth, who instantly appeared and knelt before her crying, 'Your servants are present—In what can the spirits serve their mistress?' Pï-chau-niang ordered them to bring her a thousand taels of silver. Hardly had she uttered the words, when the money was before her in twenty ingots of fifty taels each."

The Chinese idea of genii can best be given in the words of their own writers. A genie, says one of them, will live upon air, or even give up breathing the outer air and carry on the process of breathing inwardly, as they say, for days together as in a catalepsy (like an Indian fakeer buried alive?). He will become invisible: he will take the form of any beast, bird, fish or insect. He will mount up above the clouds, dive into the deepest sea or burrow into the centre of the Earth. He will command spirits and demons of all sorts and sizes and have them at his beck and call. And finally after living in the world for perhaps several hundred years he does not die (for a genie is immortal, though a spirit may not be so), but he rides up to heaven on the back of a dragon where he becomes a ruler of spirits.

The Tauist considers genii as the highest class of intelligent beings and places Shên or spirits next below them: the strict Confucianist denies their existence—

> Like cumbrous flesh: but in what shape they choose,
> Dilated or condensed, bright or obscure,
> Can execute their airy purposes,
> And works of love or enmity fulfil.
> *Paradise Lost*, IL., 24.

In Kwan-tzu, sec. 14, we find this definition:—"That which when it would be small becomes like a moth or a grub, when it would be large fills the world, when it would ascend mounts the cloudy air, when it would descend enters the deep—whose transformations are not limited by days, nor its mounting or falling by seasons, is called *Shên* (or spirit)."—The agreement of this with the description of genii given in the *Arabian Nights* is too obvious to need insisting on. Taoist genii (仙人) are thus described: "The genie is a man who had a former existence in the world of spirits, is born into the world either on account of some indiscretion or for some benevolent object, or simply by way of amusement—usually in some lowly situation. He early begins to shew a predilection for things mysterious, to receive visitors from the unseen world, to practice Alchemy and the healing art, to prepare and use certain drugs and charms of which no one knows the use or the virtue but himself, and the more advanced genii from whom he gets from time to time instruction and assistance; and then to give up human food and all ordinary human occupation." After this there is scarcely any marvellous thing which the human mind can fancy that he will not be found doing. One of the most celebrated genii alluded to in Chinese history is Chang Kwoh, who possessed a white mule which could transport him if required thousands of miles in a single day, and which when he halted he folded up and hid away in his wallet.* Another was Hu Kung, 壺公 a magician who effected wonderful cures and was accustomed to retire at sunset to the interior of a gourd hung up at his own doorpost (See *Ch. Readers' Manual*, sect. v.) Many females also are numbered in the list of such beings, one of the most celebrated being Ma Ku 麻姑. The seeds of the Che 芝 plant were reputed by the Tauist mystics to be the food of the genii, as were also the leaves of the Yoh Wang 藥王 tree which grows in the moon. The result of using this food is that the bodies of those who eat of it become pellucid as crystal.† As with the Westerns the genii possess the secret of a magic powder. They use the yellow heron (Hwang Kuh Ko) as an aërial courser.

The "Isles of the genii" San Shên Shan 三仙山 were supposed to lie pretty much where Formosa actually exists, and, like the fabled Atlantis of European superstition, they have been the subject of actual search. Su Shih or Su Fuh, a necromancer who lived about B.C. 219, announced their existence to the then Emperor, and, in accordance with his own request, was placed at the head of a large troop of young men and maidens, and set out on his voyage of discovery; but the expedition, though it steered within sight of the magic island, was driven back by contrary winds. Mr. Mayers adds to this account in his *Manual* that it is conjectured this legend has some reference to attempts at colonizing the Japanese islands. If so the parallel between the Isles of the genii and Atlantis is yet more perfect.

A very superficial comparison of Chinese and Western ideas on the subject of necromancy demonstrates their identity. The familiar stories of Jane Shore and the Countess of Soissons, accused respectively of making waxen images of the Duke of Gloucester and of Louis XIV. to compass their death; the less known account of the death of Ferdinand Earl of Derby, whose death by poison in the reign of Elizabeth was by popular credulity attributed to witchcraft, "a waxen image with hair like that of the unfortunate earl being found in his chamber and reducing every suspicion to certainty;" King James' remarks in his *Daemonology* (Book II., Ch. V.) "that the devil teacheth how to make pictures of wax or clay, that by roasting thereof, the persons that they bear the names of may be continually melted or dried away by continual sickness";—these and the host of similar stories recorded in our own and continental annals all find an exact reproduction in China.‡ There is a well-known legend amongst the Cantonese of a builder having a grudge against

---

* *Chinese Readers' Manual*, p. 6.
† *Chinese Readers' Manual*, p. 284.
‡ The Aymara Indians believe that witches make waxen images of those they wish to injure, and stick thorns in them. They dislike any one having in his possession a portion of their body, hair, &c., such ownership conferring on the posses- sor the power of injuring the original owner. An Indian will pay a large sum to get back hair or other substances, which have thus passed into other hands. See *Eth. Review*, Vol. II., No. 3, p. 236.— The Chinese superstition, based on a similar belief, is that amputated limbs, &c., should be buried or burned.

a woman whose kitchen he was called upon to repair—(builders, as already noted, are believed to often practice witchcraft.) The repairs were duly completed, but somehow or other the woman could never visit the kitchen without feeling ill. Convinced that witchcraft was at the bottom of it, she had the wall pulled down, and sure enough there was discovered in a hollow left for the purpose "a clay figure in a posture of sickness." It may be noted that a reflex of the old English superstition that drawing blood from a witch renders her harmless is suggested by the Chinese belief regarding images such as that above described. Builders or plasterers are supposed to cut a gash in some part of their bodies whence the warm blood is injected into the interior of the image thus making it alive! Nor does Chinese superstition confine itself to clay images only. It is believed that certain wizards are able to endow with life figures cut out of paper with similar effects. In other cases these paper mannikins become the wizard's familiars and obey all his orders. There is also a widespread superstition that the feathers of birds, after undergoing certain incantations, are thrown up into the air and being carried away by the wind work blight and destruction wherever they alight.

References to necromancers who have at various times enjoyed a large amount of popular reverence abound in Chinese history, though it is somewhat difficult to distinguish between the historical "magician" and the mythical "genie." In Mr. Mayers's very comprehensive *Manual* are notices of, amongst others, Hsien Yuan chi, who (A.D. 847) played the part of Cagliostro, pretending to the gift of perpetual youth and the power of transforming lovely damsels into wrinkled harridans and *vice versa*; of Li Shao kun (*Circa* B.C. 140), who professed to know the secrets of transmutation and immortality; of Lu-Pan, the patron saint of Carpenters, who carved a genie which of three years inflicted drought on the people of Wu; of Lu Yen (A.D. 755), who for 400 years wielded a magic sword with which he traversed the Empire, slaying dragons and emulating the deeds of the knights of Western chivalry; of T'u Yü and Yü Lui, renowned for their magic control over evil spirits; and of Tso-Tzŭ, who in the second century practised magic. It is noteworthy that throughout all this mass of legend there runs the same vein of search after the elixir of youth and the philosopher's stone which forms so prominent a feature of our own mediæval history. "Men of the four seas are all brothers," says one of the tritest of Chinese apothegms; and so it would seem.

The vast extent of the Chinese Empire has allowed the natives to allot a portion of its territory to a tribe of magicians called *mao shan*; and it is to this country that those desirous of acquiring magical arts proceed, to place themselves under the instruction of its diabolical inhabitants. Adepts in their lore can, it is asserted, make fowls which, being placed outside houses it is desired to rob, will during the night open its doors so as to admit the robbers. Another belief refers to the existence of invisible necromancers called *shan ching kwei* 閃青鬼. People who have been deeply wronged and are unable to otherwise avenge themselves can by practising certain spells become *shan ching kwei*. The most efficacious way is to dig up a coffin, and, after removing the body it contains, to sleep in it for several nights in succession. At the end of so many days the sleeper becomes invisible until dawn, and can thus gratify his revenge without fear of detection.

A belief in demon monsters somewhat resembling the genii of the *Arabian Nights* exists in full force in China and dates back to respectable antiquity. One of the Emperors who flourished about 700 A.D., having been taken ill, dreamt he saw a blue half-naked devil coming into his palace. He stole the empress's perfume bag and also the emperor's flute which was made of precious stone, and flew off with them to the palace roof. Suddenly there appeared another blue devil, but of giant stature, having a black leather high boot on one foot, the other being bare. He had on a blue gown. One arm was like his foot, bare, with which he wielded a massive sword. His mouth was like that of a bull. This fierce looking monster seized the little one and with a blow made an end of him. The Emperor asked this monster demon what his name was. He said his name was Tsung Kwei, and that he was a military M.A. when in the body, but that now he had become a sort of colonel-commandant over all imps, ogres, wraiths, hobgoblins and the like under heaven. The emperor was greatly flattered at being visited by such a distinguished although unearthly personage, and waking up found his illness gone. He called a painter to paint for him what he had seen in his dream; and it was executed so faithfully that the emperor ordered two hundred ounces of gold to be given him and that copies of the painting should be distributed throughout the whole empire, so that all the people might know and pay due respect to this blue bull-headed demon. To this day he holds a conspicuous place in the temples of the people.

*"Although this monster demon ranked high, he was low when compared either to the ancient or present head of the vast host which abounds in the air, the earth, or the infernal regions. All mermaids of the deep, all satyrs of the forest, all needle-necked starving ghosts, the weak and the strong, whatever forms they take, whether birds, fishes, beasts or men, or a combination of some or all of them, make nondescript monsters of demons. All are said to have existed in the time of Fuhi, and immediately after that time under the rule of the harpy Nü-kwa 女媧. She had a human face with the body of a bird. It was she who mended the visible heavens for us, but unfortunately it was not completed. There is a little hole in the north west corner, and to this day the wind from that quarter is colder than any other.

"The present head of the demons was a Tquist priest named Chang Tau Ling, who lived when the kingdom of Wei was powerful. At sixty years of age, he ate the pills of immortality, after which, Lautsze, the founder of Tauism, appeared to him and gave him supreme power over all demons. When he was thus appointed to be the modern head of the demon kingdom, Lautsze gave him a book of charms and spells together with two magic swords. Chang Tau Ling lived to the age of 123 years, when he ascended in the light of day to his onerous

---

* The quotations which here follow are from Mr. Gardner's article. I have however taken the liberty of occasionally altering the text.

duties of ruling the devils. After this many of the Tauists for a time actually called themselves devils; the name evidently had become respectable.

"Having dealt with demons in general, let us now proceed to a special class of *human phenomena* which the Chinese attribute to the influence of demons. Firstly, then, is their power to produce diseases. There is no disease to which the Chinese are ordinarily subject to that may not be caused by demons. In this class the mind is untouched; it is only the body that suffers, and the Chinese endeavour to get rid of them by vows and offerings to the gods. The subject in this case is an involuntary one.

"Next come those who are possessed by the indwelling of the evil spirit. These the Chinese distinguish from the lunatics both by their appearance and language. There is more of a cringing nature in the possessed, and the patient's manner is perfectly consistent with his or her new consciousness, and which is said to be the demon's. When questioned as to his home, the demon answers, it is in the mountain or desert, generally in some cave. Sometimes he says that the person whom he had possession of before is dead, and having no abode, he takes up his quarters with a new victim. Sometimes he says he is travelling or has only come to pay a visit to a brother or sister, to a father or mother, and that after a short stay he will go away. Those possessed range between 15 and 50 years of age—quite irrespective of sex. Possession comes on very suddenly—sometimes in the day, sometimes in the night. The demoniac talks madly—smashes everything near—possesses unusual strength, tears his clothes into rags and would rush into the streets or to the mountains, or kill himself, unless prevented. After this violent possession, the demoniac calms down and submits to his fate, but under the most heart-rending protests. These mad spells which are experienced on the demon's entrance return at intervals and become more frequent the longer possessed and generally with more intensity, so that death at last ensues from their violence.

"A Chefoo boy aged 15 was going on an errand. His path led him through fields where men were working at their crops. When he came up to the men and had exchanged a word or two with them he suddenly began to rave violently, his eyes rolled, and he made for a pond which was by. Seeing this, the people ran up to him, stopped him from drowning himself and took him home to his parents. When he got home he sprang up from the ground several yards, manifesting superhuman strength. After a few days he calmed down and became unusually quiet and gentle, but his own consciousness was lost. It was that of another. He spoke of his friends in Nanking. After six months the demon departed, and the boy got back his own consciousness. He has been in the service of several foreigners in Chefoo since. In this case no worship was offered to the demon.

"Now we come to those who are involuntarily possessed but who yield to the worship of the demon. The demon says he will cease from tormenting the demoniac if he worships him and will reward him by increasing his riches. But if not, he will punish his victim, make heavier his torments and rob him of his property. People find that their food is cursed, and that whenever they prepare any, filth and dirt comes down from the air to make it uneatable. Their water is likewise cursed, their wardrobe is set on fire, and their money very mysteriously disappears. Hence arose the custom of cutting off the head of the string of cash that it might not run away. The 999 cash of the thousand is made to return to the one left in the following manner. The blood of a fly called Fu-chien (蚨蟬) sprinkled on the one cash left at home and the fly's eggs are put on the 999 cash that are laid out. Tradition says (and Kanghi's Dictionary perpetuates it) that the young flies in the eggs, although fastened to each cash, will all find their way back again to their mother, bringing the cash with them. When the people's faith in these and similar antidotes fail, they yield to the demon and say, 'Hold! Cease thy cursings, we will worship thee.' A picture is stuck up on the wall, sometimes that of a woman, sometimes of a man and prostration is made to it twice a month. Being thus reverenced, money comes mysteriously *in* instead of going *out*. Even millstones are made to move in at the demon's orders and the family at once becomes rich. But it is said that no luck attends such a family; it will eventually be reduced to poverty. Even officials believe these things. Palaces are known to have been built by them for these demons, whilst the latter are obliged to bo satisfied with humbler shrines from the poor."

Stories of persons being possessed by demons are so common that it is difficult to choose from the selection which offers itself. I quote the following as illustrating one phase of the common belief. It relates to animal possession, and is as follows:—"At Ningpo, some religious Budhist published a tract with a picture of a buffalo, a frog and a dog, and some Chinese characters. It tells how a native of Ningpo, who used to catch and kill frogs, was possessed by the spirit of his victims, how his body broke out into blotches, how he squatted like a frog, and finally was impelled to spit himself in the very manner he had spitted these innocent little reptiles."

The other story is a translation from the Chinese,* and runs as follows:— In Funghua district a literary man surnamed Woo had a slave girl of fifteen or sixteen who was black and ugly, but his wife was fair and beautiful. The slave always slept in the wife's apartment, till suddenly one day she was missing and could not be found for two or three days. At last an old female servant on going to fetch firewood and opening the coal-hole heard an inexplicable chirping noise and turning aside some of the firewood found the girl standing like a stump in the middle of it. She was perfectly inane and on being pulled out, though she walked, would answer no questions. They gave her a dose of hot ginger and water, upon which the threw up a basin full of mud. Then she began to speak and said, "There was an old man like a genie in green clothes and square cap came and called me away, the other day, I know not where. When I wanted food he gave me cakes to eat. But now I am very hungry." They gave her some rice and that night she slept in her mistress's room. But everything in the room was being pulled about, so that the master and mistress got up to look. They called the girl, but she did

* *Che-wan-luk*, Sec. xviii.

not answer, and as the doors and everything were in their usual state they said nothing about it. Next day the girl was missing again, and searching for her in the old place they found her exactly as before. On giving her three slaps with the hand she came to herself, but while they were in the act of scolding her lo! there was what she called "an old man like a genie" up in the caves of the house, holding a white fan and in appearance neither old nor young but middle-aged. They went up to the room above and tried to strike him, but they could not hit him nor make him move. In the midst of the hubbub he suddenly disappeared. But as suddenly it was reported that fire had broken out in the kitchen. This was extinguished, and then all was quiet. But afterwards every night either the slave or her mistress muttered or talked in the bedroom, or else there was heard the sound of people eating, or doing something out of the way. The master did not know what to do. One day he went and got some brave men to keep guard around the room with fire-arms, but then a fire broke out down stairs, and while all the people were putting it out the mistress and slave seemed perfectly unconscious that anything was going on. Next day, when the rice was cooked, on opening the pot they found that it was all mixed with dirt, and uneatable. There was no end to annoyances of this kind. At last they called in a Tauist priest to fast and say requiems. At the same time a "Fragrant Feast" of fine things was prepared as if for a great visitor. The master of the house put on his best clothes and also knelt down while he presented the wine and the viands: and the whole family small as well as great worshipped one whole day and night. But the trouble went on exactly as before. The genie himself would make his appearance at odd times; and in the dark there would be talking and conversation indistinctly heard, so that nothing could be definitely made out of them. One day the mistress took the slave girl, and fled with her to her (own) mother's house; and then everything was out of joint there. There were sounds and movements, and dashing and breaking of things, and clothes burning. So they fled next to a small quiet Buddhist nunnery. But bad as things were before, here they were worse; and the master was at his wits' end, all his means being exhausted to no purpose. After about half a year of this he took the girl and sold her to a villager in the neighbouring district of T'sze K'e, and his wife had peace at last. The villager however found the girl an intolerable nuisance, and when he wanted to sell her no one would buy her; so he drove her out into the street. But nobody would have anything to do with her there either, and she turned to begging. Then her master had peace and quietness.

There are many more stories about the *Woo-tung-shên* (五通神). It appears from the Tsze-pu-yu (子不語) that in one village in Sze-chuan he required a young girl for a wife every year, and that the girl chosen became possessed by this evil spirit.

The active possession which induces a sort of ecstatic frenzy, and vents itself by bodily exertion is quite familiar to the Chinese. Persons under this influence are known as "devil dancers," and to a great extent act the part of media for those who desire to make enquiries from the other world or induce the assistance of spirits to heal the sick. When devil dancers are called in, a feast is prepared in their honour. The head dancer, accompanied by pupils who are learning the art, presents himself at the house and having done justice to the viands provided commences by burning incense, while enquiries are made as to what is amiss. Some of the attendants then seat themselves with drums, bells, &c., and begin a sort of musical accompaniment to which the dancers keep time. Presently the music quickens; the dancers increase their speed until the whole party are almost convulsed with their efforts. Suddenly the leading dancer falls exhausted to the ground. Here for a few moments he lies as if lifeless. Presently he raises himself up and begins to speak. Questions are put to him and he describes the disease of the sick man, the remedies he ought to adopt, &c. When all the questions are answered he again falls as if exhausted, and is gradually brought back to ordinary consciousness.

Mr. Gardner states that in Manchuria "they do not ordinarily observe the custom of inviting their neighbours' spirits, but the devil-dancers are far better skilled in their art. The chief, with a belt of bells, stands up to dance with two of his pupils on each side. If he has not four pupils, some from the family must make up the number. The devil-dancers present many varieties and various ways of calling on the spirits. Thus, for instance, the chief says his demon is a white tiger. A whole pig must be cooked for him. He must get two children, one in each hand, to go with him to eat pig out of the boiling caldron. He assumes himself to be a tiger and thrusts his head down to his neck in the boiling water, and bites a mouthful off for his young whelp in his right hand, then a thrust and a bite for the whelp in his left hand, and finally a thrust and a bite for himself. This over, he commences the dance. Most of the class just described are men, but there are women also who are devil-dancers. They never condescend to go about. Those who seek their assistance must go to them. In seeking their aid, the suppliant takes with him presents of incense and paper money to worship the demons, besides valuable presents of bread, red cloth, and red silks. These neither dance nor beat drums nor ring bells, but sit and commence a slow shaking as from ague; then yawn, gape, and at last shake so violently that the teeth rattle in their gums; then they fall into a fit, like the former class. They tell the suppliant to return home and place a cup on the window outside, and the right medicine will be put into it by a spirit. The suppliant is at the same time made to vow that he will contribute to the worship of the particular demon, whose power and intervention they now invoke, and that he will also contribute towards some temple in the neighbourhood."

The impostors who gain their living in the way above described are of course mere ordinary mortals whose power of simulating hysteria and epilepsy easily imposes upon the masses. But the Chinese believe in the existence of a class who are human only in their outward appearance. They are supposed to be veritable demons specially sent from the spirit world to warn mankind of the consequences which may follow indulgence in evil. A Minister of State during the time of the T'ang is alleged to have been one of these demons, and legends illustrative of his powers are still to be met with in the collections of popular tales to be found in every book-stall. It does not appear that the old English belief as to witches was very remote from this demon theory. In one case we read of a witch being hunted for in a salt box, it being supposed that she possessed the diabolical power of changing her shape to any extent. But the whole subject of Western witchcraft is so wide that space forbids my even entering upon it—to say nothing of the fact that most readers are fully acquainted with the subject.

It is somewhat odd to find—and one is puzzled to know whether the fact is complimentary to Christianity or the reverse—that in those parts of China to which missionary effort has penetrated, a popular belief exists in the power of Christian exorcism. Missionaries of all denominations know of cases in which either they or their converts have been called in " to cast out the devil" supposed to possess a patient. Were this to be accepted as a tribute to their powers as real intercessors with the Creator, the fact would be gratifying; but it is to be feared that the confidence thus evinced turns rather on the popular belief that Christian relations with the Satanic hierarchy are uncommonly intimate. Be this as it may, the fact remains that converts are classed with the native exorcists. Most places of any pretension have demon shrines to which the friends of those afflicted resort in the first instance. Offerings are here made to demons of all descriptions—not merely to those which take possession of men, but to those of floods, drought* and pestilence. It is when supplications at such shrines are useless that exorcists are consulted.

Exorcists are of various kinds. Spiritualists, such as those already described, are frequently called in, their success being various. Taoist priests find more favour with some people, and their pretensions are not one whit inferior to those of the more orthodox media. Conjurors of this sort, says a writer before quoted, "sit on mats and are carried by invisible power from place to place. They ascend to a height of 20 or 30 feet and are carried to a distance of 4 or 5 *li*. Of this class are those who, in Manchuria, call down fire from the sky in those funerals where the corpse is burnt. These conjurors not only use charms but recite incantations, make magic signs and use some of those strange substances which the astrologer uses to keep away evil influences." The class of so-called doctors also enjoy the reputation of being able to cast out out evil spirits, and their *modus operandi* is thus described:—" They use needles to puncture the tips of the fingers, the nose, and the neck. They also use a pill made out of *ai tsau* 艾草 and apply it in the following manner: The thumbs of the two hands are tied tightly to each other. The two big toes are

---

* "The P'oh of drought is doing mischief."—The P'oh is the *Shên* of drought. In the South there is a man of two or three feet high, naked and having his eyes in the top of his head. He runs like wind. His name is P'oh. Where he appears there is drought. Another name is "the Mother of Drought." It belongs to the class of elves.—*Book of Poetry*, Ta Ya.

When the *shên* of mountains and rivers caused floods or drought or pestilence they made a special sacrifice to drive them away. This was called Ying.—*Tso-chuen*.

also tied to each other in the same manner. Then one pill is put on the two big toes at the root of the nails and the other at the root of the thumb nails. At the same instant the two pills are set on fire and there they are kept until the flesh is burnt. Whether in the application of the pills or in the piercing of the needles the invariable cry is—'I am going, I am going immediately. I'll never dare to come back again. Oh have mercy on me this once; I'll never return.'"
All the above-mentioned practitioners may however fail, and as a last resort a professional exorcist, neither medium, priest, nor doctor, is called in. The men who follow this as a profession pretend to singular experiences. As the recognized enemies of evil spirits these latter never cease to persecute them. They are mysteriously pinched and beaten by the Puck-like emissaries of ghostly tormentors. Stones are thrown at them by unseen beings, and spirit hands seize and attempt to drown them if they incautiously venture into running water. To counteract these influences they always carry about their persons amulets of which the spirits stand in dread. Their first act when called in is to paste written charms upon the windows and doors of the room in which they operate. They then recite certain formulæ and are sometimes answered by the spirits, who promise to cease troubling the patient in future.

As with us there is a sovereign Chinese charm against witches. Sir Walter Scott, in his *Old Mortality*, refers to the popular belief that they can only be shot with silver bullets. A Chinese receipt given in the *Rites of Chow* is as follows: " If you wish to kill this *Shên*, take a certain piece of wood with a hole in it: insert a piece of ivory in the hole, making the form of a cross and throw it into the water: thus the *Shên* will die and the deep become a hill." Certain officers were in old times appointed to "hoot at," "shoot," and "kill" those spirits (*shên*) which were injurious.

The popular identification of the cat with matters pertaining to witchcraft in Europe is well known, and it is interesting to find that the Chinese assign to it a somewhat similar connection. As with us the vulgar believe that witches can change themselves into cats,* though the hare, and more especially the fox,

---

* Do you remember the German story of the lad who travelled "*um das gruseln zu lernen*" (to learn how to tremble)? Well, I, who never *gruselte* (quaked) before, had a touch of it a few evenings ago. I was sitting here quietly drinking tea and four or five men were present, when a cat came to the door. I called "*bis, bis,*" and offered milk, but puss, after looking at us, ran away. "Well dost thou, lady," said a quiet sensible man, a merchant here, "to be kind to the cat, for I dare say he gets little enough at home; *his* father, poor man, cannot cook for his children every day." And then, in an explanatory tone to the company, "That is Alec Nasseeree's boy Yussuf—it must be Yussuf, because his fellow twin Ismaeen is with his mule at Negadeh." *Mir gruselte* (I shivered), I confess; not but what I have heard things almost as absurd from gentlemen and ladies in Europe; but an "extravagance" in a *kuftan* has quite a different effect from one in a tail-coat. "What! my butcher's boy who brings the meat—a cat!" I gasped. "To be sure, and he knows well where to look for a bit of good cookery, you see. All twins go out as cats at night, if they go to sleep hungry; and their own bodies lie at home like dead meanwhile, but no one must touch them, or they would die. When they grow up to ten or twelve they leave it off. Why, your own boy Achmet does it. Oh, Achmet!" Achmet appears. "Boy, don't you go out as a cat at night?" "No," said Achmet, tranquilly, "I am not a twin—my sister's sons do." I inquired if people were not afraid of such cats. "No, there is no fear, they only eat a

are reputed to be their more favourite disguises. But the demoniacal attributes of a cat's ghost are more singular. In Section I. of the Che Wên Luh (誌聞錄) occurs the following notice*: "At Leong Chow in the province of Kansuh the people sometimes do homage to the ghost of a cat. The same thing is mentioned in the history of the North. The way they proceed with this monstrous thing is first to hang the cat, and then perform certain ceremonies of fasting and requiems for seven weeks, when the spiritual communication is established. This is afterwards transferred to a wooden tablet, and put up behind the door, where the owner of the cat honours it with offerings. By the side of it is placed a bag about five inches long, intended for the cat's use. From time to time it goes and steals people's things, and then, about the fourth watch of the night before cock crowing, the bag is amissing. After a little while it is hung up on the corner of the house, and the person uses a ladder to fetch it down. When the mouth of the bag is opened, and the bag inverted over a chest, as much as two hundred catties of rice or peas are got out of it, so much does the depraved imp manage to make the little space hold. Those who serve it always get rich very fast."

A certain prefect once received a birthday present of rice from a friend. It weighed over a thousand catties and was put into a large cask. Several days after the prefect sent a man to divide it out, when it was noticed that the top of the flour was all in a crust like paper, while below it was clean gone. The man, in a fright, told the prefect, who sent an officer to enquire into the matter. It was then found that behind the prefect's residence there was a person who practised sacrificing to this kind of cat. The officer found out the image and severely chastised it in the hall with forty blows, and also flogged its owner. He then laughed and sent them off. After this, as the story goes, the *Shin* had no efficacy. Choo-tzu says—"The spirituousness (Ling) of *Shên* is the result of the accumulated earnestness of the people—there is really no *Shên*. When one turns his back upon it the spirituousness is immediately dispersed. Therefore while the people honor it the *Shin* keeps its place, but you may scatter it with a kick."

Tigers also figure as demoniacs or ghosts. In the same work as that above quoted from a story relates how a benighted traveller suddenly observed amongst the brushwood a brilliant light and a man in red clothes, with a golden crown and armour of rare brightness, and before and behind him a regular retinue of followers. The traveller was astonished, and, wondering what mandarin it could be, hid himself in the wood. Next day he asked the little of the cookery; but if you beat them they will tell their parents, next day, 'So and so beat me in his house last night,' and show their bruises. No, they are not Afreets; they are *beni Adam;* only twins do it, and if you give them a sort of onion broth and camel's milk the first thing when they are born, they don't do it at all." Omar professed never to have heard it, but I am sure he had, only he dreads being laughed at. One of the American missionaries told me something like it, as belonging to the Copts, but it is entirely Egyptian, and common to both religions. I asked several Copts, who assured me it was true, and told it just the same. Is it a remnant of the doctrine of transmigration? However, the notion fully accounts for the horror the people feel at the idea of killing a cat.—*Lady Duff Gordon's Last Letters.*

* Chalmers.

natives of the place who it could have been. They told him it was the tiger ghost of the mountains. "When he wishes to eat people up he puts off his clothes and is changed into a striped tiger. He then advances with a great roar and the traveller is instantly torn in pieces." "You," said they, "have had a wonderful escape."

Nor are tigers alone in this regard. The ghosts of the "green ox" and "black fowl"* are mentioned in native legends; while a yet more fantastic extract narrates that "the carp as soon as its scales number 360 is caught and carried away by dragons; but if every year a shên be placed to guard it, it cannot be carried away. This shên is a tortoise."†

Dragons again furnish their quota of ghostly representatives, and the following legend accounts for the popular belief. "During the reign of an emperor of the T'ang dynasty, the dragon god of rain had greatly offended the Supreme god, and orders were consequently given to the prime minister to behead him on such and such a day. On the night before the execution, the dragon god of rain appeared in a dream to the Emperor and begged him to intercede on his behalf and exercise his influence over his minister. The Emperor promised he would. The following day the Emperor invited his minister to play chess with him. He hoped he would forget the time, and that the dragon god would thus be saved. As the hour drew nigh the minister got very sleepy. The Emperor seeing this, said nothing about the dragon god, but let the minister sleep. Suddenly, the latter jumped up and said, "I must behead immediately;" and right between them a dragon's head fell from the sky. The King fell back with fright and was taken ill. That night the dragon's ghost appeared to him in a dream and threatened him severely for this breach of promise, insisting on bringing the case up before the judge of the lower regions. The Emperor explained, begged forgiveness and made a promise, the results of which remain to this day. He engaged to honour the dragon god by having all his high officers and the great people of the land to carry the dragon above their heads. The plan adopted was to place a dragon's head on every palace roof, so that when the gentry and officials were at home, they had a dragon's head over them. The head seen so often on temples and palaces is said to have had this origin." In those days, adds the account from which the foregoing is quoted, the demons had such unlimited power to transform themselves that a son would not leave his father, or a husband his wife, without secret tickets, which they carried about with them and compared on meeting. If a person was unable to produce the ticket he was believed to be a demon in human form. This is the origin of the proverb: "If your ticket be lost, you are hopeless."

But of all known animals the fox plays the principal part in Chinese demonology. European folk-lore assigns a prominent place to the were-wolves (Germ. *Wehrwolf*, Port. *Lobis-homem*), which are even now believed by the superstitious peasantry of many countries to haunt their native forests.

* 談徵 (*t'an chêng*.) Sec. IV.   † 逑異記 Shuh E Kê.

Well, in China we find the same idea in a slightly different form. The fox takes the place of the wolf, and "fairy foxes" play an important part in every native collection of supernatural tales. The belief in their existence dates from remote antiquity, though more prevalent in Northern than in Southern China, the inhabitants of the latter taking the doings of genii more especially as the basis of their fairy lore. There is however this difference between the were-wolf and the fairy fox:—that whereas the former is invariably malicious, the latter may be either beneficent or malignant. In many of the tales the fox is only transformed (as in the well-known nursery story of "Beauty and the Beast") into human shape *after* making acquaintance with its host. "At the age of 50 the fox can take the form of a woman, and at that of 100 can assume the appearance of a young and beautiful girl. When 1000 years old he is admitted to the heavens and becomes the celestial fox."*

In and about Peking the belief in foxes having power to assume a human shape flourishes perhaps more thoroughly than in any other part of the empire, though similar stories are told throughout the eighteen provinces. The *Liao-chai-chih-yi* (聊齋志異), a collection of tales published in 1765, abounds with narrations of this nature, many of the most curious, unfortunately, being unsuitable for publication in an English dress. But the whole subject has been so fully dealt with in accessible publications that the extended notice which the subject would permit is unnecessary. Dr. Birch, of the British Museum, wrote an interesting paper on the subject of Fairy Foxes† in No. III., of the *Chinese and Japanese Repository* (1863), which was followed by a notice from the pen of the well-known sinologue Mr. W. F. Mayers, in No. III., of Vol. I., of *Notes and Queries on China and Japan* (1867). The most complete essay on the subject, however, which has yet appeared was written by Mr. T. Watters, and read before the North China Branch of the Royal Asiatic Society in March 1873. That accurate and painstaking scholar thus opens his remarks on the subject:—

"Chinese philosophers seem to be agreed in attributing to Reynard a long life, some making the number of his years 800 and others extending it even to a thousand. This power of prolonging life they suppose to result from the animal's living in caves and holes where it is shut out from the sun. The vital powers can thus operate free from disturbance and the wearing effect of the sun's heat and light. The fox, badger, mole and some other cave-dwelling

---

* *Chinese Readers' Manual*, p. 61.

† A specimen of the still pervading superstition respecting the Fox, comes from Minatomura, in Ibaraki Ken, Japan. A man found a fox's hole in his garden. At the same time his wife dreamt that she had seen a fox whom she was satisfied was none other than Inari-sama. Full of dread, the man put this and that together, and came to the conclusion that the hole must be the abode of Inari-sama, and he forthwith had a small temple put up over it. He then called for the Shinto priest; and after much ado, the matter got abroad, and crowds came to worship at this temple. At last the Saibansho officials of the Ken heard of what was going on, and sent for the man and his wife. The interview must have been somewhat disappointing to them, for the judges told them such superstitions now became criminal; and the punishment due for such follies was 40 days' imprisonment. As, however, in this instance, it was clearly the result of extreme ignorance on the part of the interesting pair, they were let off with a fine of 3 yen.

animals are all grouped together as enjoying long life. The Chinese are not alone in thus regarding the exclusion of light and air as tending to prolong existence. Not to refer to others, our own Bacon says:—' A life in caves and holes, where the rays of the sun do not enter, may perhaps tend to longevity; for the air of itself unexcited by heat has not much power to prey upon the body. Certainly on looking back, it appears from many remains and monuments that the size and stature of men were anciently much greater than they had been since, as in Sicily and some other places; and such men generally lived in caves. Now there is some affinity between length of age and largeness of limbs. The cave of Epimenides likewise passes current among the fables.'"

The use of the several parts of the fox's body in the Chinese pharmacopeia is followed by an account of the Chinese opinion of his cunning, in which we read as follows:—

"Like most Western nations the Chinese ascribe to the fox a cunning, crafty disposition by which he can disarm suspicion on the part of the very animals which constitute his prey. . . . The notion about the fox's caution is put to practical use in the North of China, for it has been observed that when he is crossing a frozen river or lake he advances very slowly and deliberately, putting his head down close to the ice and listening for the sound of water beneath. Accordingly when in the early spring the traveller fears the stability of the ice, if he observes on its surface traces of the fox's footsteps he may proceed any without apprehension. One can easily see what an opportunity is presented here again to the Chinese mind for the exercise of myth-making ingenuity. Below the ice is the region of the *Yin* or female element—the dark world of death and obscurity—while above it is the region of the *Yang* or male element—the bright world of life and activity. Accordingly it has come to pass that the fox is represented as living on the debatable land which is neither the earth of life nor the Hades of death. His dwelling place on the earth is among the tombs, or actually, rather, within the tomb, and the spirits of the deceased often occupy the body. Thus he enables ghosts of the dead to return to life or himself performs their terrible behest—visiting upon living men and women the iniquities they have committed against those now dead, and by this means bringing peace and rest to the souls of the latter which would else be travelling and troubling for ever."

From the numerous stories given by Mr. Watters in illustration of the popular belief in the fox's powers of transformation, I take only the following:—
"It is as a pretty girl that the fox appears most frequently and does most mischief. Disguised as a woman it is always young and handsome, generally wicked, but on rare occasions very good. At times it puts on the garb and appearance of some one well known, but who is either dead or at a great distance. An accomplished scholar who resides in a village about twenty miles from Foochow told me not long ago a story which affords an illustration of this personation of particular individuals. A friend of his had ill-treated and, as was supposed, secretly killed a pretty young wife and married another. Soon after this latter event the house was reported to be haunted and no servant

would remain in the family. The first wife's apartments were the worst of all, and this part of the premises had to be abandoned. Now one day my friend was reading with the master of the house in the works of Chuhsi, and they came to the passage which treats of ghosts and spirits. They then ceased reading and entered into a conversation on the subject, and the story of the haunted chambers was related. My friend laughed at and reproached the weakness which made a scholar believe in ghosts, and finally the two agreed to remove to that portion of the dreadful rooms. Before they had been seated here a long time, strange sounds became audible and soon the pit-pat of a woman's steps was heard. The door opened without any noise, and in walked the murdered woman clothed as of old. The blood forsook the two men's faces, speech fled their lips, and had it not been for the law of gravity their pigtails would have stood on end. There they sat paralyzed with mute awe and gazing on the spectre, which went pit-pat over the boards looking neither to right nor left until it reached the corner in which was a small wash-hand-stand with a basin of water. She took the basin in her hand and walked steadily with it over to the man who had been her husband, presenting it to him, when he instantly uttered a terrible scream and fell backwards. Then the spectral woman walked away and her patter was heard along the boards until she reached the outer door. My friend summoned up courage to go out and make investigation, but no human creature had been stirring, and only the fox which came almost daily had been seen on the premises. The house has been abandoned, the owner has gone elsewhere, but my friend believes that the ghost of the murderer's wife will torment him by means of a fox daily until it brings him to the grave."

It would be easy to multiply stories of this nature, but their narration would unduly swell the limits of the chapter, while those who are curious on the subject can easily refer to Mr Watters's paper. I prefer therefore to turn to the analogies with Chinese belief presented elsewhere. Neither amongst the Semitic nor Aryan races can I find, in the authorities at my command, that any demoniacal power has ever been attributed to the fox. No reference to the animal appears in Brand, and in Continental Europe the wolf alone figures in fairy tales as the dangerous and crafty enemy of man. But we learn on the authority of Dr. Macgowan that "when the Pilgrim Fathers landed in Massachussets, they found the Indians, especially those of Naragannset, deeply imbued with fox superstitions, many of them similar to those mentioned above." Notices of these are found at considerable length in the works of the Rev. Mr. Elliot, known as the "Apostle of the Indians." In Japan, again, we find fox-myths a mighty power in the State. Dr. Macgowan describes a primer—the first book put into the hands of Japanese children; it was, profusely illustrated with wood-cuts, in which was depicted in full detail the progress of the Fox's courtship. Thus, even in the education of childhood, the fox-myth weaves itself into the texture of Japanese thought. The fox was understood to be most mischievously inclined, and was especially mischievous in its domestic relations. It was believed, in Japan, to be no uncommon incident for a fox to transform itself into a charming young woman, who got married to some loving Japanese swain and had a family. By-and-bye something went awry in the domestic experiences, on which the mischievous fox-elf resumed her foxhood, and all her progeny did the same, and scampered off to their homes in dead men's tombs, leaving the late happy husband and father desolate and wretched. A recent newspaper paragraph, by the way, describes a murder committed at Chikuzen in which the murderer was discovered to be insane. Different members of his family, for three generations back, had gone mad, it was said, in consequence of one of their ancestors having injured a fox!—So much for the fox, thus summarily dismissed inasmuch as other writers have dealt so fully with his alleged powers.

Leaving the animal, for the mineral, world we note that even stones possess the reputation of being inhabited by spirits. A well-known Taoist legend relates that Chang Liang, a counsellor of the founder of the Han dynasty, derived his knowledge from a sage who was eventually metamorphosed into a yellow stone. Another legend tells how one of the immortals kept a flock of sheep who were changed to stone, but reassumed their proper shape at a word from their shepherd. Mr. W. F. Mayers, in his article on Canton in the *Treaty Ports of China and Japan*, thus describes the Legend from which Canton derives it soubriquet of the "City of Rams":—" In the temple of the 'Five Genii' were until lately the stone images of five (supernatural) rams, but these latter were destroyed in a conflagration which consumed the rear building in which they stood some three years since. The legend with reference to the foundation of this temple is that, some twenty centuries ago, five shepherds were seen on the site where the building now stands, who suddenly became transformed into an equal number of rams, while these again instantly changed into stone, a voice being heard at the same time proclaiming that, so long as these supernatural objects should be worshipped on this spot, the prosperity of the adjoining city should endure. From that day forward (runs the story) these images have remained on the identical spot, and it is certain that from time immemorial they have been looked upon with superstitious reverence, nor is it the less remarkable that the destruction of their shrine should coincide so closely with the actual decline in the prosperity of the city. The stones were almost shapeless blocks of granite, about eighteen inches high and the same in length, with some rude attempt at sculpture in the form of a ram's head. From them and their attendant legend Canton derived its soubriquet of the City of Rams (羊城), but the legend itself is traced by Chinese philosophers to an accidental resemblance between the word signifying 'ram' or 'sheep' and the ancient designation of the province of Kwangtung. This is a striking corroboration of Professor Müller's dictum that all myths are merely amplifications of some forgotten sound."

A popular superstition recounts that in L'ien-chow, in the province of Kwang-si, when any person walking, happens to hit his foot against a stone, and afterwards falls sick, his family immediately prepares an offering of fruit, wine, rice and incense; and proceeding to the spot, bow down and worship, after which the person gets well. They imagine that the stone is possessed by a demon. Gamblers frequently pray to stones thus possessed for "luck."

IX.—ELVES, FAIRIES, AND BROWNIES.

An accurate definition of the Chinese idea of elves and fairies is somewhat difficult. In many cases the word *shin* 神, spirit, or, as some will have it, God—can only be translated by "elf" or "brownie," while on other occasions one is puzzled under what category to place creatures who play too important a part in Chinese belief to be omitted from these pages, while strictly answering to nothing known in the West. China, at all events, boasts an infinity of beings who are alleged to possess the general characteristics of our local sprites. As with us they are sometimes malicious and sometimes merely playful. But I fancy that, in the main, a more stern air of purpose runs through Chinese than through European fairy legend. The wildest native inventions have never endowed the fairy community with, "houses made all with mother-o'-pearl, an ivory tennis-court, a nutmeg parlour, a sapphire dairy-room, chambers of agate, &c., &c."* Still less do we find anything resembling Shakespeare's Queen Mab:—

> "Her waggon spokes made of long spinner's legs,
> The cover of the wings of grasshoppers,
> The traces of the smallest spider's web
> The collars of the moonshine's watery beams,
> Her whip of cricket's bone, the lash of film."†

We hear little amongst the Chinese of fairy sprites whose highest aim is mere amusement, their action being usually, as with a certain class of brownies in our own fairy pantheon, malignant. It is, by the way, interesting to note that while the words *alp* and *alf* (Swedish and English *elf*) equally signify a mountain, or demon of the mountains,‡ the Chinese most frequently assign a mountainous locality to the homes of their fairy folk. The celebrated mountain Kw‘ên Lun (崑崙) (usually identified with the Hindoo Kush) is said to be peopled with fairies who cultivate upon its terraces the "fields of sesamum and gardens of coriander seeds" which are eaten as ordinary food by those who possess the gift of Longevity. Here too is the "Lake of Gems" on whose borders dwells the fairy mother *Si wang mu* (西王母) and beside whose waters flourishes the *k‘iung shu* or tree of life, described as 10,000 cubits in height, 1800 feet in circumference and supposed to bear fruit only once in 3,000 years. This fruit is bestowed by the fairies on their favourites, who thus become immortal. Other receipts for the "Elixir of Life" are peach-tree gum mixed with the powdered ash of the mulberry, and *tan* 丹 the elixir of gold, or *tan sha* 丹砂 the common name for cinnabar.

There are some curious resemblances between Chinese and Western superstitions on the subject of storm-fiends or fairies. Thus the storm-raiser in China is not unlike his prototype in Scotland. Sir James Melville in his *Memoirs*

---

* Brand's *Antiquities*, Vol. II., p. 499, quoted from Randolph's *Amyntas*.

† Mercutio's speech, *Romeo and Juliet*.

‡ Brand's *Antiquities*, Vol. II., p. 476.

tells us that "the spirit or devil that helped the Scottish witches to raise a storm in the sea of Norway was cold as ice, and his body hard as iron; his face was terrible, his nose like the beak of an eagle, great burning eyes, his hands and legs hairy, with claws on his nails like a griffin." The Chinese demon of the storm is thus described in the Shan hai ching 山海經. "In Daylight mountain dwells the *shên* called Ke-mung. His shape is like a man with a dragon's head. He wanders about continually in the depths of the Chang river, and whenever he comes over or goes in there is sure to be a violent storm and rain."

Fairies in China indeed, as with us, usually possess the attribute of beauty. A well-known Chinese legend relates how two friends wandering amongst the ravines of their native mountains in search of herbs for medicinal purposes come to a fairy bridge where two maidens of more than earthly beauty are on guard. They invite them to the fairy land which lies on the other side of the bridge, and the invitation being accepted they become enamoured of the maidens, and pass what to them seems a short though blissful period of existence with the fairy folk. At length they desire to revisit their earthly homes and are allowed to return, when they find that seven generations have lived and died during their apparently short absence, they themselves having become centenarians.* Another version of the story is found in the *Liao chai chih yi*. About A.D. 60 or 70 two friends named Yüan Chao and Liu Ch'ên when wandering amongst the T'ien-t'ai mountains lost their way, and after wandering about for some time at length came upon a fairy retreat where two beautiful girls received them and fed them on *hu ma* 胡麻 (hemp, the Chinese *haschisch*). After spending what seems only a few days with their hostesses they return home and find to their astonishment that seven generations have passed away since they made the acquaintance of the maidens.† I may here remark that this Rip Van Winkle sort of story takes several forms in China, and a slight digression on this subject may be pardoned. A legend, related of Wang Chih, one of the patriarchs of the Taoist sect, involves him in a similar catastrophe with less obvious excuse than in the case of the two friends above mentioned.‡ Wandering one day in the mountains of Kü Chow to gather firewood "he entered a grotto in which some aged men were seated intent upon a game of chess. He laid down his axe and looked on at their game, in the course of which one of the old men handed him a thing in shape and size like a date stone, telling him to put it into his mouth. No sooner had he tasted it than 'he became oblivious of hunger and thirst.' After some time had elapsed, one of the players said, "It is long since you came here, you should go home now!" whereupon Wang Chih proceeding to pick up his axe found that its handle had mouldered into dust. On repairing to his home he found that centuries had passed since the time when he had left it for the mountains, and that no vestige of his kinsfolk remained. Retiring to a retreat among the hills he devoted himself to the rites of Taoism, and

---

* Quoted in Sir J. Bowring's *Flowery Scroll*, p. 27.
† *Ch. Reader's Manual*, p. 289.
‡ *Ibid.*, p. 239.

finally attained to immortality—a very un-Van-Winkle-like termination to the legend.

The striking resemblance of these to legends popular throughout Europe needs no demonstration, they being in fact identical with Erse, Gaelic and Teutonic stories yet related in their respective neighbourhoods. The bridge in the first story is described as the "Azure bridge," the fairy home being known as the "Jaspar city." "*Yao chi*" or the "Jaspar lake" is the name given to a sheet of water which it is believed forms one of its chief attractions, and to speak of a Chinese lady as "a nymph of the Jaspar lake" is to pay her the highest compliment for purity and beauty.

The somewhat particular, and at times pugnacious, "Brownie" is supposed to exist in China. Readers acquainted with our north-country folk-lore will be aware that a practice exists in many parts of the country of setting out milk &c. for the consumption of some household brownie, who performs willing labour for the benefit of its entertainer, the one proviso being that the brownie's operations are never to be overlooked by mortal eye. It is curious, in this connection, to find such a Chinese legend as the following recorded (*T'an ching* 談徵, vol. 4):—"In the Ts'ê dynasty there was one Chang Ching, who went out one night and saw a woman on the south corner of his house who beckoned him to come to her; and when he came she said: 'This is your honour's mulberry ground, and I am the *shên* of this place. If you will make next year, in the middle of the first moon, some thick congee, and present it to me I will engage to make your mulberry trees a hundred times more productive.' Having said this she disappeared. Ching made the congee and afterwards had a great crop of silkworms. Thence arose the practice of making thickened congee on the 15th of the first moon." Of the more truculent class of brownies we also hear a good deal in China. In an article on "Gunpowder and arms in China," published in a recent volume of the N. C. B. R. A. S. Transactions, the author, Mr. W. F. Mayers, quotes from the *Shin-i-king* the following: "Among the hills in the Western parts [of China?] there exist beings in human shape, a foot or more in height, who are by nature very fearless. If attacked [or offended] they cause men to sicken with [alternate] heat and cold. They are called *Shan sao*." It was to frighten these brownies that the practice of burning bamboos, now-a-days substituted by fire-crackers, (as already alluded to,) was adopted. Another account makes the *Shan-sias* or *Shan-sao*, to be a species of bird which when attacked summons tigers to its aid and burns down dwelling houses. In any case these beings bear many points of resemblance to our own sprites, especially those that are malignant. A curious story, which may serve as the type of many such, is also given in the same volume as that from which the above is derived, the *locale* given being Lew-chew, which until very lately was deemed a dependency of China. It relates how a fairy in the guise of a beautiful woman is found bathing in a man's well. He persuades her to marry him, and she remains with him for nine years, at the end of which time, despite the affection she has for their two children, she "glides upwards into a cloud" and disappears. We find a very similar story in the Arabian nights, and both Germany and the Shetland islands give us an almost identical legend.

A large proportion of the fairy tales of all countries are of course what grave scholars denominate "puerile"; but I need hardly apologise for giving the two following, which illustrate both the idea of diminutive stature attributed to fairies and the yet more common endowment of animals and insects with fairy power. In the work *(T'an ching)* above quoted from we read that the Emperor Yuen Tsung of T'ang had imperial ink called Dragon fragrance. One day he saw in the ink little Taoist priests like flies walking about, and they called to him, "Live for ever! Your servants are the spiritual essence of ink, the ambassadors of the black pine. Whoever in the world has literary cultivation must have twelve of us dragon guests in his ink." This is not badly matched by the following: "A youth while sleeping was accosted by a maiden who asked him to accompany her for protection against some menaced danger, telling him she was a princess in disguise; but he turned away from her. Soon afterwards he heard the noise of humming and saw entangled in the web of a spider a bee about to be devoured. He released the bee, placed it upon the ink-slab, when by the impression of its feet it left the character "Grateful" and flew away. He followed it with his eyes and saw it enter a honey-comb suspended above. The disguised princess was the bee." Sir John Bowring, who gives this story in almost the same words, adds, "It is easy to fancy that the character or sign meaning 'Gratitude' could be made by the impress of a bee's feet." I fear that the learned ex-governor of Hongkong was in this instance indulging in an exaggeration not unusual with him.

Chinese popular stories also abound with references to "kelpies" such as in Scotland are reported to haunt fords and ferries. A not less popular belief credits the monkey tribe with peculiar attributes as being possessed by fairies who make woman-stealing an ordinary avocation—thus affording a curious parallel to a South-African superstition. In the *History of the White Monkey*, by Kung T'sing, we read that a man of Leang, who had a very pretty wife, was travelling and came to pass some time at Chang-toh. Warned by the people of the place that a local *shên* was given to stealing females he conceals his wife in an inner room: but, despite all his precautions, on the second night in the fourth watch she is abducted. After seeking her high and low amidst great perils he at length comes to a stone door in a mountain facing the East, and learns from women passing in and out that his wife is within. To effect her deliverance he is advised to provide two kilderkins of spirits, ten dogs and several pounds of hemp. With this the women in the cave promise to attempt the *shên's* capture. The *shên* accordingly sees and devours the dogs and drinks the spirits, when he is securely bound with the hemp. The husband being called in, finds an enormous monkey bound hand and foot to the bed, and Ngau-yang Hih (the husband) kills him, thus releasing all the females in his power.

Fairies who embody the powers of nature are firmly believed in. "The

Emperor Liang when tired fell asleep in the sunshine and dreamed that he was visited by a woman of celestial beauty. He asked whence she came and who she was. 'I live on the terrace of the Sun on the Enchanted Mountain. In the morning I am a cloud, in the evening a shower of rain.'" The popular credence which this legend obtains argues a very deep-seated belief in the fairy-like attributes of representatives of the powers of nature, and shows a close analogy to the Western legend of the "Spirit of the Mist."

But the Chinese people other spheres with Fairy inhabitants; and there is a touch of the imaginative in such beliefs which rather induces sympathy with than hostility to their tenour. The universal legend of the Man in the Moon takes in China a form that is at leasts as interesting as the ruder legends of more barbarous peoples. The "Goddess of the Palace of the Moon," Chang-o, appeals as much to our sympathies as, and rather more so than, the ancient beldame who in European folk-lore picks up perpetual sticks to satisfy the vengeful ideas of an ultra-sabbathaical sect. Mr. G. C. Stent has aptly seized the idea of the Chinese versifier whom he translates:—

> "On a gold throne, whose radiating brightness
> Dazzles the eyes—enhaloing the scene,
> Sits a fair form, arrayed in snowy whiteness.
> —She is Chang-o, the beauteous Fairy Queen.
> Rainbow-winged angels softly hover o'er her
> Forming a canopy above the throne,
> A host of fairy beings stand before her
> Each robed in light and girt with meteor zone."

Making every allowance for the polish of translation, the foregoing verses intimate a delicacy of perception that raises Chinese fairy folk-lore to the level of our own. It is scarcely necessary to quote, from European sources, verses which in sentiment express a similar idea.

Fairy Tales abound in Chinese resembling those in Arabic folk-lore. A very well-known legend relates how a celebrated musician, aspiring to wed a princess who played so exquisitely on the flute that all the birds, even to the eagle, came down from heaven to listen to her, was accepted, on shewing proof of this ability as her husband. "Too good to live," however, the pair were transformed into genii, and still occupy a place in the somewhat vast arcana of Chinese gods. Other legends relate to animals becoming endowed with the gift of speech. Thus Chwang-tzŭ, the hero of a story which has been popularised by Mr. Stent under the heading "Fanning the Grave," is related to have reached a river, the banks of which were almost dry. Various small fishes thereupon petitioned him to restore their much-needed element—water—representing that if he did not do so, they would all perish; and their request was acceded to. Ireland and Germany both give us similar legends.

To sum up, I am inclined to the conclusion that no very real distinction obtains in Chinese folk-lore between the various beings described in the West as demons, genii and fairies, though, as I have endeavoured to shew, supernatural creatures, possessing the attributes of each, are fully believed in. The constant application of the term *shên* 神 in this connection seems to me an argument against its adoption by Christian missionaries to express our own conception of the Creator. It is singular, by the way, to find that just as we use the word "spirit" in two different senses when we say "God is a *spirit*" and "He is a man of spirit," the Chinese in like manner make the word *shên* do double duty. Of course the argument cuts both ways; but its inapplicability to the Chinese side lies in the fact that the language provides no word for the *one ultimate cause*. Whatever word our missionaries agree upon must do some violence to the native idea. The subject is, however, too wide to be more than incidentally touched on here. Suffice it to say that both in the everyday language of the people and in popular literature *shên* conveys the idea of *gods, spirits, fairies* or *demons* only. A careful consideration of this fact is imperative in any discussion as to its adoption in Christian books to express the Hebrew "Jehovah."

X.—SERPENTS, DRAGONS, FABULOUS ANIMALS AND MONSTERS.

The part played in the mythology of the Aryan and Semitic races by the Serpent and Dragon would have led one to expect a similar concurrence in the Legendry of China, even if the well-known designation under which its government is so frequently referred to did not at once direct attention to the fact. The land of the "Dragon Throne" is indeed by no means singular in its beliefs in this connection. To say nothing of the Biblical narrative, the Brahminic Krishna, under his two aspects of Krishna serpent-wounded in the heel and Krishna standing triumphant on the head of his arch-enemy, the classic stories of Hercules and the Hydra, Appollo and Python, Cadmus and the Dragon, the Teutonic myth of Sigurd and Fafner, or our own legend of St. George, and others which will be referred to in their proper place, combine to give the serpent and his congeners an universal celebrity. "Among different forms in use as an old symbol (says a recent reviewer) none is more mysterious than the serpent. The animal itself glides out and into holes and corners, and as it glides you only, perhaps, see a coil of the reptile; so, with its symbolism, the facts are most difficult to be got at, and the understanding of them is more difficult still. All nations seem to have had the serpent as a symbol in some form or another. Perhaps one of the strangest forms of this creeping thing was that of the Christian Ophites, who kept a serpent which crawled over the bread of the sacrament on the altar, and this they considered to be the act of consecration." It is hardly necesssary, however, to tell students of Chinese literature or folk-lore that our own assortment of popular legends and beliefs touching the serpent tribe shrink into insignificance beside that of the "Middle Kingdom." The brazen serpent of Moses has been the lineal progenitor of a succession familiar indeed to the sons of Han.* Confining our attention in the first instance to serpents proper, let us glance at the vast array of legend which greets the most superficial enquiry into Chinese beliefs on the subject.

And, before dealing with its supernatural characteristics, let me note the healing qualities ascribed to the serpent's flesh. The skin of the white spotted snake is used in leprosy, rheumatism and palsy,† while the flesh of other varieties enter largely into the often filthy prescriptions of native doctors. Though I am not aware that the figure of a serpent has ever been used in China as with the classical Esculapius and Hygia, who are represented as bearing a staff round which is coiled a serpent, as a symbol of health, the snake is a popular item of the show-part of every native drug store, and the virtues attributed to its body are at least a reminder of the Western legend. As a drug, however, it ceases to possess supernatural qualities. To the living animal are attributed powers not less potent than to the gods themselves. And the writer encountered an instance of this superstition when endeavouring some months since to induce his Chinese assistants at the Hongkong Museum to kill and prepare a fine specimen of the boa tribe which had been caught on the island.

That evil spirits or human beings compelled by enchantment can assume the form of snakes, is a deeply-rooted belief, as is also its converse that mysteriously-gifted serpents can at will present themselves to the public eye as ordinary mortals. In the "Thunder-peak Pagoda" novel, already referred to, we find the heroine of the story to be a white snake who possesses the power of assuming the human form. In the Cavern of the Winds situated on the Green Mountain near Ching-to-foo in Sze-chuan "there was," says the story, "reputed to be a monstrous white female serpent, who had been there from time immemorial. In this cave also grew strange flowers and wonderful shrubs. This serpent had existed for eighteen hundred years, and had never yet done harm to any living thing. On account of her great age, this white serpent had attained to a vast degree of knowledge, and was able to work marvellous spells, and to take the form of a woman, in which condition she adopted the name of Pī-cheu-niang." Her servant, like herself, was a serpent and the scene in which the two are for the first time introduced to each other is described in a way worthy of the Arabian nights:—

"Hang-chow is a most beautiful place. The residences of princes and nobles are

---

* See Kitto's *Cyclopædia of Biblical Literature*, Art. *Serpents*, too long for transcription in this place, but giving a most interesting sketch of serpent worship. Briefly summarized, it touches on the Naga Kings of Hinduism; the astronomical fables of the serpent Ananta, or the Milky Way, and the sun-and-moon-devouring dragons; the Scandinavian legend of the water serpent of the deep; the Celtic, Basque and Asiatic legends of the dragon guardian of riches. "These fables were a residue of that antique dragon worship which had its temples from High Asia and Colchis to the North of Great Britain and once flourished both in Greece and Northern Africa—structures with avenues of upright stones of several miles in length whereof the ruins may still be traced at Carnak in Brittany, Abury in Wiltshire and Redruth in Cornwall.". . . . The author refers to the sect of Christian heretics known as Ophite or Ophiani, who were professed serpent worshippers; and he gives some curious details of the Egyptian Python worship, emblems of which have even been discovered in British Archæology.

† F. Porter Smith's *Chinese Materia Medica*, Art. *Snakes*.

hero, and beautiful flower gardens and ancient temples are scattered all over the place. Among these, the garden of Prince Chow was pre-eminent for beauty; but Prince Chow had long been dead, and his beautiful garden was deserted by mankind. In it were altars, pavilions, and mountains almost equalling in splendour the gardens of the imperial palace. Here there resided a huge black serpent, which had been in this place for more than eight hundred years,—and could also ascend into the clouds, and take the human form; and when she saw the white serpent coming in, she hurried to prevent her entrance, saying, "Whence comest thou thus to invade the privacy of my garden? Dost thou not fear my wrath?" The white serpent, who had assumed the human form, as had the other, merely smiled, and said, "Don't talk about your power, but pay attention to what I am going to say—I am a powerful white sepent, come from the mountain cavern of the winds, where I have resided more than eighteen hundred years; but because I am not so powerful as I could wish, I have determined to change my abode, wherefore you must let me take up my residence in this garden— besides this, why should we quarrel, being both spirits in the form of serpents?" But the black snake was not so easily pacified, and angrily exclaimed, "This is my garden, and you are a spirit from some distant place—How then do you dare thus to deprive me of mine own? If, moreover, you think yourself more powerful than I am, let us contend together three times for the mastery." The white serpent smiled slightly, and said, "It is no desire of mine that we should contend together, as I do not wish to injure one of my species; but since you so much wish it, I *will* contend with you, but upon this condition only that whoever shall be victorious in the strife, shall become the mistress, and that the conquered one shall always act as a slave.

The black snake, still angry, snatched a sword and cut at the white serpent, but she, drawing two swords, put them before her in the form of a cross. In a few minutes the superior talent of the white serpent became evident, for by muttering a powerful spell, the sword was snatched from the hand of her adversary by some invisible means, and she was left defenceless. The black serpent at this was very much frightened, and kneeling down, respectfully addressed the other, saying, "Do not contend any longer—I acknowledge you as my superior, and am willing to serve you as your slave." Matters being thus settled so satisfactorily, the mistress and servant entered the garden together."*

The adventures of these two serpent women and the scrapes into which an unlucky attachment for the mistress led the hero of the tale, form the principal features of the plot. I cannot, of course, here follow that out; suffice it to say that the enchantress brought grief to all connected with her. But the story presents certain analogies with an old English legend that are worth noting. The "worm of Spindlestone Heugh" in Northumberland, was, so the legend says, a beautiful girl transformed by her step-mother into a loathsome serpent, until her brother should come to her rescue from beyond the seas. This of course he eventually does, and the charm is broken.

> "He quitted his sword, and bent his bow,
> He gave her kisses three;
> She crept into her hole a worme
> But out stept a ladye."†

The well-known Linton worm or dragon‡ supposed to inhabit the borders of Roxburghshire, gives us another parallel between a British and a Chinese belief. From his cave on Linton hill this monster "could with his sweeping and venomous breath draw the neighbouring flocks and herds within reach of his fangs." Again we read, "such was the dread inspired by the monster's poisonous breath" that the villagers were beside themselves with terror. Now we have only to go back to 1867 to find a story extensively believed through-

---

* *Lei-fung-ta,—Chinese & Japanese Repository*, Feb. 1864.

† Henderson's *Folk-Lore of the Northern Counties*, p. 255.
‡ *Ibid.*, p. 257.

out the Fuhkien seaboard, in which the poisonous character of a serpent's breath is an important element.* It was to the effect that a party of tiger-catchers near Foochow discovered in the cage which they had constructed to receive the tiger a monstrous snake with two large horns. Although somewhat frightened at their unexpected prisoner, they decided on taking him on board their junk with a view to eventually selling him. A few days after they had put to sea a thunderstorm came on, and a flash of lightning struck the junk, breaking open the cage. Away slipped the monster into the hold, which, being stored with rice and other edibles, was a decided change for the better in his position. As, however, the captain and crew were bound to deliver their cargo intact, the former offered $1,000 to anybody who would go down and kill the snake. Two men were found to venture, but no sooner did they approach the animal than "raising his head a little, he hissed out a vapour on them and they lay dead." Of course captain and crew immediately deserted the junk, and she is still reputed to be, like the flying Dutchman's ship off the Cape, cruizing around the neighbouring coasts; and so great is the fear of the serpent's breath, that no one who has heard the story dare board a castaway Foochow junk to this day.

Something more than mere traces of serpent worship are to be found throughout China. The *San-chieh* temples (三 界 廟) at Canton are also known by the name of *Ch'ing Shê Miao* or "Green serpent temples," the origin of which name is thus given in a compilation by the well-known author Chao Yi.† "When offerings were made to the god a serpent came out and ate or drank what was laid before the altar. If any person made a vow and did not afterwards fulfil it, although he might be hundreds of *li* away, serpents would come and claim fulfilment of his promise. These were commonly called Green Serpent Messengers. At present the most famous of these temples is that at Wuchow-fu, where scarcely a day passes on which plays are not performed or sacrifices offered, at the expense of traders who thus celebrate the fulfilment of their entreaties at the shrine. At the time of sacrifices being offered a green serpent does in reality issue forth from the sanctuary or make its appearance from the rafters, or from within the garments of the God, to drink the wine and devour the eggs that are placed there without being deterred by the sight of the persons standing by. After finishing its meal the creature quietly glides away."‡ Monsieur de Beauvoir, in his recent work describing a visit to the East, speaks of a temple at Canton within the enclosure of which was a clump of trees near an altar, the residence of a sacred serpent. "A crowd of worshippers were pressing round the sacred bushes, bringing gifts to the ugly reptile, a snake two feet long, which crawled about close to some hot ashes." I have not identified the temple, but the account is probably accurate, as native informants confirm it. Yet stronger evidence of the hold which serpent-worship has over the Chinese mind is afforded

---

* *N. & Q. on C. & J.*, Vol. III., p. 74.
† Note on the San Chieh Miao: *Notes & Queries on China & Japan*, Vol. III., p. 76, by W. F. Mayers.
‡ Mr. Waring quotes from the "Plutus" of Aristophanes a passage which alludes to the keeping of tame snakes in the Greek temples. The author thinks that it "was regarded rather as a symbol of Power, Wisdom, and Life, than as an actual deity."

by the fact that during the height of the Tientsin floods, in the autumn of 1873, Li Hung-chang, a man distinguished for his clear common sense and administrative ability, joined in offering worship to a miserable little snake which had been picked up and placed in one of the temples, afterwards extolling, in a memorial to the Throne, the divine favour exhibited by the appearance of the wretched reptile. And in the following year the *North-China Herald* related an even more absurd instance of faith in the supernatural attributes of the serpent tribe. "In this case also," says the journal in question, "the memorialist is a man of distinguished ability, which he has given evidence of both in connection with Foreign and Chinese matters. He reports wonderful miracles on the part of the river gods, in saving embankments and helping the men who were at work on them, over and over again. Apparently the Taiwang are credited with power to make the waters abate just at the critical moment, but not to avert such unfortunate crises altogether. The river god is, in every case, a small water snake, which popular fancy has converted into a deity. The story of Chen Ching-lung Chang-chün, one of the deities mentioned, is that he was inspector of the Yellow River, and being unable to repair a breach in the embankments, on account of the strength of the current, he in despair threw himself into the river. The water ceased to rise, the current slackened, and the breach was repaired. Chen was transformed into a River God for his noble devotedness, and constantly appears in the shape of a water serpent, to work miracles on behalf of his more fortunate successors in the difficult duty of checking the outburst of 'China's Sorrow.'"

That snakes contain in their heads certain precious stones is an old belief common to most branches of the human family.[*] A story in a native book of anecdotes relates how a foreigner passing a pork-butcher's shop asks the master what he will take for the bench on which the pork is exposed. The answer, given in fun, is "fifty taels." The foreigner offers to pay the money. This convinces the butcher that there must be something valuable in the bench, so he declines to sell it, and carefully puts it by. The foreigner leaves the place and returns after a year's absence. Seeing the butcher he asks after the bench, and, in answer to a very natural enquiry why he deems it so valuable, informs him that, lodged in a cavity within it, is a snake, holding in its mouth a precious gem. He further adds that the snake lives on the blood that soaks through the wood from the raw meat exposed on it, and that when this supply is cut off the snake will die, and the gem become worthless. Cursing his own stupidity, the butcher seizes a hatchet and splits the bench open, finding the snake dead, while the jewel it undoubtedly holds in its mouth is of the same colour as the eye of a dried fish. I have chosen this story as illustrating another point in native folk-lore—the mysterious powers attributed to foreigners—but may observe that constant allusions are to be found in Chinese works to the idea of snakes containing precious stones. Now, to go no further than a file of Indian papers received a few weeks ago, I find in one of them the following paragraph. "*The Lawrence Gazette* indulges in surmises as to the object of the ex-King of Oudh in collecting snakes. Perhaps," it says, "he wishes to become possessed of the precious

[*] *Notes and Queries on China and Japan*, Vol. II., p. 130.

jewel which some serpents are said to contain, or of that species of snake by whose means it is said a person can fly in the air. The jewel referred to (*nun*) has in all times been a popular myth, but located variously in the heads of toads, fishes, and even horses." The superstition therefore is not confined to the Chinese. Is it not possible that Shakespere's allusion to the toad, which,

"Ugly and venomous, wears a precious jewel in his head,"

may have been suggested by this popular belief, though now interpreted to apply only to the beautiful eye with which the animal is endowed?

The transition from the serpent to the dragon is easy, but appears to have followed much the same rule in China as in England—there being a considerable amount of confusion in the legendary lore of both countries between the two animals. It is indeed somewhat difficult to exactly say where fact left off, and fancy commenced, to contribute to the popular portrait of the dragon. China does, in fact, produce an animal—a harmless species of lizard,—which may well have sat as the original of the native monster; but its small size (only some two feet from nose to tail) deprives it of any ferocious semblance. Looking at the widespread belief in dragons there seems little doubt that the semi-myth of to-day is the traditional successor of a really once existent animal, whose huge size, snake-like appearance and, possibly, dangerous powers of offence made him so terrible that the earlier races of mankind adopted him unanimously as the most fearful embodiment of animal ferocity to be found.

Dr. Eitel, in an interesting article on the subject of dragon worship,[*] expresses his belief that it has sprung from the same form of snake or naga worship as that still existing in India, Burmah and Siam. "What strengthens this assertion," he says, "is the circumstance that I am enabled to state positively that the Chinese translators of Sanscrit Buddhist texts invariably rendered the term naga (which has been identified with *cobra di capello*,) by the word "lung" (龍) or dragon. The religious mind of China has never made a scientific distinction between snake and dragon." Suffice it to say that China is the oldest home of dragon worship, the animal being represented as winged and four-footed, each foot having four (or five) claws—the latter number being appropriated solely to pictures, embroideries or figures used by the Imperial Court. Thus a dress with a five-clawed dragon worked on it can be used by one of Royal blood only. It is noteworthy that the English dragon is also nearly always represented with wings. For those who have never read the ballad of the Dragon of Wantley I may quote his description, to enable a comparison to be drawn between him and his Chinese brother :—

> "This dragon had two furious wings
> One upon each shoulder,
> With a sting in his tayle, as long as a flayle,
> Which made him bolder and bolder.
> He had long claws, and in his jaws
> Four and forty teeth of iron,
> With a hide as tough, as any buff,
> Which did him round environ."

---

[*] *Notes and Queries on China and Japan*, Vol. III., p. 34.

The *authentic* species of dragon or *Lung*, has, according to Chinese belief, a camel's head, a deer's horns, a rabbit's eyes, a cow's ears, a snake's neck, a frog's belly, a carp's scales, a hawk's claws and a tiger's palms. The chief distinction between the snake and the dragon in Chinese eyes is that, while the former is worshipped as a real, everyday object, the latter is avowedly supernatural. A popular proverb says, "Dragons bring clouds, and tigers bring winds."* The dragon is in fact an all-pervading element of every myth relating to the powers of nature, and its worship is not, when we trace its serpent origin, surprising.

In no case however does it seem more absurd than when we find it gravely noticed in official documents. Thus a year or two since an Edict published in the *Peking Gazette* stated as follows:—" Li Hung-chang has addressed to us a memorial, stating that the River Yung-ting has filled its channel, reporting for punishment the officials who were engaged on the works, and requesting the appropriate discipline on himself. He states that much rain fell for several weeks in succession this year, and the waters in river and lake rose to an unwonted height. The officers responsible worked day and night to avert danger by opening and shutting sluices and strengthening works. On the 4th and 5th July the rain came down in bucketfuls, and it became utterly impossible to do anything; the river overflowed in several places. Li Hung-chang *last year reported that he had caged the dragon*, and it is therefore an inexcusable fault that, in so short a time afterwards, even allowing several weeks' rain, the river should have broken out!" It would be difficult to come across more convincing proof that the supernatural powers of the dragon over the phenomena of nature were fully believed in.

Domestic dragon worship again is familiar to every native. The author of the paper above referred to gives curious details of the ceremonies observed in worshipping dragon-spirits. Every hill and mountain is supposed to be inhabited by them, and whenever a new house is to be erected, a Fêng-shui geomancer is consulted to learn if the location be within the range of friendly dragon spirits. The house on being completed has a niche fitted up in it as a shrine for the individual dragon which protects the destinies of the house. He is installed with considerable ceremony, and the shrine is worshipped at the same periods as sacrifices or prayers are offered in the Ancestral Hall. In the case of houses which have been built for the space of one hundred years (at the expiration of which period the original virtue and efficiency of the tutelary dragon is supposed to need reinvigoration) more elaborate ceremonials are necessary. Three days are devoted to preparation, and on the fourth the exorcism of evil influences commences. This consists in magical incantations mumbled in unintelligible language, accompanied by offerings of frankincense, wine and paper, the whole accompanied by the beatings of drums and gongs and the blowing of a horn. The chief wizard then dips his arm into boiling oil or performs some similar feat to justify his claims as an exorcist; one of the com-

* 龍從雲虎從風.

monest being to walk unharmed through an enormous fire of blazing charcoal. Another performance consists in ascending a ladder of swords. One or all of these being accomplished, the wizard repairs, attended by the neighbours, to the nearest hill and invokes the dragon spirit to return, and after announcing his arrival professes to entice him back to the house. The curious reader will find the ceremonies described at length in the article from which this is summarized.

The following dragon legend was communicated to the same periodical by Mr. T. Sampson of Canton, and is worth preservation: "It is a common expression in Canton, to say that extremely violent gusts of wind during a typhoon are caused by the passage of a *tün mi lung* 斷尾龍 or "bob-tail dragon," and it is sometimes averred that this animal is actually seen on such occasions passing through the air; generally however it is, among educated people, nothing more than an expression signifying a violent gust of wind, and the story connected with it, if known at all beyond the district of Sun-ui where it has a local circulation, is classed with such fables as that of the great sea serpent which was so long that when at rest a junk had to sail for several days to traverse its length, and which, on being cut in two by a steamer, was several hours in discovering the fact, in consequence of the immense length of the nerves which had to convey to the brain the sense of the injury inflicted.

"The story however of Ah-Tseung and the dragon, as narrated to me by a native of Sun-ui, is as follows: In ancient times there was a certain studious rustic whose name was Ah-Tseung, but whose surname has unfortunately not been handed down for the benefit of posterity; this youth having found a young snake took it home with him, and as long as he lived it was his chief delight to nurture this animal; he made a nest for it in his book-case, and after every meal he secretly conveyed food to it; it shared his bed, and was his constant companion; the boy for a long time kept the matter secret from his parents, but his teacher having observed his many visits to the book-case, wished to find out what was the attraction, and on opening it he observed to his great surprise and alarm, a huge snake filling one of the shelves, for by this time the snake had become full grown. A few months after this Ah-Tseung died, whereupon his parents drove the snake away to the neighbouring hills; on every occasion of ceremonial mourning held by the parents, and on every anniversary of his death, the snake visited the home of his departed friend, and after going several times round the house returned again to the hills; the neighbours felt a natural repugnance to these periodical visits, and remonstrated with Ah Tseung's mother, who herself anxious to get rid of so unwelcome a visitor, forbade the snake coming to her house any more; heedless of this command the snake did return; whereupon the mother, with the intention of frightening it away, brandished a knife at it in a threatening manner, but in doing so the knife accidentally came in contact with the animal's tail and severed off several joints of it. After this the snake never returned; it retired however to the Kwai-fung-shàn in the district of Sun-ui, where there is a lake of about a *mau* (⅓d of an acre) in extent and of unfathomable depth; indeed it is asserted by the inhabitants of the neighborhood, that its waters communicate subterraneously with one of the mouths of the great rivers of Kwangtung, the Ngaimun, and that any substance thrown into the lake will reappear in the ocean near that embouchure. In and round this lake Ah Tseung's snake has lived to the present day, and its appearance on the distant hill top, sometimes as a man clothed in white, and sometimes as a white dragon (an instance of progressive development without natural selection, its flight through the air causing dragonic development from the pristine type of an ordinary snake), or the foaming disturbance of the waters of the lake when he indulges in a bath, are considered sure indications of an approaching storm.

"Such is the story of Ah Tseung and the dragon. Fabulous as it undoubtedly is, there may nevertheless be, as is often the case with the most outrageous fables, a grain of scientific truth in it; the range of hills in Sun-ui of which the Kwei-fung-shan forms a part, must exert some influence on typhoons; they are in the track of these circular storms, and probably their height effects an attractive influence over them, and their conformation diverts the course of the storm as it impinges upon them. Hence the fact in the natural history of typhoons, that they, owing to these causes, frequently pass over Sun-ui and disturb the waters of the lake in the Kwai-fung hills before they reach other parts of the common delta of the Kwangtung river, may be the grain of scientific truth which has given rise to the story of Ah Tseung and the dragon with an abbreviated caudal extremity."

If we have no Western legend to answer to that just given, a very close parallel to a Serpent or dragon myth which has spread throughout Europe can be found in China. Our popular story of St. George and the Dragon has numerous parallels in Western folklore. The stories of the laird who slew the "worme of Linton," of the knight who killed the Lambton worm, of the Champion Conyers who delivered Sockburn in Durham from "a worm, dragon or fiery flying serpent," and of the plucky Scot named Martin who in Forfar achieved a victory over a dragon which had devoured nine maidens, embody the same story in other words. Scandinavian Folk-lore too abounds with similar stories. But one is hardly prepared to find the legend existing in China, with a change of sex indeed on the part of the champion, but otherwise the same in its general features as our own. Mr. W. F. Mayers, writing in November 1867, drew attention to this fact and furnished the now extinct periodical so frequently referred to on previous pages with the following translation from the *Kwang-po-wu-chih*, a thesaurus of excerpts compiled towards the end of the sixteenth century:* "In the eastern regions of Yueh Min (the present Fuhkien) there exists a range of mountains called the Yung Ling, many tens of *li* in height, in the north-western recesses of which there abode a mighty serpent, seven or eight *chang* (seventy or eighty feet) in length and ten feet in circumference, which was held in great awe by the people of the country. At a certain time it signified either to some person in a dream or to those versed in the art of divination that it lusted to devour a maiden of the age of twelve or thirteen; and the governors and men in authority of that region, equally alarmed respecting

* *Notes and Queries on China and Japan*, Vol. I., p. 148.

the monster, sought out female bond-servants and the daughters of criminals to satisfy the serpent's appetite. In the morning of the day in the 8th moon, after offering sacrifices, the victim was taken to the mouth of the serpent's cavern; and at night the serpent suddenly issued forth and devoured its prey. Year after year this happened, until at length nine maidens in all had been offered up; and a fresh demand was being made, but no victim could be obtained. At this time Li Tan, Magistrate of Tsing Lo, had six daughters and no sons. His youngest daughter, named Ki 奇, responded to the call and was ready to proceed (to the cavern), but her parents refused consent. She urged, however, that she was unable to be of use to her parents, as was Ti Ying (the faithful daughter of olden times), and being a mere source of useless expense might as well bring her life to a speedy close, and only requested to be supplied with a good sword and a dog that would bite at snakes. In the morning of the day of the eight month she visited the Temple, with the sword beside her and the dog provided. She had also previously prepared several measures of boiled rice mixed with honey, which she placed at the mouth of the cavern. At night the serpent came forth, its head as large as a rice stock and its eyes like mirrors two feet across—when, perceiving the aroma of the mess of rice, it began to devour it. Ki forthwith let loose her dog which seized the serpent in its teeth, and the maiden hereupon hacked the monster from behind, so that after dragging itself to the mouth of its cave it died. The maiden entered the cavern and recovered the skeletons of the nine previous victims, whose untimely fate she bewailed. After this she leisurely returned home, and the prince of Sueh, hearing of her exploit, raised her to be his Queen.

"Other versions of this history may exist, but the above is the only one I have met with. The occurrence of a female as the hero is somewhat remarkable, but in other respects the fact that filial piety and dexterity in stratagems replace in the Chinese legend the masculine purity and dauntless courage with which our own traditions invest St. George, as also the minuteness in detail of the events recorded, are highly characteristic of the Chinese turn of mind. In any case, this is probably the earliest existing version of the famous legend."

So much for dragons, dismissed perhaps with almost too scant notice, but scarcely needing more elaborate discussion. The third heading of the present chapter refers to fabulous animals of another description, and of these Chinese folk-lore presents us with a fair variety. The Phœnix, for instance, enjoys its classical reputation amongst the inhabitants of the Middle Kingdom, while tigers, monkeys and elephants also enjoy the reputation of a wisdom which goes beyond instinct and more than verges on the domain of humanity. Tailed men and mermaids furnish native tradition-mongers with numerous stories; and the unicorn of Chinese myth-land is to all intents and purposes identical with the celebrated animal mentioned in our nursery rhyme, relating how

"The Lion and the Unicorn
Went fighting for the Crown;"

and still "supporting" our royal arms. The *ki lin*, or Chinese unicorn, has a stag's body, a horse's hoofs, the tail of an ox and a parti-coloured skin, while from its forehead proceeds a single horn with a fleshy tip. In this case there is however but little mystery in the resemblance. So far from agreeing with Dr. Williams as to "the independent origin of the Chinese account,"* there can, I fancy, be no question that both we and the Chinese alike derived the idea of the unicorn from Central Asia, where we have almost historical proof such an animal once actually existed, if indeed it does not still inhabit the vast steppes of the continent.† The chief superstition connected with the unicorn in China proper is that one makes its appearance when a sage is about to be born.

Phœnixes also act as harbingers of the birth of great men,‡ but it is somewhat difficult to define their shape and colour. Popular native proverbs allege that "The Phœnix will only alight where there is something precious." Another saying declares that "when the phœnix comes there is prosperity." The following account of this universally-believed-in bird, given by Mr. Mayers in his *Readers' Manual*, embodies an admirable resumé of Chinese legend on the subject. The *feng* or phœnix is, he says, "a fabulous bird of wondrous form and mystic nature, the second amongst the four supernatural creatures. Very early legends narrated that this bird made its appearance as a presage of the advent of virtuous rulers, whose presence it also graced as an emblem of their auspicious government. One writer describes it as having the head of a pheasant, the beak of a swallow, the neck of a tortoise and the outward semblance of a dragon; to which another version adds the tail of a fish; but in pictorial representations it is usually delineated as a compound between the peacock and the pheasant, with the addition of many gorgeous colours. It sate in the court of Hwang-ti while that sovereign observed the ceremonial fasts; and according to the *Shu King* it came with measured gambollings to add splendour to the musical performances conducted by the great Shun. The female is called *Hwang*, and this name, combined with that of the male, forms the compound *Feng Hwang* which is usually employed as the generic designation for the wondrous bird. It is translated phœnix by many writers. Among the marvels related respecting this creature, it is said that each of the five colours which embellish the *Fêng-hwang's* plumage is typical of one of the cardinal virtues; and a name is given to each of the many intonations ascribed to its voice."

* *Middle Kingdom*, I. p. 266.

† Whilst writing the above my attention has been directed to the following interesting paragraph in the Calcutta *Englishman:* —"A long discussion is being carried on in the last papers received from the Cape as to the existence or non-existence of the unicorn. Mr. G. R. Blanche, who has travelled extensively in Namaqualand, mentions that in some large stone-caves on the banks of a river called Makapwe, he saw pictures drawn by Bush-men, which included elephants, rhinoceroses, unicorns, and gemsboks, and one old Bushman told him that he had actually seen the animal alive, and that it was very fierce. None, however, had been seen for some years. The Macacas stated that to the north of their town, on the river Teoga, large numbers of unicorns are still to be seen, and Mr. Blanche considers that in the vast region of unexplored territory between the Zambesi and Lebaby's country they may still be in existence. Mr. Thomas Baines, another well-known African traveller and naturalist, says that the existence of such an animal has never been disproved, and that it might be found in this unexplored country, for else where did the bush-men obtain the subject for the pictures they have drawn?"

‡ Dr. Legge's *Chinese Classics*, Vol. III., pt. I. pref., p. 108.

An animal occupying an intermediate position between fact and fiction—its existence being the one, and its alleged qualities the other—is known as the Sing-sing 猩猩, a very large species of baboon found in Cambodia. Its blood is supposed in China to be useful as a dye; but inasmuch as it of course dries up if the animal is killed, the Chinese allege that artifice is resorted to by hunters to induce it to submit to the process of bleeding, and the natives quaintly describe the (very imaginative) operation. The story is evidently the production of some Chinese Æsop, containing as it does an admirable satire on the temptations of the wine cup. But, nevertheless, the animal is really believed by the vulgar to possess supernatural powers. The account given is as follows:—" The *Sing-sing* is remarkably fond of wine ; so the blood-hunters lay a trap for him thus:—Having found the tracks he frequents, they place in some position where he is sure to see them a pailful of some intoxicating liquid and a cup, and then conceal themselves in the vicinity. After a time the *Sing-sing* discovers the pail; but after inspecting it mutters, 'Ah! this is put here by the blood hunters, but I shan't be fool enough to drink it; it's nothing but poison.' Moving away for a short time it presently returns, observing, ' After all wine is a good thing in itself, if one doesn't take too much; it's very nice, and I shall just try one cup.' The animal accordingly takes one cupful and walks away, soon however returning for a second and a third, finally drinking itself helpless. The hunters then seize it and place it in a cage, and on its recovery begin to bargain with it for its liberty. Its blood, to be of any service, must be voluntarily given, so the hunters demand so many cupsful as the price of its release. After a good deal of palavering this is settled; the animal then himself opens a vein, measures out the quantity agreed on and is released, again to fall a victim to similar temptation." The assumption that the baboon can, if it will, hold converse with mankind is noteworthy as common to most countries whence the monkey tribes take their origin.

Of course our old friend—I might almost say, in view of the latest published accounts, our American friend—the Sea Serpent, turns up on the coasts of China, and the description given of him does not greatly differ from that recorded elsewhere. According to a popular legend the Chien Tang river was at one time infested by a great *Kiau* or sea serpent, and in 1 129 A.D., a district graduate is said to have heroically thrown himself into the flood to encounter and destroy the monster. His wife forthwith put an end to her existence also, from devotion to him, and their virtues were commemorated by a temple erected for their worship.* It has been already noted that most of the river gods are supposed to appear in the form of water snakes, and that the *sea* serpents noticed in Chinese records have always infested the mouths of rivers. From a tutelary deity to one purely malevolent is no great step. Other remarkable animals are noted by the writer above quoted (Dr. D. J. Macgowan) as stated to have visited the same river: In 488 A.D. a salt inspector discovered near its mouth a "sea-fish which the tide had left behind. It was more than 300 feet long, of a black colour, without scales," and was eaten by its captors. About 120 years ago,

* Transactions N. C. B. R. A. S., 1853, p. 36.

again "a huge sea-fish appeared off Chapoo; it followed the vessels in with the tide and at ebb was unable to return. It measured one hundred feet in length, was ten feet high and twenty wide." This is probably an exaggerated story of a whale, but as the Chinese have a distinct name for the whale, with which they are fairly familiar, there remains a possibility of the animal in question being something unknown to naturalists.

A very singular coincidence between two legends relating to fabulous fish is to be found in the following. A recent visitor to Nanking thus describes the basin which formerly decorated the top of the celebrated porcelain pagoda: "We happened to discover among the ruins an immense cast iron basin, 39 feet in circumference, which is connected popularly with the above account of the thunder spirit. This basin was placed with its mouth upwards on the summit of the pagoda, and hence would constantly be full of rain water. A bird perched upon the edge of the basin one day dropped a fish into the water, which grew and grew till it became a strange monster, exercising such an evil influence over the neighbourhood that the God of thunder was at length compelled to attack it, and in doing so struck the tower and partially destroyed it. It was finally destroyed by the rebels in 1856." Now if we turn to Henderson's *Folk-lore of the Northern Counties*, p. 248, we find the following story of the "Heir of Lambton." Fishing one day in the river Wear he felt something tugging at his line and thought he had secured a fine fish. But to his horror he found that he had only caught a worm of unsightly appearance which he hastily tore from his hook and flung into a well close by. "A stranger of venerable appearance passing by asked him what sport he had met with. To which he replied, 'Why truly I think I have caught the devil himself. Look in and judge.' The stranger looked, and remarked that he thought it boded no good . . . . . Meantime the worm remained in the well till it outgrew so confined a hiding place. It then emerged and betook itself by day to the river, and by night to a neighbouring hill round whose base it would twine itself; while it continued to grow so fast that it soon could encircle the hill three times. The monster now became the terror of the whole country side, &c." The feat of arms by which this "Lambton Worm" was finally killed has been before alluded to. But the coincidence between the Chinese and English legend, in other respects, seemed worth additional notice.

Some of my readers may perchance be interested to learn that the original home of the mermaid (Ch. sea-woman 海女 *hai nü*) is almost within sight of the room in which these notes are being written. The only specimen of a veritable mermaid I ever saw was Barnum's celebrated purchase from Japan, which, so far as could be judged, consisted of a monkey's body most artistically joined to a fish's tail. But the author of a work entitled *Yueh chung chieh wên*, or "Jottings on the South of China," compiled in 1801, narrates how a man of the district of Sin-an (locally *Sin-on*) captured a mermaid on the shore of Ta-yü-shan or Namtao Island. "Her features and limbs were in all respects human, except that her body was covered with fine hair of many beautiful colours. The fisherman took home his prize and married her, though she was unable to talk and could only smile. She however learned to wear clothes like ordinary mortals. When the fisherman died the sea-maiden was sent back to the spot where she was first found, and she disappeared beneath the waves." The narrator quaintly adds, "This testifies that a man-fish does no injury to human beings," and he moreover informs us that these creatures are frequently to be found near Yü-shan and the Ladrone Island—so that any adventurous Hongkong canoeist may still have a chance of making a novel acquaintance. Another case recorded by the same writer speaks of a mermaid of more conventional form than the lady already noticed. "The Cabinet Councillor Cha Tao being despatched on a mission to Corea, and lying at anchor in his ship at a bay upon the coast, saw a woman stretched upon the beach, with her face upwards, her hair short and streaming loose, and with webbed feet and hands. He recognised this being as a mermaid (or man fish) and gave orders that she should be carried to the sea. This being done, the creature clasped her hands with an expression of loving gratitude and sank beneath the waters."

The Straits of Hainan are regarded by the Chinese as the chief habitat of monstrous fishes of strange shape, ruled over by the God of the waters, a sort of Chinese Neptune. And it is quite possible that the opening of the principal port of the island to foreign trade may (on the ground that nearly all such legends have a faint substratum of truth) reveal to the eyes of the naturalist new and undreamt-of inhabitants of the deep. It is but a few years since the ridicule excited by M. Victor Hugo's "devil fish" has given way to a sober recognition of the fact that the octopus of real life is a monster but little differing from the fanciful sketch given of his congener. And he would now-a-days be rash who ventured to assert that the Chinese have less ground for asserting the existence of very real monsters to our eyes than is possessed by the hardy fishermen of the coasts of Northern Europe.

XI.—SUPERSTITIONS REGARDING THE POWERS OF NATURE.

The beliefs to be noticed under this head are such as those familiar with Asiatic ways of thought would expect to find. The sun, moon, and stars, thunder and lightning, wind, water, and fire are each supposed to exist and exercise their powers under the directions of particular deities or spirits. As with ourselves, the moon enjoys amongst the Chinese a preëminence in regard to the numerous traditions related of her inhabitants. There is an Old Man of the Moon, a Goddess, a Lunar Frog, a Toad, a Hare &c., and each myth bears more or less resemblance to legends handed down to us from our own forefathers. The sun, though in a less degree, is the object of similar beliefs. Planetary or stellar influences are devoutly believed in, stars being, as amongst the ancient

Westerns, the embodiments or homes of heroes or demons. So too with cosmical phenomena. Being unable to realize that these occur in accordance with natural laws laid down by an all-powerful Creator, the Chinese are naturally thrown back upon the pagan idea of numerous supernatural directors. That their legends regarding such matters are, however puerile, so strikingly free from aught that is obscene or (when mythology is in question) unnatural, is creditable to the purity of the popular creeds.

Dr. D. J. Macgowan, whose numerous contributions to our better knowledge of Chinese matters have placed his readers under considerable obligations, furnished an interesting mass of matter in this connection in an article read in December 1858 before the North China Branch of the Royal Asiatic Society. In his introductory remarks he thus accounts for the fulness of cosmical record for which Chinese literature is remarkable:—"According to Chinese cosmogony, man is so intimately identified with the powers of nature, being what they term ' a miniature heaven and earth,' that, in order to be conversant with the science of civil government, one must study celestial and terrestrial phenomena,—as the deviations from the course of nature are all more or less portentous of evil, excepting a few, which are regarded as felicitous. Indeed, in high antiquity they professed to have a revelation in a tabulated form, procured from the carapace of a tortoise, by which those who observed the weather and seasons might form correct opinions on the political aspect of the times. In the Shu-King, under the section Hung-Fan or Great Plan, this doctrine is summarily laid down thus:—

SEASONABLE RAIN,	indicates	*Decorum.*
EXCESSIVE RAIN,	,,	*Dissoluteness.*
OPPORTUNE FINE WEATHER,	,,	*Good government.*
LONG-CONTINUED DROUGHT,	,,	*Arrogance.*
MODERATE HEAT,	,,	*Intelligence.*
EXCESSIVE HEAT,	,,	*Indolence.*
MODERATE COLD,	,,	*Deliberation.*
EXTREME COLD,	,,	*Precipitation.*
SEASONABLE WIND,	,,	*Perfection.*
CONTINUED TEMPEST,	,,	*Stupidity.*

"From these views, which have great influence on the minds of the Chinese, it happens that a fuller account of subterranean action of meteorological wonders, and the like, are found in their records, than among the annals of any other people, anterior to the birth of meteorology as a science."

No doubt the explanation here given accounts for the attention paid by the more educated classes to natural phenomena. But, as is usually the case, popular belief has grafted upon an intelligible, if absurd, system numerous additions. The superstitious peasantry trouble themselves but slightly about the science of civil government but eagerly discuss portents which are believed to affect their little world. And as my object is rather to deal with such superstitions as they affect the vulgar, than as they influence the literati, I content myself with this mere glance at the profounder system involved in watching cosmical phenomena and pursue the humbler branch of the subject comprehended under the term "folk-lore;" though it is probable that I shall here transgress the boundaries of my subject, inasmuch as such beliefs are too closely connected with native mythology to enable a strict line to be drawn between the two.

The Chinese "Old Man in the Moon" is known as *Yue-lao* and is reputed to hold in his hands the power of predestining the marriages of mortals—so that marriages if not, according to the native idea, exactly made in heaven, are made somewhere beyond the bounds of earth. He is supposed to tie together the future husband and wife with an invisible silken cord which never parts so long as life exists. Readers of Mr. Baring-Gould's "Curious Myths" will remember the various legends attaching to the Man in the Moon, none of which however endow him with any power over sublunary affairs. The parallel between an English and Chinese superstition regarding the Queen or *Goddess* of the Moon is closer. This still exists in parts of Lancashire and is the basis of numerous legends in China. Regarding these latter I cannot do better than quote the remarks made by Mr. W. F. Mayers,* though, as will be observed, he does not notice the Lancashire superstition. He says:—"No one can compare the Chinese legend with the popular European belief in the 'Man in the Moon,' as sketched, for instance, in Mr. Baring-Gould's 'Curious Myths of the Middle Ages' (First Series, p. 179), without feeling convinced of the certainty that the Chinese superstition and the English nursery tale are both derived from kindred parentage, and are linked in this relationship by numerous subsidiary ties. The idea, says Mr. Gould, of placing 'animals in the two great luminaries of heaven is very ancient and . . . a relic of a primeval superstition of the Aryan race.' A tree, an old man, and a hare, are, as Mr. Gould shews in various passages, the inhabitants assigned to the moon in Indian fable; whilst the curious notion that the human recluse condemned to an abode in the lunar regions owes his transportation thither to an act of theft or of sacrilege is a well-known concomitant of the story in all lands. In all the range of Chinese mythology there is, perhaps, no stranger instance of identity with the traditions that have taken root in Europe than in the case of the legends relating the moon; and, luckily, it is not difficult to trace the origin of the Chinese belief in this particular instance. The celebrated Lin Ngan, author (in part at least) of the writings known as Hwai Nan Tsze, is well known to have been the patron of travelled philosophers, under whose guidance he studied and pursued the cabalistic practices which eventually betrayed him to his death; and the famous astronomer Chang Hêng was avowedly a disciple of Indian teachers. That the writings derived from two such hands are found giving currency to an Indian fable is, therefore, not surprising; and there seems to be ground for suspicion that the name Chang Ngo, (or, as the dictionaries assert more properly Heng-ngo) appearing in their treatises may be the corrupt representation of some Hindoo sound, rather than connected, as the writer quoted above suggests, with the doubtful title of an office obscurely mentioned in times long anterior to the dates at which they wrote. The statement given by Chang Hêng is to the effect that 'How I 后羿, the fabled inventor of arrows in the days of Yao and Shun, obtained the drug of immortality from Si Wang Mu (the fairy "Royal

* *N. & Q. on C. & J.*, Vol. III., p. 123.

Mother" of the West); and Chang-Ngo (his wife) having stolen it, fled to the moon, and became the frog—*Chan-chu*—which is seen there.' The later fabulists have adhered to this story and amplified its details, as for instance, in the *Kwang-ki* a pleasing story of a subsequent reunion between How I and his wife is told; but in general the myth has been handed down unaltered, and the lady Chang-ngo is still pointed out among the shadows in the surface of the moon. In its etymological bearings, the legend is well worthy of further investigation." With this conclusion all readers will agree. As regards the legend concerning the hare, it is purely of Indian origin, having been introduced into China with Buddhism. Sakyamuni, the founder of Buddhism, is related to have been a hare in one of the earliest stages of his existence, living in friendship with a fox and an ape. Indra having sought their hospitality the fox and ape procured him food, but the hare could find nothing. Sooner than be inhospitable the hare cast itself into a fire in order to become food for his guest, in reward for which Indra transported him to the moon.* The lunar hare, as Mr. Mayers notes in his "Manual," is said to squat at the foot of "the cassia tree of the moon" (月中桂) pounding drugs for the Genii (Art. Kwei 桂 § 300.) A vulgar superstition asserts that the hare conceives by looking at the moon, bringing forth her young from the mouth.

The influence exerted by the moon on tides is recognised by the Chinese—a noteworthy fact in view of the strenuous denials of there being any basis of scientific truth in a belief shared by every Western sailor. The moon is, in China, the embodiment of the *Yin* or female principle influencing darkness, the female sex, the earth, water, &c. &c. A trace of a similar belief is to be found in the Isle of Skye. The Skye correspondent of a home Journal writes:—
" During the fortnight commencing on the 24th of June, when the moon was crescent, no real Skyeman would stack his peats for any consideration, believing that unless stacked under a waning moon the peats will give neither light nor heat when burned. 'A power of smoke' is all that can be expected from peats stacked under a crescent moon. In Skye the crescent is called 'fas,' and the wane 'tarradh,' and under these two terms the moon not only exercises great influence over peats, but also over many other things. In some parts of the High-lands, sheep, pigs and cows are only killed in the 'fas,' as meat made in the 'tarradh' is supposed to be good for nothing but 'shrinking' when in the pot." Native Chinese records aver that on the 18th day of the 6th moon, 1590, snow fell one summer night from the midst of the moon. The flakes were like fine willow flowers or shreds of silk.

If we except the somewhat bold speculations of certain modern religionists who place the hereafter within the fiery orb forming the centre of our system, European legend and belief have but little to say about the sun. The Chinese however have not failed to assign it as the dwelling-place of mysterious beings, one account making it the residence of a spirit named *Yuh I*, while others

---

* *Curious Myths of the Middle Ages*, 1st Series, p. 191. Mayers' *Chinese Readers' Manual*, pp. 95, 219, 288. Eitel's *Handbook of Chinese Buddhism*, Art. *Sakchi*.

allege that a three-legged bird of supernatural attributes is its ruling demon. The sun rules the masculine principle and is supposed to be the offspring of a female named Hi Ho.* Other popular Buddhistic legends allege the names of the solar genius to be—Su-li-ye 蘇利耶 or Su-mo 蘇摩. We must turn to the fire-worshippers of Persia or Mexico, to the worshippers of Baal or the sun-worshippers of Phœnicia for precise analogies in this direction. Dr. Kitto concludes that the latter worshipped not the sun itself but an astral spirit residing in it. The most singular fact in connection with the Chinese beliefs is, after all, their compatibility with an absence of any extended system of Sun-worship, though that luminary is adored as *Tai-yang-ti-chün*—the "Sun ruler" who presides over the soul of man.

The identification of the stars and planets with the dwelling places of heroic or supernatural beings prevails extensively in China. These superstitions are mostly Taoistic and strongly resemble those of the Hindoos. The Divine Tortoise 神龜 *Shên-kwai* is said to be the embodiment of the star "Yao Kwong" in Ursa Major. The Spirit of the legendary prince *Chih-yu* 蚩尤 is supposed to inhabit the planet Mars. *Yu-hwang-ti* is assigned to the pure Jade stone palace in the T'ai-wei tract of stars. *T'ien-hwang-ta-ti*, who rules the poles, and regulates heaven, earth and man, is said to reside in the pole star. *Hsing-chu*, the "Lord of the stars" resides in a star near the pole known by his name; while the spirit of the South pole has a similar celestial residence. As already noted, Kwan-Ti, the God of War, is alleged to have made himself visible, on occasions of dire political distress, within a brilliant star. Numerous examples of this sort might be adduced, but the foregoing may suffice. The constellations, by the way, are in Chinese almanacks formed into arbitrary figures as in Western astronomy, while, as is natural, the Chinaman actually associates the monster thus designed with the stars forming its supposed outline. Persons born under certain constellations are (in accordance with European Astrology) liable to good or evil luck. Apropos of this I came across a curious work from Madras† a short time since, in which the rules for building a house in compliance with stellar influences closely resemble similar beliefs in China.—"Having selected a site, the frontage must be divided into nine equal parts, five being assigned to the right and three to the left, the fourth division being reserved for the door-way. The enumeration begins on the left and thus the fourth section is in the mansion of Mercury. The occupant of such a house may become as wealthy as Kubern. A person born under Gemini, Cancer or Leo, must build his house on a line stretching east and west, the entrance being placed easterly. A person born under Virgo, Libra, or Scorpio, must build on a line running north and south, the door-way being southerly. One born under Sagittarius, Capricorn, or Aquarius must build west and east, placing the entrance westerly. If born under Pisces, Aries or the Twins, he must build south and north, the door being placed northerly. A family occupying a house built contrary to these rules will be ruined."

* *Chinese Readers' Manual*. p. 75. † Percival's *Tamil Proverbs.*

Some of the popular beliefs regarding appearances in the heavens have been alluded to under Portents and Auguries, but I may here add a word or two to the details already given. The appearance of ships, troops, &c. in the sky is of course deemed supernatural, Chinese science being as yet unacquainted with the causes of the mirage. Several well-authenticated stories of such phenomena are on record, one at Kung-shan having been visible for a whole day. That part of the sea on Hangchau Bay which lies near Kiahing often, says Dr. Macgowan, exhibits this illusion. It is more frequently seen from the opposite side. "Sea Market" is the general term by which the mirage is designated, and it is noted as occurring at different points of the coast from Canton to Shantung. It can easily be believed that such an apparent miracle, in view of two contending armies, would suffice to turn the scale of victory on the side of those expecting reinforcements. Amongst other phenomena recorded in China is the appearance of a hen without feet sitting on the sun! Parhelia, or mock suns, have frequently been seen, and the concurrence of their manifestation with important state events has of course tended to justify a popular belief in their portentous qualities. A well-known story published only a few years since, in one of the foreign papers, relates how the Changning rebels besieged one of the cities in the Yangtsze valley, and how the magistrate having first offered prayer in the temple of Tien-kung, led the troops against them and completely defeated them. The rebel prisoners all stated that when the battle commenced they saw a large flag in the heavens with the characters *Tien* 田 on it, and in the rear of the flag a host of ghostly soldiers flying through the air, smiting the rebels as they passed, and scaring them out of their wits. Thus the city was saved. The success was fully attributed to divine interposition, and the story is gratefully recounted by the people to the present time. A memorial was drawn up by the local gentry, and presented to the district magistrate with the request that the Throne should be petitioned to confer a higher title on Tien-kung. Such a request being in accordance with Chinese custom, it was of course granted.

The absurd stories told of meteors are endless. In the native Records, the most extraordinary phenomena are alleged to have been observed. A shooting star from which fell fish (A.D. 519), a meteor which after lying where it fell for some days suddenly moved of itself (A.D. 1561), and a formless body as large as a house which bounded over the dykes near Yuling into the sea, furrowing the ground as it went (A.D. 1782), are duly recorded, with a host of ordinary meteorites, as having alarmed the neigbourhood in which they appeared. "In the year 1348, a star as large as a bowl, of a white and slightly azure colour, with a tail about 50 feet long, lightened the sky, with a rumbling noise flew from the North-east, and entered the midst of the moon, the moon then looking as a reversed tile,—*i.e.* upright." The Chinese are not of course much worse (if so bad) in regard to such matters than the people of the West, and equally curious records exist amongst ourselves. As was observed in the introductory chapter the distinction between the superstitions of the Middle Kingdom and those of Europe lies rather in the more widely accorded credulity to alleged marvels amongst the former than in any actual difference of belief.

Thunder and lightning are, of course, in China the manifestations of supernatural anger.* The god of Thunder in China (Lui-tsz) corresponds to the Indian Vajrapani, and is a well-known Buddhist deity, worshipped like his numerous companions as a stellar god, and occupying in popular belief a position not unlike, though less important than, that of the Scandinavian Thor.† The connection between lightning and fire in all known mythologies is equally obvious in China. But we miss the Promethean legend so widely known in the West. Here the God of Fire wields indeed the lightning, but only to cause the conflagrations which satiate his vengeance. He is, in fact, a very everyday deity, destitute of the enormous powers wielded by his representatives elsewhere. The popular idea of his attributes is well illustrated by the following legend, kindly placed at my disposal by Mr. G. M. H. Playfair (of H. M. Consular service in China) as having been related to him during his residence in Peking:—

"The temples of the God of Fire are numerous in Peking, as is natural in a city built for the most part of very combustible materials. The idols representing the god are, with one exception, decked with red beards, typifying by their colour the element under his control. The exceptional god has a white beard, and 'thereby hangs a tale.'

"A hundred years ago the Chinese Imperial revenue was in much better case than it is now. At that time they had not yet come into collision with Western powers, and the word 'indemnity' had not, so far, found a place in their vocabulary; internal rebellions were checked as soon as they broke out, and, in one word, Kien Lung was in less embarrassed circumstances than Kwang Hsu; he had more money to spend, and did lay out a good deal in the

---

* Lei-chau, (thunder district) is a long mountainous peninsula in Canton province opposite the island of Hainan, and is celebrated throughout China for several myths respecting its thunder-storms, which doubtless reverberate through the alpine regions of that latitude in a manner which awakens awe and superstition. Standard Encyclopædias, quoting from various authors on the subject, inform us, that after thunder-storms black stones are found emitting light and a sonorous sound on being struck. At times, also, hatchet-shaped things are picked up which are useful amulets. The fields are often furrowed by thunder as if they had been ploughed. In a temple consecrated to the "Thunder Duke," the people annually place a drum, drawn thither on a carriage purposely constructed, which it is supposed he beats during a storm; and it is said that since a drum covered with paper has been substituted for one covered with leather, the peals of thunder have been less severe. Formerly the drum was placed on the top of a mountain, and a boy left there as an attendant on the thunderer —a sort of sacrifice to him.—Dr. Macgowan, in *Journal N. C. B. R. A. S.*, 1853.

† See Dr. Edkins' "Taoist Mythology" in N. C. B. R. A. S. Journal for 1859, p. 311. A North American Indian superstition is to the effect that thunder is caused by an immense bird, whose outspread wings darken the heavens. It is named "Then-cloots." The lightning is caused by a serpent-like fish of immense size, with head as sharp as a knife. When he puts out his tongue it makes the lightning. Its name is "Ha-hake-to-ak," and the thunder-bird catches it for food. The bird is in shape like an Indian, but of great proportions and strength. It lives on the top of the mountains. An Indian once found the nest of a thunder-bird and got one of its feathers which was over 200 feet long!—*American Magazine.*

way of palaces. His favourite building, and one on which no expense had been spared, was the 'Hall of Contemplation.' This Hall was of very large dimensions; the rafters and the pillars which supported the roof were of a size such as no trees in China furnish now-a-days. They were not improbably originally sent as an offering by the tributary monarch of some tropical country, such as Burmah or Siam. Two men could barely join hands round the pillars; they were cased in lustrous jet black lacquer, which, while adding to the beauty of their appearance, was also supposed to make them less liable to combustion. Indeed, every care was taken that no fire should approach the building; no lighted lamp was allowed in the precincts, and to have smoked a pipe inside those walls would have been punished with death. The floor of the Hall was of different-coloured marbles, in a mosaic of flowers and mystic Chinese characters, always kept polished like a mirror. The sides of the room were lined with rare books and precious manuscripts. It was in short the finest palace in the Imperial city, and it was the pride of Kien Lung.

"Alas for the vanity of human wishes! In spite of every precaution, one night a fire broke out and the Hall of Contemplation was in danger. The Chinese of a century ago were not without fire-engines; and though miserably inefficient as compared with those of our London fire brigades, they were better than nothing, and a hundred of them were soon working round the burning building. The Emperor himself came out to superintend their efforts and encourage them to renewed exertions. But the wall was doomed; a more than earthly power was directing the flames, and mortal efforts were of no avail. For on one of the burning rafters Kien Lung saw the figure of a little old man, with a long white beard, standing in a triumphant attitude. 'It is the God of Fire,' said the Emperor, 'we can do nothing:' so the building was allowed to blaze in peace. Next day Kien Lung appointed a Commission to go the round of the Peking temples in order to discover in which of them there was a Fire god with a white beard, that he might worship him and appease the offended deity. The search was fruitless; all the Fire-gods had red beards. But the Commission had done its work badly; being highly respectable mandarins of genteel families, they had confined their search to such temples as were in good repair and of creditable exterior. Outside the North gate of the Imperial City was one old, dilapidated, disreputable shrine which they had overlooked. It had been crumbling away for years, and even the dread figure of the God of Fire, which sat above the altar, had not escaped desecration. 'Time had thinned his flowing locks,' and the beard had fallen away altogether. One day some water-carriers who frequented the locality thought, either in charity or by way of a joke, that the face would look the better for a new beard. So they unravelled some cord, and with the frayed-out hemp adorned the beardless chin. An official passing the temple one day, peeped in out of curiosity, and saw the hempen beard. 'Just the thing the Emperor was enquiring about,' said he to himself, and he took the news to the palace without delay. Next day there was a state visit to the dilapidated temple, and Kien Lung made obeisance and vowed a vow.

"'O Fire God,' said he, 'thou hast been wroth with me in that I have built me palaces and left thy shrine unhonoured and in ruins. Here do I vow to build thee a temple surpassed by none other of the Fire-gods in Peking; but I shall expect thee in future not to meddle with my palaces.'

"The Emperor was as good as his word. The new temple is on the site of the old one and the Fire god has a flowing beard of fine white hair."

Some odd superstitutions connected with the spread of fire come under my notice at this moment. The Chinese are cautious of provoking the "God of Fire" or "Fire Principle" either by ill-timed allusions to his powers or by other acts, and the Tientsin correspondent of a Shanghai journal refers to this fact in noting that, in view of an existing drought, and the closing of the South gate of the former City as a stimulus to rain, the Fire Principle might revenge itself by an outbreak. On the 19th of May last the correspondent writes:—
"Almost as soon as this ill-timed suggestion had an opportunity to get itself considered, the Fire Principle proceeded to act upon it; the consequence is that a large quantity of combustible material, and several rather incombustible mud houses, now 'slumber in the valley.' The houses at the foreign settlement a mile and-a-half distant were illuminated by the lurid light, before which even the full moon paled its ineffectual fires. The inevitable 'fire pigeon;' whose indeterminate circles and final flight are watched with close and most superstitious awe, did not fail to appear, and having indicated by his course that the fire would spread across the wall into the city, caused the most intense excitement there. Fortunately the wind was comparatively light, and the damage done, considering the terror inspired, was trifling. The next day in a violent gale another conflagration broke out at the south-west corner of the city, destroyed the grass intended for horses and donkeys, but no houses." The "fire pigeon" here alluded to is nothing supernatural. Most cities in North China are frequented by large flocks of pigeons, and the light of a conflagration generally attracts a number who wheel in circles round the burning house. The bird nearest the flames is looked upon as affording an augury of their spread—not always, as is above evidenced, of the most reliable description.

Mountains in China as in Europe have their demons or presiding divinities. The God of T'ai-shan in Shantung *Tung-yoh-ta-ti* regulates the punishments inflicted on sinners in both this world and the next. Four other divinities rule over the principal chains in other portions of the Empire.

The formation of islands by natural causes in the vast streams which water the empire is of course the basis of numerous legends. A gentleman who explored the West River near Canton, some ten years since, gave the following instance, showing how easily a popular belief springs into being. "Pau Man-ching, who was Departmental Magistrate (some eight hundred and twenty-five years ago) of what was then known as Tün Chau now Shiu Hing Fù, is said to have been a man of remarkable administrative powers and possessing the most sterling integrity. He filled his term of office in such an acceptable manner, that on its expiration he was immediately transferred to a position of honor and trust in the capital. Illustrative of his great virtue it is recorded, that when he arrived at Shiu Hing, the Department City, he found the officers were in the habit of practising gross abuses of power, and set himself immediately to the work of reformation. Particularly were they accustomed to require the people to furnish ten-fold more than the lawful tribute from the ink-stone quarries, which are regarded as the best in the Empire. The surplus thus acquired was secretly distributed among the high officers at the Court, in order to secure special favor. He at once put a stop to the practice, and would allow no more tribute to be levied than was actually sent up to the Emperor. In this one respect he was so strict that he did not carry away a single stone for himself when he left. Now tradition amplifies the idea and says, that of the many testimonials of gratitude and respect offered him by the people on his departure, he only accepted an inkstone, lest there should seem to be even the shadow of bribery or corruption chargeable against him. When he arrived at the above-mentioned point in the river on his voyage down, a violent storm arose, which threatened to overwhelm the boat. The inkstone became a burden to his conscience, and Jonah-like was hove into the stream; whereupon the storm immediately ceased and an island rose up, known to this day as 'Inkstone island.' Another form of the legend is, that in the midst of the storm he fell into a passion, upbraided the Gods of the country for thus rewarding a man who had endeavoured to do his duty, and then cast away the stone, the act being followed by the above result. If either of these were true, it surely might be said that this was one of the most productive inkstones in China." It should be added that the better-read literati of the neighbourhood simply refer the name to the fact of the inkstone being cast overboard opposite the island, but the more miraculous version is firmly accepted by the unlettered peasants. I need scarcely refer to well-known European legends to find parallels to the above.

The belief that violent winds or typhoons are caused by the passage through the air of a "Bob-tailed Dragon" has been before adverted to, and the superstitions connected with water, whether in the shape of rain, sea, or river, are equally quaint. The rain god Yü-Shih 雨師 or "Master of rain" is a divinity identified by the ancient cosmogonists with a son of Kung Kung bearing the name 玄冥 (Hsuan-ming). He is identified with the constellation 畢 (Hyades) and is held as personifying the aqueous influences of the atmosphere.*
One of his effigies occupies an honoured position in a temple some ten miles from Peking, and about a hundred and fifty years ago fell under the displeasure of the then Emperor for his persistent neglect to send down the much needed showers. A chain was put round his neck and he was ignominiously dragged to the Mongolian frontier, when a lucky deluge delivered his godship from his unpleasant position. He was taken back in great state, and the Emperor himself bestowed on him a yellow dress, which still adorned the idol at the time of my visit.

As a specimen of the form in which the popular superstitions in this con-

---

* Mayers' *Chinese Readers' Manual*, p. 283.

nection are evidenced the following from a correspondent at Tientsin deserves record. Writing to a Northern journal in May last he says, "The season continues excessively dry, in spite of the liberal petitions to every god by all people whatsoever. The most recent sensation story relates to a Buddhist priest who has conceived the idea of doing a little temple building at the expense of the public credulity, and has accordingly, after interviewing the high officials for permission, announced that he will pray for rain for a period of six or seven days, on an altar for that purpose erected near the Sung Wang Miao, and if within the specified time rain does not fall, he will be burnt alive." A general curiosity was manifested to know whether this foolish bargain would be kept. Happily for the enthusiast, or impostor, a slight shower which fell an hour or two before the date expired was considered sufficient to save his reputation and his life, Chinese officials not liking to be trifled with in such matters. For the rest, praying for rain is an every-day matter in China where drought is one of the most serious of disasters. By native custom the Emperor is deemed responsible if the drought be at all severe, and numerous are the self-condemnatory Imperial edicts on this subject published in the pages of the venerable *Peking Gazette*. In extreme cases the Emperor, clothed in humble vestments, sacrifices to Heaven and entreats its benevolence. No touch of superstition this, however,—rather a glimpse of Chinese humanity at its best, conscious of its subjection to a higher will and openly confessing its shortcomings!

Tides share with rain a superstitious belief in their regulation by supernatural beings. The most remarkable phenomenon in connection with this subject to be witnessed in China is the *Eagre* or bore of the Tsien-tang river which debouches into the sea at the extreme eastern portion of the coast, the city of Hang-chow being situated at its mouth. The Eagre at times causes a rise of tide to the extent of some forty feet opposite the city, and a writer already quoted, in a paper on the subject read before the China Branch of the Royal Asiatic Society so long ago as 1853, gives some interesting details of the superstitions connected with it. The Chinese, he says, regard the Eagre as one of the wonders of their world, and it gave its name to the province. "As might be expected, therefore, it is blended with their mythology. It is not a little remarkable, however, that it should be popularly ascribed to the spiritual energy of a 神 *shên* (or god,) who lived so recently as five hundred and forty years before our era, or about twenty years before the birth of Confucius. At that period the Tsien-tang was the boundary of two belligerent kingdoms, Wú and Yueh. Fu Chai, king of the former, incensed against his minister Wú Tsz' Si, for opposing the terms of a treaty, submitted by Chung, ambassador of Ku Tsien, King of Yueh, sent him a sword, with which, understanding his master's will, he committed suicide, by cutting his throat, a method still pursued by sovereigns in China towards officers of distinction who have incurred their displeasure. This incident in ancient history is recorded in the spring and autumn Annals of Confucius; but in a work, entitled ("Spring and Autumn Annals of the States of Wú and Yueh) a historical novel, written several hundred years after, a prevailing myth is superadded to the authentic narrative, which the author himself seems to credit, and which to the present day is received as verity."

"Wu Tsz' Si's corpse, which was thrown into the Tsien-tang, after being carried to and fro by the tide for some time, tunneled a passage through the hills on the Yueh side, as far as the tomb of the quondam ambassador Chung, whose cadaver he took with him to the estuary. Since that period, it is stated Wú Tsz' Si has been the god of the Eagre, his periodical indignation being exhibited by its violence; hence the sacrifices and prayers officially presented at appointed seasons to propitiate his anger. Monarchs of almost every dynasty have honoured him with titles, so that they are recorded."*

The superstitions connected with that class of phenomena referable to Volcanic agency are numerous. The many earthquakes which have visited the empire are frequently alleged to have been accompanied by the appearance of white hairs on the ground. As a similar appearance has been observed in Mexico the allegation is doubtless true, and is probably explainable by natural causes. Some scientists are of opinion that these hairs are caused by the mixture of some salt of the soil with a certain gas. But whatever the true reason, the Chinese commonly view them as supernatural productions emblematic of serious disaster. Another very frequently recorded appearance at such times is that of blood falling from the sky, issuing from the ground, or otherwise appearing in unusual places. The following legend regarding lake Man in the prefecture of Sungkiang is related in the native topography of the district. This lake was in former times the site of a flourishing city called Chiang-shui. A report, said to have originated with the children of the place, ran to the effect that whenever blood should be seen upon the gates of the city it would disappear and the site become a lake. Now there lived at Chiang-shui an old woman who being deeply impressed by the possible danger used to come daily to see if blood was on the gates; and some of the soldiers on duty thought in an idle moment that it would be fine fun to hoax her; so they killed a dog and smeared the gates with his blood. The old woman immediately left the place amidst the jeers of the jokers. But their laughter was short-lived. A few days only had elapsed when a flood took place; a fearful noise was heard, and, with scarcely a moment's warning, the entire city sank into the earth, the resistless waters filling up the hole and forming the lake now visible. The fact appears to be historical, and similar instances of sudden sinking are alleged to have occurred in the same neighbourhood.

Records of sudden fissures in the earth (due it may be safely alleged to volcanic action) are plentiful enough in Chinese annals, but are, of course, always accompanied by other portentous occurrences. A favourite legend

---

* "The Tidal King Temple is near Hangchow. Its *shên* (or god) was an official, who in 828 A.D. undertook the restoration of a dyke, which an Eagre of unusual violence had overthrown; and failing in the construction of the foundation, drowned himself from chagrin. He afterwards became a *shên* and three centuries later, on the occasion of a combat between the people and rebels, who were attempting to capture Hangchan, his name was seen inscribed on a streamer in the darkened sky, where also unearthly noises were heard. The enemy instantly succumbed."

relates to the emission of a *shên* or chiao 蛟 which eventually becomes a dragon. The fissures are due to its efforts to escape from the earth's interior. "The *Shên* is popularly described as an embryotic dragon, or a dragon in the first stage of existence. It is formed by the perspiration of that animal falling from the sky upon terrestrial beings. Animals thus affected become *Shên*, sink into the ground and remain there, some say thirty, some an hundred years, emerging in heavy rains as a Kiau."* Other legends record the emission of fragrant vapours from the rents thus made, the issue of blood from springs in place of water, &c. These latter occurrences may have been due to a gush of water through oxide of iron beds, but Chinese records are too unscientific to allow aught save conjecture in this respect. Trees also are recorded as giving forth blood, an appearance due in all probability to the presence of minute insects in exudations from the bark.

Waterspouts are usually spoken of in native annals as dragons, and when more than one is seen they are described as fighting in the air. Nine dragons fighting at sea are recorded as having been seen at Shanghai in the year 1519. The following list of such occurrences is from the authority already quoted—

A.D. 1605.—A couple of dragons fought at Whampoa and tore up a large tree, and demolished several tens of houses.

A.D. 1608, 4th moon.—A gyrating dragon was seen over the decorated summit of a pagoda; all around were clouds and fog; the tail only of the dragon was visible; in the space of eating a meal, it went away, leaving the marks of its claws on the pagoda.

A.D. 1609, 6th moon.—A white dragon was seen at Whangpu; on its head stood a god.

A.D. 1452, 6th moon.—A dragon at the Tsan stream taking up water, lifted a boat, and transported it to the middle of a field; rain fell to the depth of several feet, soaking plants to death.

A.D. 1667, 6th moon, 14th day.—Dragons were seen fighting in the air; there was a violent wind and excessive rain; the canal rose four or five feet; many houses were destroyed, a tree above ten armlengths in circumference was torn up &c.

A.D. 1773, 7th moon, 20th day.—A group of dragons burnt paddy in the field, drew houses into the air and travellers also; hail-stones of two or three catties weight fell, killing houses and animals.

A.D. 1739, 9th moon, 3rd day.—Dragons fought at Man lake, and went off S. E. to the sea, destroying the paddy as they went.

A.D. 1787, 7th moon.—Dragons fought; a great wind overturning houses, and carrying off, no one knows where, half a stone bridge.

It is satisfactory to be able to identify the very mythical dragon (as usually deemed) with a tangible force. The popular superstitions regarding it acquire a certain amount of respectability in view of this fact—first pointed out I believe by the ingenious writer above quoted.

* See Dr. Macgowan's article, before alluded to.

Popular beliefs concerning human beings being metamorphosed into stone have been already touched on under the heads of Witchcraft and Demonology, the "stone rams" of Canton being cited as an example. But similar legends, though of less supernatural complexion, exist in all parts of the empire. Shiu Hing Gap 肇慶峽 on the West River is more properly called Ling Yung Hap 羚羊峽 i.e. "Chamois Gap," since tradition asserts that some such animal was thereabouts transformed into stone. Not far from the same spot, says a traveller who visited the place some ten years since, "The Woman looking for her husband" 望夫石 is pointed out. Two thirds way up the mountain, in a slight depression between a secondary peak and the main peak above and beyond, and at the head of a ravine which, from a point on the river a little further up, inclines down the stream as it ascends the face of the hill, there is a rock apparently only a few feet in height, which presents a striking resemblance to a woman seated on the ground and looking towards the west. In ascending the pass the view is not fully obtained until you have passed slightly beyond the position, when a good binocular reveals a fine side view of the head and body of a woman, the coiffure being quite distinct and the general appearance tolerably true to life. The legend connected with the rock-freak is that in ancient days the wife of a military officer who had gone to Kwang-Si and fallen in battle, came here day by day to look for his return. Being ignorant of his fate, her vigils were protracted until they were finally rewarded by the transformation of her body into this rock, a conversion into her own monument."

Such then are a few of the cosmical facts or phenomena in which Chinese superstition finds room for indulgence. I may fitly conclude this chapter by noting an incident in this connection which reflects credit on the Emperor to whom it alludes. A secretion (probably of animal origin) is occasionally found to fall like the manna of old from the sky, and such an event being rare a report of it is always made to the authorities. In the year 1788 a notice that sweet dew had fallen for three days in the Sung Kiang prefecture was sent to the Emperor Yung Ching. The memorial stating the fact "attributed it to the virtues of the monarch, which called down this signal manifestation of heaven's favor. His Majesty gracefully declined taking the honor to himself, as it did not fall in the palace; but ascribed it to the goodness of the officers and people of the palace, and enjoined on them the duty of acknowledging and proving themselves worthy of the heavenly token." Pagan gratitude to Heaven, though it sometimes takes queer forms, is not an unknown sentiment in China.

XII.—LEGENDS OF LOCALITY, HOUSEHOLD TALES, &c.

All who possess the slightest acquaintance with the legendary lore of the Celestial empire will readily credit the assertion that any attempt to even cursorily notice a tenth of the vast number of legends current throughout its population would be a task far beyond both the scope of these pages, and the average reader's patience. In touching therefore on the subjects embraced under the above heading, an attempt must be made to deal chiefly with those which are typical of numerous variants, while at the same time offering resemblances to legends current in the West. Few countries present a larger field for curious enquiry in this respect; and any shortcomings in demonstrating the fact must rather be referred to the fault of the writer than to paucity of matter.

In an interesting article on the "Legends of the Yang-Tsze River" the *North China Herald* recently drew attention to the wealth of material at the disposition of any one willing to gather it, in the following well-chosen words: "The Romish Church has been said by a great Catholic authority to be 'hung with miracles,' and in the same way the whole of China is hung with legends. The most industrious and materialistic race in the world attest the resolution with which the imaginative faculty suggests itself, by the wild variety of the legends that linger about its austere mountains and winding dells. The rocks, tapestried with creepers, the fountain sparkling in the winding vales, and the rude rocks or tawny islets that abound in the large streams, all have their presiding fairy or their romantic tale of magic and glamour. The names of the various elevations that the voyager meets with, suggest all manner of curious enquiries. We hear of 'Yellow Ox Hill,' 'Golden Yoke Cliff,' 'Flying Phœnix Mountain,' 'Ascending Dragon Peak,' and 'Filial Maiden Precipice.'" The writer indeed admits that though the legends connected with the Yang-Tsze, its tributaries and lakes, are full of interest, the wildest and most romantic stories and the richest historical associations do not gather about the Yang-tsze-kiang but about the Yellow River. But his remarks will, it may be hoped, stimulate research in both directions, and I can only regret that no chance of exploring this rich mine of Chinese legend presents itself to me before giving these pages to the press. Enough however is at disposal to render selection difficult.

Most nations have, or have had, a reputed gate of Purgatory or Hell situated somewhere within their borders, more especially if the country they inhabit include vast tracts of mountainous country, amongst whose gloomy recesses popular superstition finds it easy to locate an entrance to the nether world, unchecked by the ridicule of educated visitors. Thus the

Hörselloch cavern in the Hörselberg, between Eisenach and Gotha, was supposed by the peasantry of Thuringia to be the entrance to Purgatory, and moans and shrieks were believed in former times to be nightly heard issuing from its ghostly portals.* I need scarcely refer classical scholars to the legend of the cave of Acherusia, nor will most students of ethnology be unaware how widespread is the belief that a door to the infernal regions is accessible to mortal gaze. But the fact of a similar belief existing in China may be new to many. The location of this entrance to the Chinese purgatory is by native writers placed not far from Têng Chow, of which Chefoo is the Treaty Port, celebrated throughout the length and breath of the Empire from its proximity to the birth-place of Confucius. The demons of Têng Chow are classed, according to a Chinese proverb, as one of the wonders of the world—as well they might be, did they exist. Popular tradition avers that at stated periods the ghosts of the departed, who are sent to Têng Chow to await judgment, are allowed to again revisit their earthly haunts; which, as the native chronicles naively observe, fully accounts for the mysterious doings common in the neighbourhood.

Nobody who has read the *Arabian Nights* (and who has not?) will have forgotten the story of the "City of Silence," in which the hero goes in search of "the bottles of brass stopped with molten lead and sealed with the ring of Suleymán the son of Dáood." The story goes on to tell how these bottles were frequently drawn up by fishermen in their nets and how, upon their being opened, genii were liberated who had been imprisoned by that all-powerful potentate as a punishment for their disobedience. The hero, after undergoing various extraordinary adventures, finally reaches the City of Silence and at last obtains the coveted bottles for his Sultan. Now the powers herein conferred upon the mighty Suleyman are oddly recalled by a legend (communicated to *Notes and Queries on China and Japan* by Mr. T. Sampson in 1867) which may quite rank with its Arabian prototype, with the difference that it has a local interest and, in native eyes, accounts for certain historical events. It runs as follows :—

"Many generations ago, the Prefect of Shiu-hing dreamed a dream. In his dream he saw myriads of devils who in answer to his enquiries, told him that they were going to overthrow the ruling dynasty; the Prefect expressed disbelief in their power to do so, but the devils still asserted their power and their purpose. The Prefect desired some distinguishing mark by which to recognize the devils in any altered form which they might assume in carrying out their threats, and the latter consented to allow him to mark each of them with a red spot on the forehead as a token of recognition; this the Prefect did.

"When he awoke he was much troubled, not knowing whether his dealings with the devils were a reality or an idle vision. He went out to consult wise men on the subject; but what was his surprise, on returning to his yamên, to find it strewed with small round stones, on every side of which

* *Curious Myths of the Middle Ages*, first series, p. 197.

was a red spot. 'These,' thought he, 'are surely the devils I marked last night, and what a good opportunity is this for me to get them in my power.' Accordingly he caused all the stones to be collected, to be firmly secured in earthenware jars, and then to be locked up in a strong room in his yamên. But before they were finally secured they entered into a parley with the Prefect, the result of which was an agreement on their part to submit to incarceration till a certain tree in the yamên should come in blossom, when they were to be released. The wily Prefect knew, but the devils did not know, that this particular tree never did blossom in the latitude of Shiu-hing, and thus he congratulated himself on having saved the Government from these powerful enemies. It was understood however that to render their imprisonment valid the door was to be sealed with the Prefect's seal, which was to be renewed by each successive holder of that office.

"Prefect after Prefect for some generations occupied the yamên, and each of them on assuming office faithfully resealed the door of the devil's prison, until at length the story began to be forgotten or disbelieved; and one unlucky Prefect surnamed Luk, forgetting or carelessly neglecting to perform this duty, the door was thoughtlessly left open and a jar of devils broken. At the moment this occurred it happened that an official retinue were in the yamên, and the followers had hung their red-tasselled caps on the tree, the blossoming of which was to have been a signal for the release of the prisoners.

"Perceiving that their release was the result of accident, mistaking the red tassels for flowers, and assuming that the tree had thus flowered every year during their long confinement, the devils were much incensed at this breach of faith in the matter of their promised release, and in retaliation they caused the city to be submerged below the waters of the river. And it was not until they (the story saith not how) were captured, and the door resealed that the city again came above water. Taught by woeful experience, each succeeding Prefect was from that time careful to reseal the door on assuming office, and thus the devils were long restrained from doing mischief.

"Time passed on, and with the same result as before. Faith in the necessity of sealing the door was shaken, and in 1854 a Prefect surnamed M'a assumed office, utterly despising the story of the devils. Not only did he omit to seal the door, but he caused the red-spotted stones to be taken from the strong room, and to be thrown away. What was the result? In that very year the red-turbaned rebels—the devils with red marks on their foreheads, now appearing in human form—captured the city!

"Here ends the legend. Whether the devils have been recaptured, or whether they are still abroad devising schemes for the release of a few remaining jars of their comrades which escaped Ma's destruction, or whether they ceased to exist when their human personifications were killed, the legend saith not; but so far as it goes, it is vouched for, at this day, by the inhabitants of Shiu-hing, who declare that the sealed strong room may be seen any day, and that no man surnamed Luk or M'a would now be allowed to be Prefect of Shiu-hing."

It would be interesting to know if the classical legend of the golden cup given by the Sun-God Helios to Hercules, who used it as a ship to convey him across stretches of ocean, owed its origin to the same source as a popular legend in South China. We want however in the latter case the connecting link between the original myth and the vulgar version so ingeniously shewn by Mr Kelly in his well-known work.* A tea-cup here takes the place of the more valuable utensil, but is credited with similar powers of transport. Pei Tu (杯渡) "The Cup Traveller" was a renowned Buddhist priest who lived some five or six hundred years ago, and was accustomed to wander at will over the Canton province, his magic cup serving him as a ferry-boat whenever he had to cross water. On one occasion he carried off a golden idol belonging to the house where he had passed the night. Pursuit was given, but the priest, though walking on foot, easily outstripped the fastest horse of his pursuers, who, at length seeing him carried over a river in his tea-cup, abandoned the chase. The mountain not far from Hongkong, known to foreigners as "Castlepeak," was named after this priest, Pei-tu (or in the local dialect Poi-tou). Can this legend be a dim reproduction of the Western myth?

The legend connect with the valley of the White Deer near the Poyang Lake —so named from the story that the Philosopher Choo Tzu employed such an animal to bring him provisions from the neighbouring market—recalls home tales in which deer are gifted with human attributes. Sclavonian folk-lore has many references of this nature. The Vilas or mountain nymphs of Servia are sometimes represented in their popular songs as comforting the sorrows of enamoured deer. They are usually, says Mr. Keightley, represented as "riding a seven-year old hart with a bridle made of snakes." Deer horns are, as everybody knows, supposed in China to possess all sorts of wonderful properties.

The Icelandic Troll who plays so conspicuous a part in the story of the "Shepherd of Silfrunarstadir"† possesses attributes closely resembling those with which the Chinese endow the female spirits of the gorges to be found in the vast mountain chains of the Empire. In both cases they are beneficent spirits. The great Yu is said to have been indebted to the being who watches over the Wushan gorge in Szechuan for the power to carry out his labours. The "Wild women" of Germany, who are supposed to frequent the Wunderberg, possess analagous qualities but have no dominion over the powers of nature. The Breton *Korrigan*, again, bear certain resemblances to supernatural beings believed in by the Chinese. They are described (Keightley, page 432) as short and humpy, with shaggy hair, dark wrinkled faces, little deep-set eyes but bright as carbuncles; and woe to the belated traveller who is forced to join in their fairy revels! Their breath is reported to be deadly. The Chinese legend of the Lin-lu mountain recounts the existence of a mysterious arbour inhabited by a demon and numerous companions who are in reality dogs transformed for the nonce into the semblance of earthly beings. As with the Korrigan, whoever passed the night with them was sure to die. A Sage, possessed of a magic mirror, once put up with these elves, but being warned by the mirror of the

* *Indo-European Tradition and Folk-lore*, p. 216. † *Legends of Iceland*, p. 140.

quality of his companions, stabbed the nearest, when the rest ran away. Similar stories are told of numerous localities, but this may be taken as a type of the whole.

The fantastic exaggerations of geographical facts and fancies which form so prominent a feature in oriental tales (such, for instance, as the *Arabian Nights*) are freely reproduced in China, though it is only fair to say that they seem in great part to be derived from Hindoo sources. Thus all that is recounted of the celebrated lake supposed to be the source of the Hwang-ho, with its bottom covered with diamonds &c., &c., is simply adapted from the Sanscrit. The Kwên Lun mountain, in which this lake is supposed to be situated, is, in Taoist legend, alleged to have growing upon it trees of jade-stone and pearls, the tree and fountain of life, &c., the sources of these wonderful stories being similar. Native writers have, indeed, expanded the original accounts, but the legends are substantially the same. Chêng Cheng Shan, near the capital of Sze-chuan, is supposed to be a mountain in whose caves the gods and genii assemble. Allusion has already been made to the "Isles of the Genii" supposed to exist in the Eastern sea opposite the Chinese coast. It may suffice to say that there are few such extravagances recorded in Western literature which do not find counterparts in Chinese belief.

A Western superstition, which I cannot now trace, but of which I have seen mention, that a human being or human blood cast into a smelting furnace ensures a satisfactory casting, forms the basis of a legend connected with the Bell Tower of Peking, narrated by Mr. Stent in his recent paper on Chinese legends. Briefly summarised it tells how the Emperor Yung-lo of the Ming dynasty, having built the tower, ordered a mandarin named Kuan-yu to cast a bell of the proper size. Two attempts were made to carry out the order, at intervals of some months, but without success. In both cases the casting was "honey-combed," and the enraged Emperor declared that if the third attempt failed he would behead the unfortunate official. Now Kuan-yu had a beautiful daughter aged sixteen, named Ko-ai, to whom he was tenderly attached and who did all she could to comfort her distressed parent. One day it struck her that she would go to a celebrated astrologer to ascertain the cause of her father's failures and what means could be taken to prevent their recurrence. From him she learned that the next casting would also be a failure if the blood of a maiden were not mixed with the ingredients. She returned home full of horror at the information, but resolved to immolate herself sooner than that her father should fail. She obtained leave from her father to be present at the casting; and the catastrophe is thus described. "A dead silence prevailed through the assemblage as the melted metal once more rushed to its destination. This was broken by a shriek and a cry of 'For my father,' and Ko-ai was seen to throw herself head-long into the seething hissing metal. One of her followers attempted to seize her while in the art of plunging into the boiling fluid but succeeded only in grasping one of her shoes, which came off in his hand. The father was frantic and had to be kept by force from following her example; he was taken home a raving maniac. The prediction of the astrologer was verified, for on uncovering the bell after it had cooled it was found to be perfect, but not a vestige of Ko-ai was to be seen; the blood of a maiden had indeed been fused with the ingredients." But the sequel recounts how the sonorous boom of the bell when struck was followed by a low wailing sound like the cry of a human female voice in great agony distinctly saying the word *hsieh* (shoe)—a sound still heard after every stroke; and to this day people when they hear it say " There's poor Ko-ai calling for her shoe."

The idea of self-sacrifice to ensure some public good has ever been popular in China, and ages before the heroic Roman Youth leaped his horse into the earthquake chasm for the sake of his countrymen, Chinese patriots are recorded as having exhibited a similarly noble spirit. An instance of this was afforded by a tea-merchant at Hang-chow who some hundred and fifty years ago cast himself into the river Tsien-tang as a sacrifice to the spirit of the dykes which were constantly being washed away. Numerous instances of similar devotion appear in Chinese annals, each being of course the basis of a legend more or less accurate in its adherence to facts.

The cave of Kwang-siu-f'oo in Kiang-si is the reputed scene of a legend or household tale recalling a portion of the well-known " Ali Baba and the Forty Thieves." There was in the neighbourhood a poor herdsman named Chang, his sole surviving relative being a grandmother with whom he lived. One day, happening to pass near the cave in question, he overheard some one using the following words:—

石門開, 鬼谷先生來

Shih mun kai, Kwai ku hsien shêng lai. " Stone door open; Mr. Kwei Ku is coming." Upon this the door of the cave opened, and the speaker entered. Having remained there for some time he came out and saying " Stone door close; Mr. Kwei Ku is going," the door again closed and the visitor departed. Chang's curiosity was naturally excited, and having several times heard the formula repeated he waited one day until the genie (for such he was) had taken his departure and essayed to obtain an entrance. To his great delight the door yielded, and having gone inside he found himself in a romantic grotto of immense extent. Nothing however in the shape of treasure met his eye, so having fully explored the place he returned to the door, which shut at his bidding, and went home. Upon telling his grandmother of his adventure she expressed a strong wish to see the wonderful cavern; and thither they accordingly went together next day. Wandering about in admiration of the scenery they became separated, and Chang at length, supposing that his grandmother had left, passed out of the door and ordered it to shut. Reaching home he found, to his dismay, that she had not yet arrived. She must of course have been locked up in the cave, so back he sped and before long was using the magic sentence to obtain access. But alas! the talisman had failed, and poor Chang fell into an agony of apprehension as he reflected that his grandmother would either be starved to death or killed by the enraged genie. While in this perplexity the genie appeared and asked him what was amiss. Chang frankly told him the truth, and implored him to open the door. This the genie refused to do, but told him that his grandmother's disappearance was a matter of fate. The cave demanded a victim. Had it been a male, every succeeding generation of his family would have seen one of its members arrive at princely rank. In the case of a woman her descendants would in a similar way possess power over demons. Somewhat comforted to know that he was not exactly responsible for his grandmother's death, Chang returned home and in process of time married. His first son duly became Chang tien shih 張天師 (Chang, the Master of Heaven), who about A.D. 25 was the first holder of an office which has existed uninterruptedly to the present day. So says one popular legend. An equally credible (or incredible) version of the birth of this prodigy, however, says nothing of the magic cave, but refers the event to a visit made to his mother by the spirit of the Polar star, who gave her a fragant herb called Hèng wei which caused her to become enceinte.* Be the authentic version what it may, however, the fact remains that Ali Baba's cave has its mythic representative in China.

The apparently magic power possessed by the loadstone has in China, as elsewhere, been pressed into legendary service. Stories of magic tombs also were common amongst European peoples in mediæval ages, and here we have a native legend which in many respects recalls their details. In the mountain of Ting Chün is the tomb of Chu-ko-liang 諸葛亮 or Kung-ming 孔明 celebrated in ancient annals as the wise councillor of Liu-pei and reputed during his life-time to have employed, by means of magic arts, wooden oxen and mechanical horses to aid in the military operations of his time. As was but natural, the burial-place of so renowned a man was, like that of "Wonderous Michael Scott," credited with mysterious contents. It is alleged that the Emperor Hung-wu, the founder of the Ming dynasty, once finding himself in company with the Councillor Liu Pei-wên, in the neighbourhood of this tomb, determined to visit it. Iron armour was then still in use in China, and the Emperor and his attendant were habited in the then usual way. Having obtained an entrance and passed through the anti-chamber, which contained an inscription to the effect that whosoever visited the tomb should have his hands bound by the defunct—a prediction verified by the fact that in squeezing through the entrance the visitors had to so wedge themselves as to be virtually incapable of using their arms—they broke open a second door. Within the room thus entered were several figures built of loadstone, which attracted the armour of the unbidden guests. Terrified at the unknown force which was dragging them forwards they hastily cast off their armour and fled—not before noticing however another inscription which may be rendered in doggrel:—

<blockquote>
Ill strip off the skin
Of who ventures in
To open this my grave.
</blockquote>

The practical experience of the mysterious power residing in the loadstone figures was quite enough for the Emperor, who did not stop to see if anything

---

* *China Review*, Vol. II. p. 226.

worse might befall him. The tomb was closed, and the tradition of Hwang-wu's visit is still recounted by the story-tellers of the neighbourhood.

Another and perhaps better-known version of the (doubtless) same story refers it to the tomb of Confucius who was buried in the hill of Keu-fau in Shantung. His disciple Tze-kung is related to have covered the coffin of the great philosopher with loadstone. When the Emperor Chin gave orders to open the tomb the pick-axes were attracted by the magnetic fluid, as was also the armour worn by the soldiers, so that it was found impossible to proceed with the work. Hence the tomb of Confucius has never been violated. Absurd as both stories are they point to a belief in the powers of the loadstone which was readily accepted by mediæval Europe.

The principle that good deeds generally bring a substantial reward, underlying so many legends and tales in all parts of the world, is sedulously encouraged by Chinese folk-lore. The Servian story entitled "Animals as friends and enemies,"* in which the hero is rewarded for not killing the fox, bear, wolf, hare &c., has numerous variants in native lore. A proverb referring to "The bird which brought the yellow flower" tells how a Chinese, seeing a bird fall to the ground wounded by an arrow, draws out the weapon and nurses the bird until it has recovered. Some time afterwards the man falls sick and is about to die, when the grateful bird brings him some yellow flowers in its bill, assuring him that if he makes and takes a decoction of their petals his life will be saved. Another story tells how another bird, rescued from the talons of a more powerful companion, rewards its preserver by bringing him four silver bracelets; while a third recounts how (in flat contradiction to the Æsopian fable) the Emperor Ho-ti 和帝 found a wounded serpent in his path and, having cured and released it, was rewarded by a carbuncle of exceeding brightness brought to him by the snake. Chinese story books abound with tales similar to the Servian story, "One good turn deserves another," in which a supernatural being is imprisoned by a certain king, whose son having released him secures the being's aid in all his undertakings.

The saying of the English Queen that when she died the name of Calais would be found engraved on her heart reminds us of a popular Chinese tale concerning an enamoured boatman, who being obliged, while plying his daily avocation, to pass beneath the window of a beauteous maiden, fell violently in love with her. His passion was reciprocated, but after a time the young lady died. On being opened (the idea of a Chinese post-mortem on a disconsolate maiden is, by the way, quite as wonderful as anything else!) her heart was found to be of iron, upon which was painted or engraved a picture of the boat, the window, and the two lovers.† This being shewn to the bereaved boatman he instantly expired, his body turning to ashes! We are gravely informed that this event happened about B.C. 350.

Like the Italian original of our own popular and faithless Punch, his Chinese brother has a legendary origin. Punch and Judy shows, indeed, are, in some quarters, alleged to have been introduced into Europe from China.

* *Servian Folk-lore*, p. 295. † *C. & J. Repository*, Vol. I., p. 345.

Be that as it may *Po-tai-hsi* (布袋戲), so called because the showman used to cover his head with a linen bag in order that his face might not distract attention from the puppets, date back to at least 260 B.C. The received legend asserts that about this date a lady named *Oh*, (閼) wife of a general named Mao-tun, was besieging the city of Ping in Shen-si. Its defender Chan-ping knowing the lady to be of a very jealous disposition, invented a puppet in the shape of a wooden woman, which was made by strings and springs to dance on the battlements of the beleagured town. As he intended, Mrs. *Oh* became alarmed at the idea of so fascinating a creature falling into her husband's hands and becoming an addition to his seraglio; and she consequently raised the siege! In memory of this "happy thought" similar, but smaller, puppets were constructed whose antics have for two thousand years amused the Chinese populace. The principal puppet used to be known as "Kwoh, the bald" in memory, as it is averred, of a man of that name who having lost his hair in sickness began on his recovery to jump and dance.* Rather hazy and contradictory ideas indeed prevail in China of the origin of the amusing vagabond, different stories being told at different places. So simple an explanation as that of some ingenious native having determined to turn an honest penny by reproducing in miniature the jokes of the stage, seems however to have been ignored. I may in passing note that Lord Macartney, in his *Journal*, speaks highly of these exhibitions. The pandean pipe of the drummer is in China replaced by that most ear-splitting of instruments, a native clarionet.

That so important a shrub in Chinese eyes as that which produces tea should have a legendary origin is hardly surprising. The virtues of the cup which "cheers but not inebriates" have been sung by the Cowpers of China from time immemorial, and of this fact most people are aware. It may be less generally known that a vulgar (Buddhistic) legend attributes the production of the first plant to Bodhi-dharma, the 28th Indian and first Chinese patriarch of the Buddhist hierarchy. He brought the famous *patra* (almsbowl of the Buddhist mendicant, regarding which Indian legend has some wonderful accounts) to China, which he reached in the year 520 A.D.† Kœmpfer, in his well-known Dutch work on Japan, thus tells the story.‡ "About A.D. 519 this Dharma came to China. His object was to bring the inhabitants of this populous country to the knowledge of God and to preach to them his Gospel and service. . . . . He went further and strove by godly grace to lead a most exemplary life, exposing himself to all the hardships of the storm and tempest; chastising and mortifying his body and bringing all his passions under subjection. He lived only upon the herbs of the fields, and considered it the highest degree of holiness to pass the day and night in an uninterrupted and unbroken *Satori*, that is the contemplation and meditation of the godly essence; to deny all rest and recreation to his body and to dedicate his soul wholly and entirely to God

* See *N. & Q. on China & Japan*, Vol. I. p. 140.
† Eitel's *Handbook of Buddhism*, Art. Bodhidharma.
‡ Translated by G. Phillips, Esq., of H.B.M. Consular Service in China.

was in his opinion the truest penance and the most eminent degree of goodness to which human nature could attain. After many years of this continual watching he was at length so weary and tired by his work that he fell asleep. On awaking the following morning and seeing that he had broken his vow, he determined to do penance to show his sincere sorrow; and that this misfortune should not occur again he cut off both his eyelids as the instruments and servants of his crime and threw them on the ground.

"Returning to this place on the following day he remarked a wonderful change, and that each eyelid had become a shrub; and the same which we now call tea, whose virtues and use were at that time as unknown as the plant itself. Dharma, on eating the leaves of this plant (fresh and green, for infusing them in water was unknown), found with astonishment that his heart was filled with extraordinary joy and gladness, and that his soul had acquired renewed strength and power to enable him to continue his godly contemplations. This event and the extraordinary virtues of the tea plant he immediately brought to the notice of a number of his disciples, together with the manner in which it was to be used. . . . . And hence it comes that since that time to the present, the learned have made no remarks about it, and that some have considered it sufficient to attribute its origin to the eyelids of Dharma." The translator shows however that tea was not unknown in China in the third and fourth centuries, so that the legend bears the impress of modern invention. Its existence is repudiated by modern Buddhist scholars, and it is essentially a mere vulgar tale. But, accepted as such, it is interesting in the hint it gives us of the Hindu myth, wherein the falcon who undertook to steal the heavenly *Soma* (drink of immortality) had a claw and a feather shot off by a demon arrow. They fell to the earth and took root, the claw becoming a species of thorn and the feather a *palasa* tree, the Indian representative of the rowan or mountain ash.* The classic origin of the hyacinth (from the blood of Ajax), the growth of mint from the body of Minthe the mistress of Pluto, the almond tree which sprang from the corpse of Phyllis, and numerous other legends familiar to our schoolboy days all embody the same idea of the human body, or a portion of it, springing up anew in the shape of some member of the vegetable world.

The cocoa-nut tree is also the subject of a fanciful Chinese legend. "The prince Liu Yeh having had a quarrel with Prince Sueh sent a man to assassinate him; this he did while his victim was in a state of intoxication. His head was then suspended on a tree, and it became metamorphosed into a cocoa-nut with two eyes on the shell. Thus the fruit acquired the name of Yueh-wang-t'ou or Prince Yueh's head."† The cocoa-nut is now known as the Ye Tzu, owing, as is alleged, to the fact that during the Ching dynasty princes have been called "Ye." The fable is not countenanced by the Pen Tsao or native herbal, but is gravely recorded by Chinese authors. It is noteworthy that vessels made of cocoa-nut shell are supposed to betray the presence of poison in the liquids they

---

* *Indo-European Traditions & Folk-lore*, p. 158.

† Mr. T. Sampson in *N. & Q. on China & Japan*, Vol. III. p. 147.

contain, either ebullition taking place or the vessel bursting. Spoons made of the same material are in Ceylon supposed to possess similar virtues.

An interesting parallel to Western beliefs is found in the legendary virtues attributed by the Chinese to mercury and its preparations. The native term for Quicksilver—water-silver—is the equivalent of the Greek and Latin terms. Sulphide of mercury is called *hsien tan* 仙丹 of which our phrase "Philosopher's stone" is a sufficiently near rendering; and this, like the long-sought secret of western alchemists, is supposed to have the power of conferring immortality. Stories in which this substance figures as a supernatural agent are to be frequently met with in Chinese books.

Household tales reminding one of the "Judgment of Solomon" find place in Chinese folk-lore—as indeed they appear to do in that of nearly all Asiatic nations. One of the most original I have heard, introducing as it does a supernatural element, is as follows. During the time of the Sung dynasty there lived a man, a maker of marriage ornaments, and his wife, who loved each other dearly. A white dog versed in magic having seen the woman, who was remarkably good-looking, determined to win her, and in order to carry out his project transformed himself into an exact likeness of her lawful husband. Mistakenly calculating on the absence of the latter, he visited the wife just as the real husband was returning, and she was accordingly thrown into a state of the most extraordinary doubt at beholding two "Simons Pure," as they appeared to be, at the same moment. Unable to decide between them, she insisted on their at once accompanying her to the magistrate's yamên—a proposition to which, from very different motives, they both assented. Upon the parties making their appearance, the magistrate, like the wife, was at first completely puzzled. Suspecting however that one of the claimants was a dog in disguise he remembered that a tiger confined on the premises was accustomed to feed on dogs though it had never attacked men. He therefore placed both husbands in the tiger's cage. -The tiger at once flew at and devoured the dog which had assumed a man's disguise, leaving the real husband untouched; and the reunited pair left the yamên, praising the sagacity of the magistrate who had delivered them from the power of enchantment.

A version however of the real Solomonaic story is to be found in China. As in the Hebrew tale two women had each of them an infant, one of which died by misadventure, the bereaved mother claiming the surviving child. The official before whom they came did not suggest so cruel a measure as the division of the infant, but simply ordered that it should be handed to a domestic in his yamên to be brought up for official life. He rightly surmised that the real mother would gladly accept so good a chance for her offspring, while the pretended mother, who only wanted the child in order to dispose of it, would demur. Judgment was accordingly given in favour of the tearful acceptor of the proposition, and the story, which is alleged to be historical, is widely believed. The Chinese are very fond of telling stories having a similar basis, most of them being, very probably, derived from Indian or Semitic sources.

Superstitions connected with the use of bread have in China, as amongst ourselves, formed the basis of legends more or less absurd. Our Good Friday Hot Cross buns are, as is known, simply relics of the heathen custom of offering sacred cakes to the gods as propitiatory offerings. This idea underlies a story related of Chu-ko Liang, the ingenious minister before mentioned. "Returning from the conquest of Pegu and reaching a river on the borders of China he found himself surrounded by a thick fog from which proceeded groans and wailings. On enquiring from the inhabitants into the cause he was told that they were uttered by the multitude of dead killed by the pestiferous waters of the stream; and that to disperse the fog it was necessary to sacrifice forty-nine men to the river. Shocked at this barbarity he invented loaves bearing the human figure each with a head and one hand, and threw forty-nine of them into the water and so dispersed the fog; and, since that time, bread has been used for the same purpose in China." It is probable, however, that the use of bread for such purposes by the Chinese existed long before the date of the legend (about A.D. 220). The "Staff of life" has amongst all nations possessed symbolical attributes, and its sacrifice to the gods of rivers, &c., is one of the most commonly met with of superstitious practices.

Dr. S. Wells Williams, in a paper which he prepared for the N. C. B. Royal Asiatic Society in 1869, drew attention to the interesting tale from Lew Chew to which I have casually adverted in a previous chapter and which at once recalls Mr. Baring Gould's "Swan maidens." The Samojed legend in which the theft of the feather dresses is made instrumental in obtaining atonement for injuries inflicted on the family of the purloiner is not noticed by the learned author; but he reminds his readers of the story in the *Arabian Nights* in which the hero obtains the daughter of the King of T'an by carrying off her dress of feathers while bathing, and when she eventually flies away with their two children, follows her to the land of Wak Wak, and remarks that both Germany and the Shetland islands have similar legends, though in the latter case the fairy dress was a seal skin. The Lew Chewan legend is translated from the journal of a mission to that country written by the Envoy Li Ting-yuan in 1801-1803 and is as follows.

"Once in olden time a man named Ming-ling-tzŭ, a farmer in poor circumstances and of irreproachable character, but without any family, had a well of delicious water near his house. He went one day to draw some, and when at a distance saw a bright light in the well: on drawing near to see what it was, he beheld a woman diving and washing in the water, who had her clothes on a pine tree. Being displeased at her shameless ways and at his well being fouled he secretly carried off her dress. The garments were quite unlike Lewchewan in their style and were of a ruddy sunset colour, which excited his surprise so that he cautiously came back to see what change would come about. The woman, finishing her bath, cried out in great anger, "What thief has been here in broad day? Bring back my clothes, quick." She then perceived Ming-ling-tzŭ and threw herself on the ground before him. He began to scold her and asked her why she came and fouled his water? to which she replied that both the pine tree and the well were made by the Creator for the use of all. The farmer entered into conversation with her and pointed out that fate evidently intended her to be his wife as he absolutely refused to give up her clothes, while without them she could not get away. The result was that they were married. She lived with him for ten years and bore him a son and a daughter. At the end of that time her fate was fulfilled, she ascended a tree during the absence of her husband and having bidden her children farewell glided off on a cloud and disappeared." I can find no trace of any similar story in China proper, though one may exist, and the reappearance of the Keltic legend in a group of islands in the China sea is a noteworthy phenomenon. The German and Persian versions are in some sense links in the chain of connection; but if the theory of a simultaneous eastward and westward spread of legend from an Aryan source be correct, the fact is not less striking that in this case it has appeared to leave no trace in so many of the intermediate countries through which it has passed to its Ultima Thule on either hand.

Stories in which the example of Penelope is imitated by wives long deserted by their lawful husbands are sufficiently common. The following will serve as a specimen:—In the time of the Chow dynasty there lived a man named Pak-li-shi who was one of those unsettled adventurers ever longing to enjoy fresh experiences. After being married a few years to his wife, who gave birth to a son, he one day disappeared without intimating his intended route. Time passed away until over thirty years had elapsed, the runaway having meantime risen to be prime minister in a neighbouring state, while the wife and son wandered over the country in search of the missing husband and father. One day his son (who had of course arrived at man's estate) was attracted by a proclamation issued in what appeared to be his father's name. He informed his mother, who had been compelled by poverty to become an itinerant sempstress, and they at once devised a means of obtaining access to his house. Reaching the town where he resided the mother assumed the rôle of a wandering vocalist and contrived to scrape acquaintance with some of his servants, from whom she learned that their master was liable to fits of deep dejection on account of his being unable to find his family, of whom he had lost sight for many years. She suggested that some of her songs might soothe his regret and was accordingly introduced, the denouement being of course a recognition and reconciliation. Another Chinese story bearing on the marriage relations, and recalling several well-known tales of home origin, relates how a military man leaves his mother and wife for the scene of war and is compelled to remain absent many years. When at length able to return, he espies at a short distance from his house a woman who he believes is his wife. Foolishly anxious to test her fidelity he accosts her (she not recognizing him) and introduces himself as a friend of her long absent husband. Presently his manner becomes decidedly warmer than their supposed relations justify, and the woman, far from any aid, seizes a handful of sand or mud and throws it in his eyes, availing herself of his temporary inconvenience to escape to her house. Shortly afterwards, having cleansed his eyes, he likewise enters the house and makes himself known to his mother, who joyfully sends to tell her daughter-in-law that the son has returned. The wife comes out and seeing him to be the man who, pretending to be a stranger, had offered her violence, begins to upbraid him, and finally rushing from the room hangs herself. She is, however, cut down in time and at length suffers herself to be reconciled to her husband.

The still commoner story referred by Mr. Henderson to the "Genœva root" is as prominent in Chinese as in Western household lore. One native version relates how a son leaves his young wife and stepmother to look for employment at a distance from home. The latter hates the wife and in the absence of her stepson makes her perform the most menial work, crowning her evil deeds by accusing the poor girl on her husband's return of unfaithfulness. The husband, who exaggerates the Chinese sentiment that the mother's wishes or assertions rank before those of the wife, believes his step-mother, and orders his wife to commit suicide. Before the deed is consummated, however, the wicked stepmother is killed by lightning. This, in view of the wife's protestations of innocence, is accepted as a divine judgment, and the husband is reconciled to his wife.

Wives of supernatural race are reputed to be acquired in other ways than that mentioned above (see the Lewchewan story of stealing the dress). The gods are at times so pleased with the good conduct of individual mortals that they give him one of the female genii to wife. A man named Tung Yung was thus favoured and the union was a very happy one. But as in the previous case the wife's liking for mortal life could not outlast a certain term, and, on her husband reaching the highest rank to which he could aspire, she committed their son to his care and reascended to the ranks of the genii.

The classic myths relating to children being suckled by animals closely resemble similar tales from Chinese sources; but the tiger here plays the part assigned elsewhere to the wolf, &c. A well-known native story recounts how a husband and wife with their infant child fled during one of the many rebellions into a desert. While setting up their encampment a tiger suddenly made his appearance and so scared the parents that, forgetting the child, they incontinently fled, and were shortly afterward captured and put to death. The tiger picked up the infant and bore it to its cave, where (the legend says not how) it was duly nourished and in time became a well-grown young man. The tiger having taken a great fancy to its singular nursling led him to some villagers who at once took charge of him, his foster mother thenceforth disappearing. The hero lived to avenge his parents' wrongs and eventually rose to high office.

Following the example of Mr. Henderson in tabulating the "Story radicals" illustrated by his interesting work, I arrange hereunder those to which the foregoing pages have referred. To assume that they do more than indicate the direction in which further research will doubtless discover most interesting matter, would be absurd. But the list, slight as it is, may serve as the basis for a more complete illustration of the subject at a future day.

LEGENDS OF LOCALITY, HOUSEHOLD TALES, &c.

STORY RADICALS.

I. RELATING TO HUSBAND AND WIFE.

1.—PENELOPE ROOT.

The husband leaves his wife at home ;
She awaits his arrival in fidelity ;
They are reconciled after some trouble.

2.—GENŒVA ROOT.

The man goes away leaving his wife at home.
A false charge is brought against her and he orders her death.
Before she dies he discovers his mistake.
They are reconciled.

(*Variant.*)

The man leaves his wife as before.
He attempts to test her fidelity ;
It results in her death, *or*
It nearly results in her death, but they are reconciled.

3.—SVANHVIT ROOT.

A man sees a woman bathing with her charm dress on the shore.
He steals the dress and she falls into his power.
After some years she recovers the dress and escapes.
He is unable to recover her.

(*Variant.*)

A man is wedded to a woman of supernatural race.
After some years she becomes tired of earth and escapes.
He cannot recover her.

II. RELATING TO PARENTS AND CHILDREN.

4.—JUDGMENT OF SOLOMON ROOT.

Two mothers have a dispute about offspring ;
They refer it to the wisest official they can find :
He tests their *bona fides*.
The rightful party triumphs

5.—RHEA SYLVIA ROOT.

Children are exposed by accident or design ;
They are suckled by a wild beast ;
They eventually rejoin their countrymen, *and*
Are finally raised to high honour.

III. MEN AND THE UNSEEN WORLD.

6.—ACHERUSIAN ROOT.

A place accessible to mortals affords an entry to the lower world ;
Spirits enter and repass ;
A mortal visits it and learns secrets of the hereafter.

7.—CITY OF SILENCE ROOT.

Genii are imprisoned in vessels of metal or earthenware by mortals;
They are released by accident or design.
(a) They revenge themselves on those who imprisoned them, *or*
(b) They accept their release with thankfulness.

8.—MAGICAL CONFLICT ROOT.

Two persons with supernatural powers test them against one another.
They pass through various transformations;
The better or more powerful one overcomes the other.
(See chapter on Serpents, Dragons &c. for illustration).

9.—HERCULES CUP ROOT.

A mortal is presented by a supernatural being with a cup;
The mortal uses it as a means of transport;
If pursued the pursuers abandon the chase on perceiving his magic cup.

10.—ALI BABA ROOT.

A mysterious cave opens and shuts at the command of a master endowed with magic powers.
A stranger learns and uses the pass-word.
He acquires riches or advantages from his knowledge, *but*,
Some one is sacrificed to ensure his good fortune.

IV. MEN IN CONFLICT WITH NATURAL INFLUENCES.

11.—MAGIC TOMB ROOT.

A tomb possesses magnetic powers;
An attempt is made to open or enter it;
The attempt wholly or partially fails.

V. MAN MATCHED WITH MAN.

12.—QUEEN DIDO ROOT.

Strangers visit a new country;
By cunning they induce the natives to grant what they do not intend to the newcomers.

[Chinese Chronicles assert that the Dutch when they first settled in Formosa adopted a ruse similar to that of Queen Dido. The classic story is more accurately reproduced in the *Ming-shi*, containing accounts of foreign countries, in which the Spaniards, who arrived in the Phillippines about 1574, are narrated to have presented the native chief with valuable gifts, begging in return the privilege of occupying for building as much land as could be covered by the hide of an ox.—See *China Review*, Vol. iv. p. 386. At all events the story, however imported or originated, is perfectly well known to the Chinese and as such is included in my list.]

LEGENDS OF LOCALITY, HOUSEHOLD TALES, &c. 145

VI. MEN PERFORM EXTRAORDINARILY HEROIC ACTS.

13.—MARCUS CURTIUS ROOT.
 (a) Human life must be sacrificed to close a chasm, or,
 (b) Human blood must be infused into a casting to ensure its success.
  (Many variants).
 (c) A person sacrifices him or herself accordingly, or,
 (d) A person is compelled to do so by force. A successful result ensues.

VII. MEN AND BEASTS.

14.—BIRD, BEAST AND FISH ROOT, OR "ONE GOOD TURN DESERVES ANOTHER" ROOT.
 A man is asked to aid an animal to escape from confinement, to recover from sickness &c.
 He aids it with good humour.
 The man falls into trouble,
 The animal aids him in the nick of time.

VIII. PLANTS &c. SPRINGING FROM A PORTION OF THE BODY.

15.—SOMA-BRINGING FALCON ROOT.
 A being undertakes extraordinary work.
 By its own act or that of others a portion of its body is cleft to the earth;
 The portion taking root, produces a plant;
 The plant is thereafter venerated.

Necessarily brief as the foregoing illustrations of the subject under notice have been they will, it is hoped, suffice to demonstrate the general resemblance of Chinese vulgar legends to those in vogue elsewhere. Both in motive and in detail they remind us of the tales formerly told by our own firesides, and demonstrate the fact—theoretically admitted by most people, but often practically ignored—that a common humanity claims the Chinese and the Saxon. And I may take this opportunity of referring to the objections which are raised by some sinologues to treating Chinese "old wives tales" as matters worth serious record and discussion. To those who share those objections I cannot do better than quote the words of Mr. Henderson. "It is," he says, "only of late years that household tales have been regarded as of interest by men of learning. For long they were thought to be 'milk for babes' but to have nothing in them which could repay a moment's study by one who had emerged from childhood. But the great Grimm saw that in these stories for children lay fragments of ancient mythology, and he learned to trace them from land to land and thus to prove them to be precious hairlooms derived from our primeval ancestors before they parted into separate nationalities." Without asserting that all the Chinese versions of the legends above noted can be referred to a common parentage with those of Europe, and leaving what has here been dealt with in a single chapter to be further elucidated by more competent scholars, the instances given of agreement between Western and Chinese tales are I imagine sufficient to arrest attention. To a charge of having but slightly discriminated between legends properly so called and household tales I must plead guilty. But as no purpose was to be served by observing a strict distinction, the matter may pass.

XIII.—FABLES AND PROVERBIAL LORE.

The use of fables to convey some homely truth or enforce the point of some moral apothegm, to those who might turn from abstract argument with indifference, is as familiar to the household world of China as to that of the West. Strangely enough, however, it does not appear that the Chinese possess (with two exceptions to be presently mentioned) any collections of fables properly so called, though their literature abounds with them as isolated tales. The literati indeed affect to rather despise them in the abstract, as fit only for the perusal of women and children, though they do not disdain to employ them at times with considerable effect. One cause of the supercilious attitude thus assumed is, very probably, that the only known collections in the language (forming the exceptions above noted) are translations from Sanscrit Buddhistic sources, and hence exotic to Chinese thought. Your true Confucianist—the believer in the dry bones of a system (if system it be) which, its worldly ethics aside, is the least satisfying of all known beliefs—scorns Buddhistic fables as he scorns Buddhistic prayers. Few of the better-read natives will own to any but the most distant acquaintance with the two works which form almost the sole repositories of Indo-Chinese fable—the *Fu-yuan-chu-lin** and the *Yu-lin*, which are avowedly adopted from the Pali. But besides this, the officials of the Empire have a wholesome dread of the satire which a fable may point, and it is more than probable that any popular collection of the sort would bring its authors and publishers into trouble. In 1837-38 the late Mr. R. Thom translated eighty-one of Æsop's fables into Chinese. We give the result in his own words:—

"When first published in Canton their reception by the Chinese was extremely flattering. They had their run of the public Courts and offices until the Mandarins, taking offence at seeing some of their evil customs so freely canvassed, ordered the work to be suppressed. It is not the first time that we have elucidated a disputed point by referring to one of these fables having analogy to the matter in hand; nay, we remember once stopping the mouths of a party of mandarins, who insisted that England wanted to quarrel with China, by reciting the story of the goose that laid the golden eggs. The application was at once perceived and the justice of the remark admitted immediately. It will thus be seen that the Chinese officials evince no lack of appreciation about such matters." But the power found sufficient to suppress what is deemed an objectionable brochure is of course unable to touch the numerous fables which, partly in the much-revered literature of the Empire and partly by oral relation, have been handed down to the existing generation of Chinese. To disinter an entire collection would indeed be a herculean task;

---

* See Wylie's *Notes on Chinese Literature*, p. 166.

but it is easy to cite some of the best known in illustration of the contention that the Chinese mind manifests much the same characteristics as that of other and, as we deem, more civilized races.

The earliest known specimen of a Chinese fable is noticed by Mr. Mayers in his *Manual* (p. 282). In the *Narratives of the Contending States*, Su-tai, counsellor of the prince of Chao, is said to have related the following by way of illustrating the necessity of unity amongst those opposed to or by a common enemy. "A mussel was sunning itself no the river bank when a bittern came by and pecked at it. The mussel closed its shell and nipped the bird's beak. Hereupon the bittern said, 'If you don't let me go to-day, if you don't let me go to-morrow, there will be a dead mussel.' The shell fish answered. 'If I don't come out to-day, if I don't come out to-morrow, there will surely be a dead bittern.' Just then a fisherman came by and seized the pair of them." The date of this utterance is given as about B.C. 315, and, if this be correct, it certainly boasts a respectable antiquity. It is not, of course, often possible to fix the precise dates of literary invention, but it does not appear that the claims of Æsop (B.C. 620) as the father of Western fable need yield in point of antiquity to those of his Chinese representative, whoever he may have been. The latter, like the Grecian humourist, most probably contented himself with reciting his fables, but, less fortunate in his countrymen, has not had his name handed down to posterity by those who thought his witty or wise sayings worth preservation in writing. On the other hand, Chinese literature justly claims preëminence as regards the publication of written fables. Socrates is indeed alleged to have versified some of Æsop's fables when in prison, shortly before his death; but the earliest known Western collection is dated 150-100 B.C.

A fable tolerably well known (though undoubtedly of Buddhistic origin) is that of the Cat and the Mice. The most popular version relates how an old cat was sitting up mewing with half-closed eyes when two mice happened to see her. Astonished that their old enemy should be taking things so easily they said to each other, "Puss is evidently reformed; she is saying her prayers. We need have no fear." So they began to play about without noticing her. No sooner had they got within reach, however, than the cat sprang upon one and devoured him. His companion rushed home and remarked, "Who would have thought that a cat which shut her eyes and said her prayers would act like that?" The Indian version is slightly different. A man had put a rosary round his cat's neck, for fun, and the mice, taking this to be a sign of a religious mind on the part of the cat, congratulated each other and began to make merry. In a very short time the cat had caught and eaten several of the mice: upon which the survivors said "We thought he was praying to Buddha, but his piety was a mere comedy." The moral is that those who make a show of devotion are least to be trusted; or, as others have it, that "some pray and do bad actions; others don't pray, but don't do evil." Another favourite fable has given rise to a popular saying. Pigs in Corea, it avers, are generally black; but a white one having once made its appearance the king thought it worth offering to the Chinese Emperor, and accordingly sent ambassadors to present it. When they reached Peking, however, so many white pigs were to be seen that the ambassadors saw it would be ridiculous to carry out their mission. Hence "to offer a white pig to the Emperor" is equivalent to our "carrying coals to Newcastle."

Our own (or rather Æsop's) fable, in which the man who nursed a frozen snake was bitten for his pains, becomes curiously inverted in the Chinese version; the snake rewarding its benefactor in a rather more agreeable manner. Snakes figure in two other well-known fables. In one a man is represented as having struck a cobra on the head, whereupon the reptile attacked him with its tail. Striking its tail, the head forthwith assailed him, and the man then belabouring its middle, both head and tail went at the assailant. The moral of this is "Never say die," or as the Chinese word it "There's help for everything." In the other case we find a reminder of the well-known story of the stomach and the hands, wherein the latter refuse to work for ever to satisfy an organ which does nothing to earn its living:—The head and the tail of a snake quarrelled, the latter averring that it had as good a right to direct the creature's movements as had the former, which moreover got all the enjoyment of eating and drinking. So the tail was allowed to take charge, and began to move backwards. Unprovided with eyes, however, it very soon brought both ends to grief, as the snake fell into a wet ditch whence there was no means of egress, and was drowned.

The well-known French sinologue, Professor Julien, has translated from the Chinese some forty-five fables derived from Indian sources. The majority of these are so obviously foreign to Chinese customs that they cannot be cited as examples of native fable. Five of them only seem to be at all popularly known, one being that of the snake's head and tail above noticed. Of the others the Ass in the Lion's skin is probably the most familiar. The Ass takes, in another fable, the place occupied by the ambitious frog. Desirous of becoming an ox he first of all adopts the same food. After a time, satisfied that he is going on well, he essays to change his usual bray for the deep-toned low of his horned companions. Indignant at the insult they rush upon him and gore him to death.

Tigers are such favourite subjects of Chinese superstition that it is natural to find them frequently introduced into fable. The following is found in the collection translated by Mons. Julien, and is consequently of Indian origin. A tiger having seized a monkey was about to devour him; but the monkey, bethinking himself of some means of escape, suggested that he was too small to make a good meal for a tiger and offered to conduct his captor to a neighbouring hill where a far more noble prey might be captured. This was a stag, who, rightly assuming that the tiger had come for a most unfriendly purpose, concluded that his only chance was to put a bold face upon the matter, and accordingly addressed the monkey as follows: "How is this? you promised me ten tiger-skins but you have only brought one; you still owe me nine." The tiger hearing this became alarmed and instantly decamped, vowing that he never thought the monkey could be so treacherous. Two other fables in which the tiger figures are, however, purely Chinese. In one case he is about to attack an ass, but hearing his tremendous bray becomes alarmed supposing that so much noise can only proceed from one of the bravest of animals. The ass, however, shewing no inclination to fight, the tiger advances, and presently hears another bray as loud as the first. Convinced at last that he has nothing to fear, he rushes on the ass and devours him. The moral of course is that people who put forth the greatest pretensions are not most to be dreaded. The second fable teaches how sagacity is more valuable than strength. A tiger was about to devour a fox, when the latter demanded exemption on the ground that he was superior to all other beasts. "If you doubt my word, come with me and see," said the fox: so the two set forth in company. Every animal of course fled at their approach, and the tiger, too stupid to see that he himself was the cause of their terror, conceived a high respect for his crafty companion and did not dare to attack him. The foregoing is one of the many fables recorded in Chinese history as having been used to point a moral when a ready-witted man was interrogated by his sovereign.

The fable of the Geese and the Tortoise introduced into China from Sanscrit sources is essentially the same as the well-known European version. A couple of geese lived in friendship with a tortoise by the side of a pond. During the hot weather the pond began to dry up, and the geese, anxious that their friend should not suffer from want of water, offered to transport him to some other place where the precious fluid was abundant. They directed him to seize in the middle, with his mouth, a stick which they had provided, engaging to carry it by its ends to the place indicated. "But be sure," they added, "not to speak while we are carrying you." The tortoise promised compliance, and the three started on their adventurous journey. Some little boys viewing the novel sight began to shout, "Look at the geese carrying a tortoise!" and continued shouting so long that the tortoise at last lost his temper. "What's that to you!" he retorted. But alas, in giving vent to his feelings he lost his hold of the stick and falling downwards to the ground was dashed to pieces. Another fable, which teaches the moral that people should avoid unsuitable agreements, tells how two brothers bought a pair of boots between them, it being arranged that each should wear them in turn. The elder however forgot to stipulate as to hours and the younger accordingly wore them during the working part of each day. Afraid to claim his rights, but anxious not to be wholly "done" the elder brother got up every night to get his share of the bargain, and between them the boots were soon worn out. Upon the younger brother proposing that they should buy another pair the elder said "Not unless you will let me sleep at night." The satire upon unequally yoked fellows is clear enough, though some European readers have failed to see it.

The following fable undoubtedly owes its origin to Hindoo sources, but is interesting (in view of its being tolerably well known in China) on account of its obvious derivation from a root which has furnished not merely fables but "historical" anecdotes to many Western nations. Stories in which the hero presents himself to the enemies of the countrymen in a condition arguing that he has been grossly maltreated by his friends, and from motives of revenge seeks to be received by and give aid to those to whom he is naturally opposed, are to be found in the records of nearly all races. The fable of the crows and the owls adheres to the usually-received texts. Two colonies of crows and owls respectively lived in close proximity to and hated each other in the most neighbourly way. As the crows slept by night and the owls by day each in turn attacked the other when most defenceless, and the slaughter on either side was great. At length an intelligent crow remarked that this would never do; some plan of exterminating their enemies must be hit upon if they were ever to dwell in peace. On being asked what plan he proposed he told his fellow crows to peck him badly and pull out a number of his feathers, promising, if that were done, to effect the destruction of the owls. In this sorry plight he presented himself at the owl's domicile, complaining bitterly of the treatment to which he had been subjected. The owls coming out to see what was the matter he explained that he had fled to them for shelter, and one of the owls pitying his hard lot received him into his nest. For a while all went well, until at length, his feathers having grown again, he set to work to pile large quantities of brushwood round the owls' hole, explaining in answer to their enquiries that he was endeavouring to return their kind ness by heaping up for them a barrier against the cold winds. Shortly after, a snowstorm came on and all the owls crowded into the nest to escape it. Watching his opportunity the crow plucked a firebrand from the fire of some neighbouring peasants and setting light to the brushwood smothered the owls to death. The moral, "never trust a renegade," is obvious enough, and is one which, had it been kept in mind, might have saved the China of a former age from not a few revolutions. The difficulty of overcoming evil habits is also well illustrated in the same collection as that from which the foregoing is derived. A certain king possessed by a spirit of a false economy gave orders that all the horses used by his cavalry should in time of peace be employed in mills. So long as the country was at peace the arrangement worked admirably. But no sooner were the troops called out for war than the cavalry found that their horses would only go in a circular direction and they accordingly fell an easy prey to their antagonists. It is a pity that no one with sufficient influence to make himself heard ventures to apply this fable to the so-called "troops" which compose the major part of the native army.

A very fair satire upon the habit common to some people of "borrowing trouble" is contained in the following:—A certain rich man who had lived to an extreme age had assembled all his sons and grandsons to do honour to his birthday. Despite their felicitations however he wore a troubled face, until at length some one asked him what was amiss. "Nothing particular," he replied; "I was only thinking what trouble I should have in inviting my guests when my two-hundredth birthday came round." To take overmuch thought for the morrow is a common Chinese failing, and the moral embodied in the foregoing is keenly appreciated by the populace. Two other fables remind us of old friends in our schoolboy days, though they are, I believe, purely

Chinese. In one a party of robbers are related to have attacked a village and to have killed all the inhabitants, save two—one so blind that he was unable to even grope his way about, and the other so lame that by no possibility could he manage to run away. But "heaven helps those that help themselves." After a deal of trouble the blind man managed to get the lame man on his back and piloted by his eyes the pair reached a place where they were charitably provided for. The system of mutual dependence, so essentially a Chinese virtue, is herein aptly illustrated. Not bad either is another entitled "The folly of avarice." A rich priest had hoarded a fine collection of jewels to which he was constantly adding, and of which he was inordinately proud. Upon shewing them one day to a friend, the latter feasted his eyes for some time, and on taking leave thanked his host for the jewels. "How," cries the priest, "I have not given them to you! Why do you thank me?" "Well," rejoined his friend, "I have at least had as much pleasure from seeing them as you can have; and the only difference between us, that I can see, is that you have the trouble of watching them."

Despite therefore the fact that popular collections of Chinese fables are unknown, at all events to all the literary natives to whom the writer has access —fables themselves are in common use and are of much the same character as those popular amongst ourselves, doubtless indeed owning a common origin.

Turning from fables to proverbs a very different state of affairs is found to prevail. Not only are the Chinese spoken languages richer in proverbial lore than that of any Western race, but their literature abounds with that description of short pithy saying so well defined as "the wisdom of many expressed by the wit of one." I would here mention that when this series of chapters on Chinese folklore was first projected the admirable work of Mr Scarborough, "A Collection of Chinese Proverbs" had not been published, and Mr Lister's highly interesting article in the *China Review*, "Chinese Proverbs and their Lessons,"* was almost the only essay on the subject which had up to that period appeared in the language. Most works on China indeed give more or less full lists of common sayings, but Mr Lister was the first who endeavoured to direct attention to the coincidences of Chinese thought with that of other peoples. Mr Scarborough's work has so amply supplemented all that was previously available respecting Chinese proverbs, while his introductory essay gives so comprehensive a view of the whole subject that students of the subject may well be referred to the volume in question. Dealing, however, strictly with the matter of comparison between Chinese and Western proverbs, there is still room for comment. And for this purpose I shall avail myself of Mr Scarborough's handy collection.

Out of some 2,700 proverbs and popular sayings which he has brought together, about one hundred are either word-for-word, or in sense, the same as common proverbs in use amongst ourselves. Occasionally of course we find an odd inversion of thought, but in the main they coincide with curious accuracy.

* *China Review*, Vol. III., No. 3, p. 129.

The instances of agreement might be trebled or perhaps quadrupled if popular quotations from well-known writers and Biblical texts were also compared. But in the above estimate I speak merely of proverbs properly so called. On the first page we have the equivalent of our "Much cry and little wool"—*It thunders loudly, and rains very little*, another proverb equivalent to "Lots of fuss for small profit" containing a hit at the class of small mandarins. A little further on we find our "Nothing venture nothing have" transformed into *If you don't enter a tiger's den you cannot get his cubs*, and the well-known saying "A man is known by the company he keeps" becomes, *Near vermilion one gets stained red, near ink black;* a more vulgar version having it that *Near putrid fish you will stink, near the epidendrum you will be fragrant*. That "One swallow doesn't make a summer" is taught by *A single strand of silk doesn't make a thread, or a solitary tree a grove*. "Practice makes perfect" is in one Chinese version, *The boxer must not rest his fist or the singer his mouth*, while exactly the same words as our own are also in use, and "What you do, do well" becomes, *If you kill a pig kill him thoroughly*. The Chinese have a number of proverbs implying "More haste less speed," which may account for the deliberate way in which, as a nation, they ignore anything like hurry. *In hurry is error; Done leisurely done well; Slow work fine goods*, and *What is done hastily is not done well*, may be quoted as examples. But on the other hand they have a hit at procrastination "the thief of time" in precisely our own words. Another proverb has it,—*Wait till the Yellow River is clear, and how old will you be?* Our "Too many cooks spoil the broth" finds its most literal rendering in *A thousand artizans a thousand plans*, but two or three other proverbs to the same effect are to be found in the collection.

The Chinese have numerous proverbs relating to animals, but the only one that strikes me as exactly reproducing a Western idea—"Dog doesn't eat dog"—is, *The heron doesn't eat heron's flesh*. On no subject are their sayings more plentiful than trade. Every Chinaman is said to be a born cook and a born trader, and their most popular proverbs certainly give colour to the latter part of the assertion. "Use a sprat to catch a whale" finds its representatives in *Throw a brick to allure a gem*, and *If a little cash does not go, much cash will not come*. . "There's a time for all things" becomes a business proverb in China, *There's a time to fish and a time to dry nets*. "Take care of the pence &c." is not unlike the Chinese *Count cash as if it were gold and so avoid the least mistake;* while "There are tricks in all trades" is more politely expressed by *Every trade has its ways*. "A penny saved is a penny gained" is inculcated by *Never spend a farthing uselessly*. One is strongly tempted to quote some of the other numerous proverbs relating to trade and commerce such as *Cheap things are not good: good things are not cheap* &c., but the limits imposed of verbal or at least direct comparison forbid.

The advantages of dealing for ready cash and the inconvenience of debt are as strongly insisted on in China as in Europe. "A bird in the hand is worth two in the bush," say we. The Chinese put it more directly, *Better take eight hundred than give credit for a thousand cash, Better twenty per cent in ready* money than thirty on credit; to which by the way, our "A nimble nine-pence is better than a slow shilling" is perhaps the most literal parallel. "He that goes a borrowing goes a sorrowing" is enforced on the Chinese mind by an ingenious pun in one of the words of the proverb—a practice sufficiently common in China to be worth explanation. The word *Ch'ien* debt is thus written:— 欠,—the lower half of the character being 人 *jên*, signifying a man. The proverb runs "*Debt presses on the head of a man*," the *ch'ien* being supported by *jen*. Our assertion that a man "Robs Peter to pay Paul" is expressed in Chinese by, *He tears down the Eastern to repair the Western wall*.

The Chinese equivalent of "A bad carpenter quarrels with his tools" is: *All unskilful fools quarrel with their tools*,—not a quite literal but sufficiently accurate rendering. "Cobbler stick to your last" has several equivalents, such as *The teacher should not leave his books or the poor man his pigs*; *Better be master of one than jack of all trades*; *Separate hongs* (mercantile houses) *are like separate hills*, and *The river does not overflow the well*. "Two of a trade never agree" is essentially a Chinese saying, and so is our well-known aphorism that "Dress makes the man," the native version being that *Dress makes the Gentleman or Lady*, varied to the form *That as a house needs man to set it off, so man needs clothes*. Household affairs come in for a full share of Chinese proverbial philosophy. "Early to bed &c." is represented by *Three days' rising gains one day's work*. "To wash your dirty linen at home" is advised in the more prosaic *Don't spread abroad domestic foibles*, and the well-known saying, (hardly a proverb perhaps) "Alas 'tis easier far to rule a kingdom than a wife" is but the English version of the Chinese *It is easier to rule a kingdom than to regulate a family*. "A man's a man for a' that" finds exact reproduction in the Chinese saying that *A stick's a stick whether long or short ; A man's a man whether great or small;* and our popular saying that "There are as good fish in the sea as ever came out of it" is aptly paralleled by, *If there's no light in the East there will be in the West*.

The idea expressed in our "Breaking a butterfly on the wheel" is familiarized in China by the saying *He fells a tree to catch a blackbird* and *He shoots a sparrow with a cannon*, as is that of "Carrying coals to Newcastle" by *Offering the filial classic for sale at the door of Confucius;* while the Chinaman who "Buys a pig in a poke" is said *To buy a cat in a bag*. We say "Shutting the stable door when the horse is stolen" The Chinese put it, *Fighting the wall when the robbers have gone*, equally illustrative of useless effort when the danger is over. The principle that leads the world to "Give to him that hath" is evidently no stranger to Chinese practice. Mr. Scarborough versifies the native proverb as follows:

> A lucky man is stout and fair
> And men lend him service as much as he wants.
> A luckless man is burnt and spare
> And he asks for a loan which no man grants."

"To kill two birds with one stone" is pretty closely followed in the native version "*To accomplish two things at one effort*." Our "All roads lead to

Rome" is literally the same, the word Peking alone being substituted for that of Rome. A more verbose version of the proverb implies the same truth. "Strike while the iron is hot" is another instance of word-for-word agreement; and "There's a time for everything" is reproduced in *Where it's a time for drinking wine drink it, When the place is suitable cry aloud.* Our well-known "Lookers-on see most of the game" differs but slightly from *Men in the game are blind to what lookers-on see clearly.* "It's of no use crying over spilt milk" is very like the Chinese, *Spilt water can't be gathered up again.*

Happiness and misery furnish as fruitful a source for proverbs amongst the Chinese as amongst Western nations, some of their sayings being extremely terse and to the point. They assert that *Happinesses never come in pairs; calamities never come single,* a belief not confined to the inhabitants of the Middle Kingdom. Life and death, of course, come in for their share of wise (or unwise) sayings, though the former certainly predominate. When Shakespeare wrote that "all the world's a stage" he was unconsciously plagiarizing the Chinese, *Man's life is nought but theatrical performance.* That men are apt to discover secrets when under the influence of liquor ("When the wine's in the wit's out," In vino veritas, &c.,) the Chinese know as well as we do. *Wine,* they say, *is a discoverer of secrets,* and they have numerous sayings of the same kind. We assert moreover that "Walls have ears," and so do they. The recommendation to "Do in Rome as the Romans do" is paraphrased, *Meeting men or devils talk as they do,* a proverb eminently in accordance with Chinese caution. So too they adhere to the principle expressed in "What every one says must be true," the native version being almost the same.

Blind leadership is satirized in the identical words of the evangelist "If the blind lead the blind, &c." A similar reproduction of language applies to the proverb "The boy is father to the man," the Chinese saying *You may see the man in the boy.* "Good wine needs no bush" is equally well expressed by *A good-looking woman needs no rouge.* Some of the proverbs about women, by the way, are more pungent than polite. A greedy fellow is characterized in the same language in both English and Chinese as some one with *his eyes bigger than his belly.* "Every man for himself" is another cynical saying common to both countries. "Cheap and nasty" is expressed in Chinese by *If you buy cheap firewood, you burn the bottom of your copper.* So too "Cut your coat according to your cloth" becomes with a slight revision, *Cut your cloth according to your measure.* "Once bitten twice shy" is another instance of verbal agreement, except that the Chinese saying is less terse.

Most nations have a saying to the effect that the wearer knows best where the shoe pinches. The Chinese mean the same when they say *Rats know Rats' ways.* "Let sleeping dogs lie" is a worldly-wise saying which the Chinese fully appreciate, only they apply it to tigers instead of dogs. "A chip of the old block" or "Like father like son" is expressed by *Dragons give birth to Dragons and Phœnixes hatch Phœnixes.* Nor has the Wise King's saying "Spare the rod, and spoil the child" been ignored in China, the same idea exactly underlying a proverb in which the effects of due correction and spoiling are contrasted. "Two heads are better than one" is equally acknowledged in the saying, *One man's plan is short; two men's plan is long.*

Chinese proverbs regarding "Heaven" as the supreme arbiter of human affairs are more numerous than one would expect to find amongst a people so idol-ridden as the Chinese. It is noteworthy that in this connection "Heaven" is invariably used as we use it in popular sayings to imply "the one great Cause." Thus, as we say, "Man proposes, God disposes" the Chinese say *A thousand human schemes may be wrecked by one scheme of heaven.*[*] Similar sayings are so numerous, that they suggest an as yet (apparently) unrecognized belief in a one all-powerful cause. Every student of Chinese is of course acquainted with the popular acceptation of the term. But it would almost seem (if the collection of proverbs before us is to be accepted as a guide) that the word more nearly expresses the Christian idea of *the Creator* than any other in the Chinese vocabulary.

"Murder will out" say we. The Chinese intimate that a *Body buried in the snow is sure to be eventually discovered.* Our estimate of the value of time, again, is reproduced in words that match with the proverb already quoted respecting prevarication: *An inch of time is like an inch of gold.* It is perhaps scarcely accurate to quote "Mens sana in corpore sano" as a proverb. But at all events the Chinese reproduce it in *A calm mind makes a cool body.* "The poor have no friends" is another very literal rendering of a Chinese proverb, and "Money makes the world wag" is very fairly rendered by *In the presence of money all quarrels expire,* or *Money hides many offences;* while as a concluding specimen I may quote the well-known "First come first served" expressed in Chinese by, *The first who comes becomes prince, the second minister.*

It cannot of course be pretended that the foregoing is by any means an exhaustive summary of the various proverbs which imply similar intentions on the part of their inventors, European or Asiatic. But it will suffice to show how striking are the agreements on certain well-defined subjects, and, it is hoped, to support the general principle laid down in these pages that Chinese thought is, at bottom, very similar to our own. It may well be that proverbs relating to temporal welfare only, spring up spontaneously and independently in each country. But what are we to make of the monotheistic spirit pervading the numerous sayings in which the "Heaven" of the Chinese answers to the "God" of Christian Europe or the "Jehovah" of the chosen race? Is this too the spontaneous invention of an isolated people, or is it the surviving trace of a long-forgotten worship, when the ancestors of the Chinaman and the Semite worshipped at the same shrine? This is not the place to discuss such a question, but it nevertheless suggests itself, and is worth a more careful investigation than has yet been accorded to it by the enthusiastic champions of *Shang-ti* and *Shên.* In the opinion of many,

---

[*] Dr. Williams renders T'ien, "Providence Nature, Heaven, the overruling power; and though without definite personality, employed more than any other term to indicate God."

sufficient reason has not yet been adduced to justify a refusal to adopt the only phrase *acknowledged by the Chinese* to convey the idea expressed by our word "Creator" or "Almighty."

In concluding these hasty sketches of the various departments of Chinese folk-lore, the writer cannot but express a hope that each division of the subject will before long receive fuller elucidation from competent pens. Conscious of the superficial character of much that is here written he can only regret that time and opportunity have not allowed him to deal more satisfactorily with the information at command. To those who look upon the folk-lore of a people as affording a key to many curious problems concerning its origin and progress, the foregoing chapters may afford useful hints. Many subjects might be dealt with more advantageously in special volumes than within the brief limits of a single chapter. The writer will however be satisfied if his efforts tend in any way to bridge the existing gulf between the two peoples, by illustrating, even to a limited degree, the Chinese assertion that "Men of the four seas are (after all) brothers."

THE END.

INDEX.

A

	Page.
Ages Facial, the,	63
Ali Baba's Cave, its Chinese Representative,	134
Almanacks,	8
Amulets, extensive Use of,	55
,, usually Metal or Jade,	56
Animals Endowed with the Gift of Speech,	101
,, Suckling Children,	142
Apparition at Shanghai,	73
,, of a Man Drowned in the S.S. *Fusing*,	73
,, at Foochow,	74
Arrows fired at Tidal Waves as Charms,	51
Artemisia, Leaves of the, used as Charms,	51
Aryan Cradle of Superstitions,	6
Ass, the, in Chinese Fable,	148
Astrological Beliefs common to all Classes in China,	2

B

	Page.
Baboon, Cambojan, curious Belief respecting,	113
Bamboo, anti-demoniacal Powers of,	47
,, Slips, Divination by,	62
Bats, Ominous,	34
Bells, Auguries from,	37
,, Great, at Canton and Peking,	37
,, on Clothing Worn as Amulets,	55
,, of Peking, Legend of the Casting of the,	133
Betrothal, Ceremonies of,	15
Birds, Appearance of as Omens,	33, 34
,, Trained to Aid in Divination,	63
,, the Grateful,	136
Birth, Ceremonies observed after,	13
,, Hour and Day of,	8
Bittern and Mussel, Fable of the,	147
Blind Man and Lame Man, Fable of the,	151
Blood Bread, Sold at Peking,	67
,, from Trees, &c.,	127
,, Human, as Medicine,	66, 68
,, Human in Castings,	133
,, of Unborn Infants, efficacious for Magic,	68
Borrowing Trouble, Fable about,	150
Bread, Superstitions connected with its use,	140
Bride-Cake, Bread,	18
Bridges, Curious Superstitions concerning,	70
Brownies, Chinese,	99
Buildings, Charms affixed to,	48
Burial Ancient, in Position of Fœtus,	24

C

	Page.
Candle Omens,	17
Candles at Burials,	21
,, Bridal,	17
,, Burning Green in the presence of Ghosts,	73
Cannibalism, Chinese,	67
Cannon, Fired at the Peiho to Diminish a Flood,	46
Carp, Supernatural,	92
Cash in Dead Men's Sleeves, Divination by,	21
,, Lucky, as Amulets,	55
,, Swords,	48
Cat and Mice, Fable of,	147
,, to pass over a Corpse, Ominous,	20
Cats and Witchcraft in China,	90
,, Images of, on Houses,	48
,, Unlucky,	33
Chair, Sitting in a Warm, Ominous of a Quarrel,	33
Characts or Written Charms (specimen of),	52, 55
Charms Paper, Burnt and the Ashes Drank in Tea, &c.,	54
,, their extensive Use,	45
Cheap Literature, Aid to Preservation of Folk-lore,	6

INDEX.

Chêng Chêng-shan, Caves of, .. 133
Chêng-hwang, the, ... 77
Chiao, the Chinese, ... 127
Chiromancy, Chinese, ... 63
Chopsticks used at Marriages, .. 16
Chow Dynasty, Mythical Origin of the, ... 4
Christians, alleged Powers of as Exorcists, ... 89
Chrysostom St., his Protest against Superstitions, ... 2
Chu-ko Liang, Legend of the Tomb of, ... 135
Cinnabar, Children Stained with, as an Antidote to Sickness, .. 70
Classics, Chinese, Copies of as Charms, .. 51
" Divinations by the, .. 62
Clay Figures used by Wizards, .. 83
Clothes, Burial, ... 20
Cocoa-Nut, Fanciful Legend Concerning its Origin, 138
" Shell, Virtues of Vessels made of, .. 138
Cocks, Images of White, used at Marriages, ... 16
" Superstitions as to, .. 22
Coffin, Purchase of, during Life, 20
" Unlucky to Meet a, .. 38
Coins Placed under Door Sills, .. 48
Comets, Portents from, ... 35
Confucius, Legend of the Tomb of, 136
" on Omens, ... 39
Corpse, Blood from Mouth, &c., of, 71
Cosmical Phenomena in China, Records of, ... 116
Crabs, used for Exorcism, .. 11
Cradle, Superstitions as to Rocking an Empty, ... 12
Crane, Paper Image of, used 60 Days after Death, ... 25
Crooked Paths in Gardens, Reasons of, ... 35
Crow, Ominous Character of the, 33
Crows and Owls, Fable of the, .. 149

D

Days, Lucky and Unlucky, 28, 31
Dead, Implements Anciently made for the, ... 72
Dead Bodies, Position of, Reversed before Coffining, .. 21
Death, Most Common Hours of, .. 27
" Superstitions concerning, 20
Demon Flies and Cash, ... 86
" Aid to Become Rich, 86
Demons, Chinese, ... 84
" Head of the, ... 84

Demon Imprisoned in Jars, .. 131
" Power to Cause Disease, .. 85
" People Possessed by, .. 85
" Story of Possession at Chefoo, ... 85
"Devil Dancers" Native, .. 87
" How Consulted, 88
Disturbing Graves, Dislike to, .. 26
Divination and Spiritualism, .. 56
" by the Leaves of the Juniper, &c., .. 63
" like the *Sortes Virgilianæ*, ... 62
Divining Twig, the Chinese, .. 57
Dogs, Demon, Transformed, .. 132
" Hair of as Charms, .. 51
" Strange, Lucky, ... 33
Dragon, Chinese, Description of the, ... 108
" Worship Domestic, .. 108
" Legend of the, and A-Tseung, ... 109
" The Embodiment of the Storm Spirit, ... 110
" St. George and the, Chinese Legend of, .. 110
Dragons, Ghosts of, ... 92
" Derived from Serpents, 107
" Worship, ... 107
" and Waterspouts, .. 127
Dragon's Water, near a Grave, .. 25
Drawings of Animals and Reptiles used as Charms, ... 51
Dreams, Superstitions concerning, 41
" Japanese Beliefs in, .. 43
" of Deceased Relatives, Ominous, .. 77
Dress, Article of belonging to a Child's Father, a Charm, .. 13
Drowned Bodies, Discovery of, .. 64
Duck, Bamboo and Duck's Egg used 60 Days after Death, .. 24
Duck Quacking, Unlucky, .. 33

E

Earth, Scattered on Coffin at Burials, ... 25
Eclipses, Superstitions about, .. 36
Eggs, how Prevented from Breaking when Boiled, .. 70
" Setting an even number of, 35
Eitel, Rev. Dr., on Fable of Hwang-ho, ... 4
Elixir of Life, the, ... 97
Elves and Brownies, Chinese Ideas of, ... 97
Evil Eye, the, ... 49
Exorcists, Christian and Pagan, in China, ... 89

INDEX.

Eyebrows, People with Joined, their Luck, ... 38
Eyelids, Involuntary Movement of, an Omen, ... 38

F

Fable, the Earliest Chinese, .. 147
Fables, their Use in China, .. 146
  ,, Collections of, ... 146
Fairies Embodying the Powers of Nature, ... 100
  ,, Chiefly Attributed to Mountainous Localities, 97
  ,, Chinese usually Beautiful, 98
Fairy Women, ... 99
  ,, Flies and Bees, .. 100
Feet, Bridegroom Requested to Rub Bride's, ... 16
Female Apparitions before Death Unknown, ... 26
Fêng-Shuey, ... 65
Finger, Shaking of, an Omen, .. 38
Fire Crackers, as Charms, .. 46
  ,, Legend of the God of, .. 121
  ,, Superstitions as to spread of, 123
First-foot, on New Year's Day, .. 2
  ,, The, Superstitions concerning, .. 31
First Words Heard after Making a Resolution, Ominous, .. 39
Fishing Nets as Charms, .. 57
Five, the Number, ... 40
Flesh Human, Curative Powers of, if Eaten, ... 68, 66
Flowers in the Unseen World, Representing Women, .. 11
Folklore, Origin of Term, .. 6
Food, &c. Provided for the Dead, 24
Foot-measure used at Marriages, 16
Four, a Lucky Number at Marriages, ... 17
Fowl, Black, Ghost of, ... 92
Fox, the, and Demonology, 92-96
Fo-yeung-lak, Branches Hung over Doorways, ... 47
Fruit, Dried, Used at Marriages, 16
Frog in the Moon, the, .. 118
Funerals, Unlucky to Meet, .. 38

G

Gardner, Mr. C. T., Notes by, .. 25
Garlic Bulbs, Charms against Sickness, ... 70
Geese and Tortoise, Fable of the, 149
Genœva Root Stories, ... 142
Genii, how Summoned, .. 81
  ,, Chinese Description of, 81
  ,, The Taoist Definition of, .. 81
  ,, Celebrated, ... 82, 83

Genii Magic Powder of the, .. 82
  ,, Isles of the, ... 82
Ghosts, The False Ghost at Chinkeang, ... 71
  ,, The Chinese Terms for, .. 72
  ,, Shapeless Form of, .. 72
  ,, Every-day Appearance of, 72
  ,, Of Women who Die in Child-bed, ... 74
  ,, Of Suicides, ... 74
  ,, Pranks of, ... 76
  ,, Accompanied by Celestial Police, ... 77
  ,, Low Intelligence of, .. 77
  ,, Pauper, ... 77
  ,, Exorcising (A Chinese Farce), ... 78
  ,, Of Idols, ... 78
  ,, Free to Revisit the Earth, 78
  ,, Talismans Against, .. 79
  ,, Animal, ... 79
Goats used to Discover Drowned Bodies, ... 64
Goblets, Bridal, ... 17
"God," Chinese Equivalent of the Word, ... 155
Goddess of the Moon, The, .. 117
Good Deeds Rewarded, .. 136
Gorges, Female Spirits of the, .. 132
Gourd Shells as Charms, .. 51
Grass, Used to Frighten Demons, 11
Graves, Lucky Sites for, .. 25
Gymnastics, Practice of, Conduces to Immortality, ... 69

H

Hainan Straits, Reputed Home of Sea Monsters, ... 115
Hair Combing, when Unlucky, .. 41
  ,, on Body, Excess of, Illomened, ... 38
Hare in the Moon, Legend of the, 118
  ,, Superstitions concerning the, 64
Haunted Houses, Stories of, .. 75
Heart, Jumping Sensation of, an Omen, ... 38
  ,, Name Engraved on the, .. 136
Hell, Gate of, near Têng-chow, .. 130
Hens Crowing, Unlucky, .. 33
Hercules' Cup, Chinese Version of, 132
Honey at Sicilian Marriages, .. 17
Hooks, Silver, Worn as Amulets, 55
Horses and the King, Fable of the, 150
Horse's Hoof, a Charm, .. 48
Household Tales, Grimm's Opinion of, ... 145
Hwang-ho, Fable of the, .. 4
  ,, Fairy Lake, Source of the, ... 133

I

	Page
Idols Antagonistic to Ghosts,	75
Images of Animals and Reptiles used as Charms,	51
Indian Fables Translated into Chinese,	148
Invocations used by Spirit Media,	60
Iron-plates Sunk in Rivers as Charms,	47
Islands, Legends concerning Formation of,	123

J

Jars Used to Imprison Demons,	131
Jasper Lake, the,	99
Jewels and the Priest, Fable of the,	131
Judgment of Solomon, Chinese Versions of,	139
Juniper Tree Leaves Used for Divination,	63

K

Kelpies, Chinese,	100
Kettle, Spout of, must not be Turned Outwards,	65
Key of a Dyke Water Gate used as a Charm,	47
Kingsmill, T. W., on Mythical Origin of Chow Dynasty,	4
Knife, Absurd Tale of a, at a Wedding, (note),	19
,, Cash as Charms,	57
,, used to Kill a Fellow Creature, a Charm,	51
Knots "Auspicious," in Swathing the Dead,	21
Korrigan, Resemblance to Chinese Elves,	132
Ku-tu or Magic Water,	62
Kwang-sui-fu, Legend of the Cave of,	134
Kw'en-lun Mountain,	133
,, Mountains Peopled with Fairies,	97

L

Lake Măn, Supernatural Origin of,	126
,, of Gems, the,	97
Lame Man and Blind Man, Fable of the,	151
Lamps and Lanterns at Marriages,	17
Last Piece left on a Dish,	65
Legends of Locality,	129
Lewchewan Legend of the Fairy Dress,	140
Lightning, Beliefs concerning,	121
Lin-lu Mountain, Legend of,	132

	Page
Lions, Images of, Outside Houses,	48
Loadstone, Legends regarding the,	135
Locks, Silver, Worn as Amulets,	55
Lots Method of Casting,	39
Luther, Superstition of,	3

M

Magicians, Noted,	83
Magpies, Ominous,	33
Manna, Chinese Fall of,	128
Mao-shan (Magicians) the,	83
Marriage of Emperor, Superstitious Gifts at,	7
,, Superstitions regarding,	14
Marriages, Days Suitable for,	15
Mayers, on Cult of God of Literature,	4
"Measures," Worshipping the,	13
Media, Spiritualistic Chinese,	60
Mercury and its Preparations, Virtues of,	139
Mermaid, China the Original Home of the,	114
Mermaids, Chinese Legends of,	115
Mesmerism, Chinese,	62
Meteors, as Auguries,	120
Mice and Cat, Fable of,	147
Mirages, Beliefs about,	120
Mirrors, Superstitions concerning,	35-45
,, used at Marriages,	16
Money as Amulets,	55
Monkeys Reputed to Steal Women,	100
Monster of the Nanking Pagoda,	114
Moon, Beliefs concerning the,	115
,, Cakes,	28
,, Goddess of the, Legend of,	101
,, Obscured, Hakka Superstition concerning,	32
,, Snow from the,	118
Mountains, Presiding Demons and Divinities of,	123
Mourning Colours of Different Nations,	26
Murdered People, Omens from Closed or Open Hands of,	71
,, People, Blood from Mouth, &c.,	71
Murderers Haunted by Ghosts of Persons Murdered,	75
Mussel and Bittern, Fable of the,	147

N

Nails, Coffin, as Charms,	48
Name, People of the Same, Forbidden to Marry,	19
Nanking Pagoda, Monster of the,	114
Nails, Specks on,	39

INDEX.

	Page.
New-Born Children must not be near Silkworms,	71
" Year's Day, Lucky for Certain Acts,	31
"Noon Day Tea" Cakes as Charms,	70
Numbers, Even, Fortunate,	41
" Lucky,	39
Numerical Categories, Mayers' List of,	40

O

	Page.
Oil Jar, Superstition as to Upsetting an,	33
Old Man in the Moon, Attributes of,	117
Order of Subjects dealt with,	4, 5
Owls and Crows, Fables of the,	149
" Ominous,	34
Ox, Green, Ghost of the,	92

P

	Page.
Pa Kwa, the,	50
Palm, Itching of,	39
Palmistry, Divination by,	63
Paper Slips, Divination by,	63
Penelope, Story of, Chinese Tales Resembling,	141
Phœnix, the Chinese,	111-112
Philosopher's Stone, the Chinese,	139
Physiognomy, Auguries from the,	63
Pigs, White, and "Carrying Coal to Newcastle,"	147
Planchette, the Chinese,	57
Plum Tree, its Powers over Spirits,	47
Poi-t'ou, the "Cup Traveller,"	132
Portents or Omens,	33
Possession, Chinese Stories of Demon,	86
Pregnant Animal, Passing over a Corpse, Superstition about,	20
Proverbs, Coincidence of Chinese and European,	151
" Business and Social,	152
" Use of the Word "Heaven" in,	155
Pumelo Leaves used for Divination,	63
Punch and Judy, Legendary Origin of,	136
Purgatory, Gate of,	129

Q

	Page.
Quicksilver, its alleged Properties,	139
Quilt, used to Toss Cakes at Marriages,	18

R

	Page.
Radicals, Story,	143
Rain God, the Chinese,	124
" Priests,	125
Rainstones, Ancient Chinese,	69
Red Cloth and Silk as Charms,	51
" Cloth Placed on Threshold of Bridegroom's House,	18
" Cords used for Infants,	12
" Paper for Charms,	54
" Silk Threads, used at Betrothals,	15
Ridge Poles, Charms attached to,	48
Rip Van Winkle, Chinese Versions of,	98
Roof, Holes Made in to Allow Egress of Soul,	2-22

S

	Page.
Sabbath, the Chinese, Origin of,	27
Sago Palm Leaves, Charms against Sickness,	70
Salt, Thrown into Water when a Person has been Rescued from Drowning,	64
Sampans, Red Cloths Hung on, at Birth of Children,	11
Sand Spread on Table, Divination by,	58
" Strewn on Floor to Discover if Spirit of the Dead Revisits a Place,	77
Scales, Money, used at Marriages,	16
Sea-Serpents, Chinese,	113
Sedan-chair and Crane used Sixty days after Death,	24
Sedans, Marriage, Paintings on,	16
Self-sacrifice for the Public Good,	134
Serpents, Story from Foochow,	105
" Worship,	105
" Flesh, Healing Qualities of,	103
" as River Gods,	106
" Combat between Enchanted,	104
" Precious Stones in Heads of,	106
" Power of Assuming Human form,	103
" Dragons, &c.,	102
" Wide-spread Legends concerning,	102
Seven, the Number, Superstitions concerning,	27, 38, 40
" the Number, in connection with Burials,	24
Sex of Children, how Foretold,	10, 11
Shan Ching Kwei (Magicians),	83
Shan-sao, or Chinese Brownies,	99

INDEX.

Shears used at Marriages, 16
"Shōn of Offence," the, 78
Shiu-hing, Legend of, 130
Shoes, Superstitions concerning, 11, 15, 18
Shooting Stars, Omens from, 36
Sieve, used to Purify Clothes before Marriage, 16
Silkworms, Pregnant Women not Allowed to Approach, 71
Sitting on the Dress of Bride or Bridegroom, an Omen, 19
Snake, Absurd Tale of at a Marriage (note), 19
Snakes in Chinese Fables, 148
Sneezing, an Omen, 38
Solomon, Judgment of, its Chinese Version, 139
Somnambules or Media, Chinese, 59
Spirit Media, Deity Invoked by, 61
"Spirit," use of the Word in Chinese, 102
Spiritualism and Spirit-Rapping in China, 57
Spittle, Lustration by, 52
Stars, Abodes of Supernatural Beings, 119
„ Ominous, 36
Stent, on Chinese Legends, 3
Stones, Legends concerning Human Beings Metamorphosed into, 128
„ Possessed by Spirits, 96
Storm Fiends, Chinese, 97
Straw Tied Round a Pot Prevents Boiling over, 70
Styx, Chinese, the, 24
St. George and the Dragon, Chinese Version of, 111
„ Swithun's Day, Chinese, 32
Swallows, never wilfully Killed, 34
Swan Maidens, Chinese Version of the Samojed Legend, 140
Sweet Dew, Fall of, 128
„ Flag, Leaves of the, used as a Charm, 51
Swellings Cured by Hem of a Woman's Garment, 70
Sun, Chinese Beliefs concerning, 118, 119
„ God, Cup of the, 132
Svastika, the, in China, 49

T

Tea, Legendary Origin of the Shrub, 137
Teachers, Great, of China, their Influence regarding Superstitions, 6

Thom's Translation of Æsop's Fables, 146
Thor's Hammer in China, 49
Three Children at a Birth, Superstitions concerning, 12
„ the Number, Unlucky at Marriages, 17
Threshold, Bride's Feet must not Touch, 18
Thunder, the God of, 121
Tides Excessive Superstitions as to, 125
„ Influence of the Moon on, 118
Tiger Suckling Babes, Stories of, 142
„ the, in Chinese Fable, 148
Tigers as Demoniacs, 91
Tortoise and Geese, Fable of, 149
Tree of Life, the, 97
Trees, Anti-demoniacal Powers of Certain, 47
Triangles, Gold or Silver as Charms, 49
Trolls, their Chinese Representatives, 132
Trowsers, Ominous Properties of, 38
Tsien-tang River, Human Self-sacrifice to the, 134
Twitching of the Flesh, an Omen, 38
Typhoons, Legend of Origin of, 109

U

Unicorn, the Chinese, 111

V

Veils, Used at Marriages, 16
Vermilion, a Charm against Infant Sickness, 70
Volcanic Phenomena, Superstitions as to, 126

W

"Watching Spirits," Superstitions as to, 22
Watching the Dead, 24
Water, Drawn after Midnight on a Certain Date, Efficacy of, 38
„ Magic, its Use, 62
Waterspouts and Dragons, 127
Watters, on Chinese Beliefs regarding Pigeons, Doves and Foxes, 3
Waxen Images Used by Wizards, their Chinese Representatives, 83
Wedding Ring, Chinese, 14
White Hempen Cloth for Mourning, 24, 25
Willow, the, its Powers over Spirits, 47

INDEX.

	Page.
Willow Wood, Divination by Image of,	61
,, Wood, Lucky Properties of,	16
Windows, Opening of, for Egress of Soul,	2
Witchcraft, a Communicable Act,	80
,, and Demonology,	79
Witches and Wizards, Long Existence of in China,	80
,, not Subject to Violence,	80
Witches Chinese Charm against,	90
Wives, Supernatural,	142

Y

	Page.
Yang and Yin Principle, Curious Application of,	70
Yang-tsze River, Legends of the,	129
Yellow Paper, Charms on,	54
,, River, Legends of the,	129

NOV 17 1983

PLEASE DO NOT REMOVE
CARDS OR SLIPS FROM THIS POCKET

UNIVERSITY OF TORONTO LIBRARY

www.ingramcontent.com/pod-product-compliance
Lightning Source LLC
Chambersburg PA
CBHW031445160426
43195CB00010BB/861